SKYBOLT

SKYBOLT
AT ARM'S LENGTH

NICHOLAS HILL

FONTHILL

Fonthill Media Language Policy

Fonthill Media publishes in the international English language market. One language edition is published worldwide. As there are minor differences in spelling and presentation, especially with regard to American English and British English, a policy is necessary to define which form of English to use. The Fonthill Policy is to use the form of English native to the author. Nicholas Hill was born and educated in England; therefore, British English has been adopted in this publication.

Fonthill Media Limited
Fonthill Media LLC
www.fonthillmedia.com
office@fonthillmedia.com

First published in the United Kingdom and the United States of America 2019

British Library Cataloguing in Publication Data:
A catalogue record for this book is available from the British Library

ISBN 978-1-78155-704-4

Typeset in 10.5pt on 13pt Sabon
Printed and bound in England

CONTENTS

Introduction

For nearly three years, Skybolt was seen as the linchpin of the British deterrent, even when still merely a paper project. It enabled the long-hoped-for cancellation of the British ballistic missile Blue Streak and put paid to the ambitions of Avro's missile department as well as the ambition of many of those in the Royal Navy who had hoped to deploy Polaris, until the day when the Admiralty found Polaris thrust upon them as part of a crash programme. Most of all, for Westminster and Whitehall, politicians and officials, it offered a cheap, easy, and convenient way of extending the life of the British deterrent for years to come. Its cancellation came as a considerable blow to the prestige of the government, a disaster for Anglo-American relations, and a stunning blow to the RAF, who suddenly found themselves relegated from its strategic role to a mere tactical air force.

To understand how events unravelled, it is necessary to study both the technology and the politics of the missile. There have been analyses of the crisis that have focused almost entirely on top-level politics—the thoughts, words, and deeds of the men at the top, such as Kennedy, Macmillan, or McNamara. These have been written almost exclusively by students of politics who had little comprehension of the missile, its purpose, and its technology. There has been little or no study of the options left to the British Government if the Nassau Agreement to buy Polaris had fallen through, which it might well have done.

Yet, first, to the politics. The feeling of betrayal in the British Government at the cancellation was very acute. To some extent, this was entirely unjustified. The Americans had always made it very plain from the outset that Skybolt was merely a project under development, and there was no guarantee whatsoever that it would proceed through to production and deployment. There seems to have been a collective deafness at all levels of government to this statement. Macmillan, in particular, felt a sense of betrayal since he had agreed, as an unofficial *quid pro quo*, to allow the deployment of Polaris submarines in Holy Loch in Scotland. He felt that America had reneged on its agreement. Sir Robert Scott, Permanent Secretary at the Ministry of Defence, noted:

> Eventually at Nassau, after what was evident to the world as an extremely intensive negotiation, agreement was reached on the provision of POLARIS on terms which the Prime Minister was able to defend as preserving the independent British deterrent. But by then the damage had been done. Supporters of the government who might have welcomed the agreement if it had been freely offered at the outset were embittered by the feeling that America's position of strength had been used in an attempt to force Britain to accept a diminished deterrent or a less independent one. Critics of the Government felt that their long sustained attack on the whole policy of relying on the Americans had been justified.[1]

Before we can consider the politics of the missile, we need to look at the political system. In the British system of government, decisions are made by ministers, and the permanent officials of the Civil Service are there to carry out these decisions. Furthermore, being a minister is not a full-time job. A minister has to be a member of Parliament; usually, that means being a member of the House of Commons. An MP has to nurse their constituency and deal with constituency matters. At general election time, an MP defending their seat will be spending all their waking hours campaigning. Once elected, they have to spend time in the House of Commons, taking part in debates and other business of the House, as well. In the time left over, they have to run a Ministry. A lot of their work will be carried out via the Red Boxes; these are the boxes that their officials will fill with papers to take away and read later. These may contain background briefings on matters for which decisions have to be taken. These will often be worked through late at night or early in the morning. As a consequence, a good deal of the decision-making is pushed down on to officials. Thus, for example, the government collectively have decided that the UK should have nuclear weapons. The Minister of Defence is responsible for seeing that the policy is carried out effectively and efficiently. However, their grasp of the technology might be distinctly limited, and there will be a great deal that never even comes to their attention—unless, of course, something goes wrong.

This is summed up beautifully in a memo concerning a proposed British nuclear warhead, Orange Herald. This was a fairly major project, probably costing some tens of millions of pounds (at 1950s prices), each individual warhead costing around £2.5 million. One of these warheads was tested as part of the atomic weapons trials in the Pacific, codenamed Operation Grapple, which was the largest peacetime operation ever undertaken by the military. The memo begins by asking:

> Your loose minute of 31 Oct. asks what is the present status of the official requirement for Orange Herald, and whether the Minister knows of the project. I propose to answer in some detail for I think that it will be useful to record the history of the project.[2]

After nine paragraphs detailing the history of the project, the author, the Director of Atomic Warfare (Plans), concludes by saying: 'There is no evidence that the Minister knows anything of the project beyond the code word and its definition'. That is a comment that speaks for itself.

British Politicians

Harold Macmillan became Prime Minister after the Suez debacle, a position he had held for three years when he met President Eisenhower at Camp David and negotiated the Skybolt agreement, as well as the agreement for American Polaris submarines to be based at Holy Loch in Scotland. He later met President Kennedy at Nassau in the Bahamas to discuss the Skybolt cancellation and to negotiate the subsequent Polaris agreement. He resigned for health reasons late in 1963.

Duncan Sandys had been Minister of Defence in the late 1950s, notable for the 1957 Defence White Paper, when a number of aircraft projects were cancelled. Defence spending was cut, conscription (National Service) was abolished, and much more reliance was to be placed on guided weapons. An abrasive personality, he clashed frequently with the Chiefs of Staff. He was a strong advocate for Blue Streak and strongly opposed its cancellation. Sandys was appointed Minister of Aviation in 1959 until becoming Secretary of State for Commonwealth Relations in July 1960.

Harold Watkinson was Minister of Defence from the general election in 1959 until being dismissed in what was referred to as the Night of the Long Knives on 13 July 1962 when Harold Macmillan sacked seven Cabinet members. The historian Richard Neustadt says he was sacked 'for no greater offence, apparently, than dullness'. Watkinson was in some ways a slightly unusual choice as Minister of Defence. He had been a businessman prior to entering politics; indeed, he described himself as a 'self-made businessman' in his autobiography. Perhaps he was seen as a more emollient figure than his predecessor, Sandys. Watkinson was replaced by Peter Thorneycroft.

Peter Thorneycroft became Minister of Aviation from July 1960 until July 1962, following Duncan Sandys. He then became Minister of Defence following the sacking of Watkinson. He had had a rather unusual ministerial career, being appointed as Chancellor to the Exchequer by Macmillan in 1957, then resigning, together with two junior Treasury ministers, over the issue of increased government spending.

Julian Amery had been Secretary of State for Air, which at that time was a Cabinet-level appointment, being in charge of the Air Ministry, which was responsible for the RAF. He was Minister of Aviation from 1962 to 1964 following Thorneycroft's move to Minister of Defence. He was also Macmillan's son-in-law.

Hugh Fraser followed Julian Amery as Secretary of State for Air from July 1962 to April 1964. The position was abolished, together with the post of First Lord of the Admiralty (in charge of the Royal Navy) and Secretary of State for War (in charge of the Army) on 1 April 1964, with their responsibilities passed to the Minister of Defence.

British Officials

British civil servants remain in post irrespective of any change of government or minister; indeed, one of their functions is to smooth over the transition from one government to another. The most senior civil servant in any department is referred to as the Permanent Under-Secretary (PUS), or more usually, simply the Permanent Secretary. Such a position would normally carry a knighthood.

The Defence ministries obviously relied a good deal on technical and scientific advice. There would be a post of Chief Scientist or equivalent, which was one step below the Permanent Secretary. The most notable of these was Solly Zuckerman, who came to prominence in the defence establishment during the Second World War when he was involved with studies on the accuracy of British bombing. He was for a time Scientific Adviser to the Air Ministry, before becoming Chief Scientific Adviser (CSA) to the Ministry of Defence. He was involved in many of the leading defence decisions of the period, although not entirely trusted by the military, and formed an informal alliance with Lord

Mountbatten. Between them, they are widely considered to bear a large part of the responsibility for the cancellation of the TSR 2 aircraft. Some of his actions and memoranda during the Skybolt story certainly give the impression that he could be all things to all men. Sir Michael Quinlan, who worked in the Air Ministry and would ultimately become Permanent Secretary at the Ministry of Defence, spoke of Zuckerman and Mountbatten, saying that they were both 'for all their remarkable characteristics in several ways, operators whose style of doing business was such that no one (and that included the Royal Navy) wholly trusted them'.[3]

Sir Maurice Dean was Permanent Secretary at the Air Ministry from 1955 until 1964. He had been a strong supporter of the Blue Streak missile and wrote a lengthy description of events during the crisis period in December 1962.

Sir Robert Scott was Permanent Secretary at the Ministry of Defence from 1962 and was heavily involved in the Nassau talks and Polaris. His predecessor was Sir Edward Playfair.

The Controller of Guided Weapons and Electronics (CGWL) was an important position within the Ministry of Aviation. The controller was one step down from the Permanent Secretary, on an equal footing with the Chief Scientist and the Deputy Secretary. From 1959 to 1962, the post of CGWL was filled by Sir Steuart Mitchell. He was responsible for various government establishments, including the Royal Aircraft Establishment at Farnborough, the Rocket Propulsion Establishment at Westcott, the Royal Radar Establishment at Malvern, and the Signals Research and Development Establishment at Christchurch. The position was briefly filled by Air Marshall Sir Edouard Grundy after Sir Steuart's retirement.

To give some idea of the change in value of money between now and then, in the mid-1950s, the Permanent Secretary at the Ministry of Defence, the most senior civil servant, received an annual salary of £4,500. The Chief Scientist at the Ministry of Supply received a salary of £3,750, and the CGWL a salary of £3,250. Gender equality had not yet reached the Civil Service; the salaries for the rank of Chief Executive Officer was £1,030–£1,230 for men and £936–£1,108 for women. In 2016, Sir Simon McDonald, Permanent Under-Secretary at the Foreign and Commonwealth Office, was paid £410,000—not quite a hundredfold. When considering the costs of the various covered in this account, then to convert it to contemporary values, a figure fifty times as large might be considered modest.

American Politicians and Officials

Eisenhower was the President when Skybolt began; Kennedy was the President at the time of cancellation.

Thomas Gates was Secretary for Defense in the Eisenhower administration and signed the Skybolt agreement with Harold Watkinson. He became increasingly disillusioned with Skybolt; near the end of his period in office, he imposed a budget freeze.

Robert McNamara became the new Secretary for Defense in the Kennedy administration. Initially, he supported Skybolt; however, he became increasingly sceptical and realised that with Minuteman and Polaris, Skybolt was effectively redundant. Unfortunately, he failed to recognise the political implications of his decision to cancel.

John Rubel was Assistant Director of Defense Research and Engineering under Herbert York and was very much involved in the Skybolt negotiations at Nassau. He became a friend of Solly Zuckerman but was not well regarded by other British experts. At the time of the Skybolt cancellation, a telegram from Washington commented, 'Rubel knows the SKYBOLT programme fairly well but he has never been enamoured of the system and I have reason to believe that he has slanted his advice to McNamara accordingly'.[4]

In his autobiography, he claims to have been unaware by the involvement of the RAF in Skybolt:

> I was astonished to learn only after that briefing that British RAF officers had collaborated in writing the basic military 'requirements' for Skybolt in 1958, and had sat in on the selection of Douglas Aircraft as the prime contractor early in 1959, a collaboration that American officials above the Air Force level, not to mention the President, apparently knew little or nothing about at the time. It would appear, however, that British collaboration in the Skybolt initiative was well known up to the top of the British government, perhaps from its early stages.[5]

He was one of McNamara's chief advisers and was certainly no fan of Skybolt, describing it as 'a proposal of enormous complexity and dubious feasibility'. He was also less than impressed by much of the work done by the prime contractor, Douglas. While the cancellation of a project such as Skybolt can never be attributed to one particular individual, he was certainly a prime mover in the final cancellation.

Richard Neustadt was a historian and academic working for the Kennedy administration, and when Kennedy requested a report on how the Skybolt crisis had erupted, he seized the opportunity. Armed with a letter from Kennedy, he went to London and, despite initial objections from Macmillan, successfully interviewed a number of politicians and officials. He deliberately wrote a narrative rather than a managerial report, and it is certainly well-written, with some astute character judgements. It is essential reading for any understanding of the internal American politics of the time and also the judgements he makes on the impact of the cancellation on the British.

Sources

A great deal of material in this book comes from original sources, in particular, the files of those officials and ministers who were involved at a high level in the Air Ministry, Ministry of Defence, Ministry of Aviation, and the Treasury, which are now kept in the National Archives (formerly known as the Public Record Office). These can be recognised in the references as the Ministry of Defence (DEFE), Air Ministry (AIR), Ministry of Supply, which became the Ministry of Aviation, (AVIA), Cabinet files (CAB), Prime Minister's office (PREM), or the Treasury (T).

I have quoted extensively from their papers and memoranda to give the flavour of opinion at the time and to let people speak in their own voice. On the other hand, it must be recognised that this is not the complete story for two reasons. The first is that the number of files that are preserved in the archives is very small—only a tiny fraction—so we are not seeing the entire picture. To preserve all the files would be impossible, and we have only those which were selected years ago as worthy of preservation. The second point is that not all decisions are committed to paper. The following is a quote from an excellent book on the Treasury in the period concerned:

> There is not time, even if one wanted, to conduct most business on paper. Most everyday issues are settled through one of the vital phenomena of British government, 'the chat'. And nowhere has the chat been elevated into a more pervasive institution than in the Treasury. A telephone call, lunch, a chance meeting in the corridor—almost anything can occasion a chat.[6]

Of course, this is not confined to the Treasury. There is also the point that a good deal of verbal discussion may precede an important meeting so that various people can arrive with pre-agreed positions; that might not be obvious from the minutes of the meeting.

There are also several accounts of events which were written much later, as part of autobiographies. In particular, Solly Zuckerman (who was then Chief Scientific Adviser to the Ministry of Defence) and John Rubel have written their version of events many years later. Rubel's account is a classic example of how the memory of particular details fades with age; there are considerable factual errors strewn through his account. Zuckerman adroitly skirts controversial matters in the course of a fairly lengthy account. Watkinson also produced an autobiography, but Skybolt does not get a great deal of coverage, nor does one get the impression that he had a great grasp of technical matters. One of the problems with autobiographies is that they are written with a variety of motives, one of which might be setting the record straight to the author's own satisfaction.

Virtually all the writing on Skybolt has looked at it in terms of the high-level politics: Macmillan and Kennedy, British defence and nuclear policy, Anglo-American relationships, and so on. Yet underneath the surface are the men (and it is true to say that virtually every individual mentioned in this book is male) who had to make the policy work. Part of their job was to write briefings for ministers, telling them what was and what was not feasible. The ministers themselves were not technical experts; indeed, most of them would have had little or no scientific education even at school. They had to rely on the advice given by the technical and scientific advisers. Ministers were also busy people, having to deal with constituency matters, Cabinet meetings, debates in the House of Commons, and so on in addition to all their ministerial responsibilities. Much of their work was done in the red boxes in which urgent papers were put for the Minister to take home and read each evening. One of the Civil Service criteria for ministerial effectiveness was how thoroughly they dealt with their boxes.

RAF versus RN

Something else that comes out very clearly in much of this saga is the antagonism between the Navy and the RAF, which, as far as the Navy was concerned, verged almost on the paranoid. They bitterly resented the money being spent on the deterrent—that is, of course, until they took over the deterrent itself in the form of the Polaris submarine. This is no exaggeration, as this excerpt from a letter written by the Vice Chief of Naval Staff to a colleague demonstrates:

> Our trouble is that the Minister [of Defence] has been advised by interested parties, in very optimistic terms, about SKYBOLT's state and prospects. I would almost say he has been led up the garden path. I would warn you that

some of the advisers he will bring to you with him are bitterly anti-Navy and anti-Polaris, and if you see a chance you might warn [Admiral] Burke in guarded terms of this tendency.

The Minister however is extremely shrewd and we are confident that when the facts relating to SKYBOLT and POLARIS respectively come to light, he is quite capable of discerning that SKYBOLT in 1966 or '67 may be not only invalid (in terms of its aircraft vulnerability), but also nearly as expensive as a modest POLARIS programme. He will then draw his own conclusions about spending millions on a very expensive short duration stopgap, and going straight to POLARIS ... [7]

With no sense of irony at all, the next paragraph reads:

The Admiralty line (very successful too under [Admiral] Charles Lambe) is to be completely objective and rational in all these problems, in contrast to the incessant and often foolish Air Ministry intrigue and false presentation of the facts which I'm ashamed to say still goes on.[8]

On the other hand, it would also be true to say that there were times when members of the RAF were nearly as paranoid, as for example in this memorandum:

As we know the Skybolt boat is being heavily rocked in America and there are those in the Ministry of Defence who are doing nothing to dampen out the motion reflected in Whitehall. The Admiralty have not lost a moment in suggesting that, as Skybolt and X-12 are now suspect, it would be appropriate to reconsider new propositions about a Polaris deterrent. It is my information the Minister and C.S.A. [Chief Scientific Adviser, Zuckerman] have seen the Prime Minister on this issue.

It is my impression that although the minister was depressed by what Mr Gates had to tell him, he will not alter his views about the relative merits of Skybolt and Polaris in regard to a deterrent weapon for this country. Now that we have had the latest situation in Washington, as transmitted by Group Captain Fryer, there is little more we can do than perhaps put him fully in the picture of what has gone on here. For instance, I doubt whether he knows of the sinister implication of the Inspector General for visiting the Douglas Co. If you would like me to I will write a short Air Mail letter to Fryer which will be entirely secure and exclusive asking him to his inner ear to the ground?[9]

The Treasury

Under the British system of government, the only person who can authorise the spending of money is the Chancellor of the Exchequer. In practice, of course, a lot of this authority is devolved. Thus, for example, a government department may be given a budget by the chancellor, which it must not exceed. In addition, Treasury officials may take decisions on smaller sums without referring it up to the chancellor. Thus, for example, officials at the Ministry of Aviation may request money for a feasibility study and must submit this to Treasury officials for approval before it can go ahead. The main criterion used by the Treasury was: 'Has this been agreed between Ministers?' Thus, for example, if a Cabinet committee chaired by the Prime Minister authorised the study, the Treasury would have no option but to release the funds. In other cases, they may dig their heels in. An example of this was when the future of Blue Streak looked bleak, but it had not yet officially been cancelled. The Ministry of Aviation wanted money for facilities in Australia, and the Treasury refused on the grounds that the future of the project was too uncertain.

The importance of the Treasury in British Government can hardly be emphasised too strongly. It likes to see an orderly chain of decision. Thus certain officials felt that the decision to buy Skybolt had been taken in a rather cavalier fashion, and the query was raised: 'I would be grateful if you could advise us ... of the terms of Ministerial authority to proceed with the Skybolt project'. The answer received was as follows:

> It is a little difficult to answer your questions as put. The decision to buy Skybolt was not a tidy one taken in Cabinet or Defence Committee with proper papers and adequate time to brief Ministers after interdepartmental consultation at official level.[10]

That last sentence shows that the author disapproved strongly of the circumventing of normal government and Civil Service procedure. The phrase 'not a tidy one' is an example of British understatement at its best. The Civil Service approves of tidiness.

> It was more of a gradual, shuffling process. It all goes back to the Prime Minister's visit to President Eisenhower in March/April 1960. At that time four interweaving threads of policy were in the air: the question of cancelling Blue Streak as a military weapon, the possibility of taking Skybolt, the provision by the US of ballistic missiles for NATO and the establishing of the Polaris base in Holy Loch. It is difficult to disentangle the complete story from Treasury papers ... Briefly, there was an agreement in principle at Prime

Minister/President level, followed by a slightly more detailed Memorandum of Understanding at Minister of Defence level. The real decision was taken by a small group of Ministers, including the PM and Chancellor, but they never constituted a proper Committee, and their meetings were ad hoc and of varying membership. Eventually the Minister of Defence reported the upshot to the Cabinet, who accepted what had already in effect been decided.[11]

The Treasury was not very happy with the apparently *ad hoc* nature of the agreement; it offended their sense of the proprieties. Much of the cost would be in dollars, at a time when currencies were not freely convertible and dollar expenditure was to be avoided if at all possible. The memo went on to say:

> The truth is that in Ministerial eyes the problem was whether or not the U.K. should cease to have an independent nuclear deterrent, and in a question of this political magnitude the dollar consequences did not rate very high.[12]

This is typical of the sort of query that the Treasury would raise when it felt that matters were proceeding in an irregular fashion. The Treasury was also very reluctant to sanction any further expenditure on a project that it thought was ripe for cancellation. The drawback to this policy was that the lack of finance often led to delays in projects and a drop in morale of the people working on them; sometimes, this was a false economy, in that such delays, in the end, cost more money.

Another related problem was that of defence reviews. It was certainly the case that when a new government was elected, the new minister would demand wholesale reviews of all the most expensive projects. During one meeting of the Defence Research and Policy Committee (DRPC), Sir Steuart Mitchell, the CGWL, asked whether it was the intention of the Ministry of Defence to carry out another defence review in the autumn of 1960. He complained that for a number of years, such reviews had been held. While they were in progress, most major development projects were at risk; therefore, work on them tended to slow down. The result was that costs were increased and completion dates postponed.

> The Chairman of the meeting said that the need for reviews arose from the fact that the cost of the defence programme continually increased and exceeded the amount which ministers were prepared to approve. But he recognised the serious disadvantages of a system under which most major development projects were at risk; it might be possible to identify projects

which would not be questioned and to confine the uncertainty to a small number of projects. An attempt to do this would be made during the examination of the defence programme, which was now starting.[13]

It was an issue that is just as apposite today as it was sixty years ago.

Procurement

By modern standards, the system of procurement of weapons and aircraft for the RAF looks Byzantine. There was a great deal of bureaucracy left over from the wartime period, with the division of responsibility split between various ministries. The Ministry of Defence had been a relatively small organisation designed to oversee the three services, which each had their own separate minister and ministries.

The Ministry of Defence gained a good deal more importance in 1957 when Duncan Sandys was appointed and given a good deal more authority by Macmillan. This would be further consolidated, until when in 1964, the three separate ministries were all subsumed into the Ministry of Defence. In 1971, the defence functions of the Ministry of Aviation were also subsumed into the Ministry of Defence. It should not be assumed that, as a result, inter-service rivalry disappeared.

Research and development of new weapons for the RAF was carried out by yet another ministry, the Ministry of Supply, which was renamed the Ministry of Aviation after the 1959 general election. This should not be confused with the Air Ministry, who ran the RAF.

If the Air Staff—part of the Air Ministry and comprised of senior serving officers—decided that it needed a new weapon in the form of an aircraft or a missile, it would write out an operational requirement specifying the performance details and characteristics of the new weapon. This had then been submitted to a committee known as the Defence Research Policy Committee (DRPC), which was chaired by a senior scientific figure such as Sir John Cockroft, and later, Solly Zuckerman; its membership was mainly service figures and scientific advisers to ministries. Thus the Air Staff included a member known as the Assistant Chief of Air Staff (Operational Requirements), or ACAS (OR), who acted as the representative of the Air Staff on the DRPC. The DRPC had considerable authority, as a note from Watkinson to Macmillan demonstrates. Macmillan thought it would be helpful if he and the Cabinet Defence Committee had a list of all the major projects under research and development. Watkinson thought this was unnecessarily bureaucratic and told the Prime Minister the following:

All individual projects of any magnitude require first to be approved by the
Defence Research Policy Committee and then to receive Treasury sanction;
and the Defence Research Policy Committee annually reports on the research
and development programme as a whole, and in particularly on its balance,
its cost and its practicability.... I should be sorry to add further machinery,
especially as there is already, I believe, some justice in the complaints of
industry that we are late in initiating proposals for development and that
when a project has been started, we only give short-term contracts.[14]

If approved by the DRPC, the project would then need Treasury sanction
before being passed on to the Ministry of Aviation. The Ministry of
Aviation would then pass the requirement round to various aircraft
manufacturers, who would consider the requirement and produce a design
brochure which they would then pass back to the Ministry of Aviation.
The designs would be evaluated by the Royal Aircraft Establishment
(RAE), who would note their merits and demerits. The Ministry of
Aviation would then decide which aircraft manufacturer to approach (and
this was not always done in terms of quality of design; other factors were
taken into consideration, such as the existing load on the firm and the
quality of its personnel). Finally, the company with the winning design
would be given the go-ahead to start building the prototype. While much
of this was necessary, it could take up an inordinate amount of time.

The Air Staff had little or no say in any of this process, which often
led to an argument about the approach of the Ministry of Aviation. For
example, the Air Staff wanted to treat the low altitude bomber project (a
project too ambitious for its time) and its associated equipment as one
complete unit (what would today be called a weapons system). This went
contrary to the philosophy of the Ministry of Aviation, who regarded
themselves as the arbiters of which particular pieces of equipment were
chosen for the aircraft, and the Air Staff were overruled. This would crop
up time and again as new projects were being considered. An example of
this was with the TSR 2 development:

Although BAC was the main contractor, many of the sub-contractors were
developing major systems such as the engines and Nav/Attack equipment
under separate Ministry of Aviation contracts ... This meant BAC had little
control over progress on these items but it also meant they could blame
sub-contractors for any programme delays. The sub-contractors in turn
postponed reporting any delays as long as possible in the hope that either
BAC or another sub-contractor would declare a slippage and let them off the
hook. This was one reason for the reluctance noted above to be open with
each other in discussing problems.[15]

It would have been much more efficient to have a prime contractor who dealt with all the sub-contractors, instead of having to go through the ministry each time. Yet the ministry bitterly objected to any such rationalisation, since it would have removed one of their prime functions and no bureaucracy relinquishes its power willingly.

Sir Frank Cooper was working in the Air Ministry in the 1950s and '60s and went on to become Permanent Secretary at the Ministry of Defence. The following was again written in the context of the TSR 2 but could be applied to many other projects:

> There was no doubt that relations with the Ministry of Supply/Aviation and the Air Ministry went from bad to worse and that these poor relations spread increasingly to the Ministry of Defence as a whole. The breach itself was of long-standing. The basic cause was lack of trust, particularly as regards the information received by the Air Ministry. The trust was lacking because the Procurement Ministry stood between the Air Ministry as the customer, and industry as the supplier. Moreover, nothing seemed to arrive at the right time and at the right price, let alone with the desired performance. The lack of trust was exacerbated by the financial arrangements under which the Ministry of Supply/Aviation recovered production costs from the Air Ministry but was left with the research and development costs. Hence, there was no clear objective against which the supply department could assess performance and value.[16]

Ironically, Skybolt never went through this long and drawn-out procedure in the UK, although it did experience its American equivalent, which could be equally protracted.

Codenames

The point of a code name is that it should reveal absolutely nothing about the project concerned. Warheads, bombs, missiles, and other pieces of equipment in the 1950s were given codenames that consisted of a colour plus some other meaningless word. Thus Red Duster was a missile, Orange Herald, a warhead; Red Neck, a form of radar; and Blue Sapphire, an astrocompass. This can lead to problems when reading official papers since there are times when a project is referred to either by its OR number or by its codename, so Blue Streak is also known as OR1139 (and was known to de Havilland's for a time as Code 3000). Sometimes, the names chosen were somewhat bizarre; a Naval stand-off missile was known as Green Cheese. A minister objected to the name as absurd and asked for it to be changed. However, ministers often move on faster than bureaucracy, particularly if that bureaucracy decides to drag its feet; Green Cheese therefore remained Green Cheese.

The system was changed in the early 1960s to a much more mundane two-letter and three-digit code—e.g. RE179 for the Skybolt warhead, WE177 for the laydown bomb, and so on. It was debatable whether it was much more secure, but it was distinctly less colourful.

I am very grateful to the following for their help: Chris Gibson and Terry Panopolis for providing images, and John Harlow MBE and David Stumpf for their comments.

1

Background

HMS *Warspite* earned more battle honours than any other British battleship. Launched in 1913, she was badly damaged at the Battle of Jutland in 1916. Modernised between the wars, she achieved fame during the Battle of Narvik, when the giant battleship sailed into a narrow Norwegian fjord to help sink the German ships that were sheltering there. At the Battle of Calabria in 1940, she achieved one of the longest-range gunnery hits achieved by any warship at sea, when she hit the Italian battleship *Giulio Cesare* at a range of around 26,000 yards (13 nautical miles). At the Battle of Cape Matapan, together with her sister ships *Valiant* and *Barham*, she helped sink three Italian heavy cruisers.

On 16 September 1943, she was assisting the Allied landings at Salerno, bombarding German positions ashore, when she was attacked by three Dornier bombers, which released glide bombs known as Fritz X. One of the bombs cut through the ship and made a 20-foot hole in the bottom. Another, a near miss, ripped open the torpedo protection bulges on the side of the ship. The *Warspite* was lucky to survive.

What was new about the attack was that the Fritz X bomb was radio controlled—one of the first ever stand-off weapons. This was not the first time that Fritz X had been used; earlier in September, the battleship *Roma* was sunk using the weapon, and her sister ship *Italia* was heavily damaged. Three days later, the American cruiser USS *Savannah* was hit by a Fritz X and had to return to the United States for eight months' worth of repairs. The British cruiser HMS *Uganda* was also hit, the bomb passing straight through the ship and exploding underneath.

The attack had been conducted at arm's length; the era of the stand-off weapon had arrived. It would develop from these primitive radio-controlled glide bombs to an almost invulnerable ballistic missile carrying a nuclear warhead.

The world's first and only nuclear weapons dropped in anger were released over Japan in August 1945. However, the conditions under which they were used would act as no precedent for the future. At the time, Japan was unable to mount any form of effective anti-aircraft defence. The skies were open to the Allies, and so the bombers were able to operate in broad daylight and take their time to find their aiming point. Even so, despite these advantages, one of the two bombs was dropped some distance away from its intended aiming point.

For at least the next ten years after 1945, there was no alternative to the bomber, carrying a free-fall bomb as a means of long-range delivery. The first British test, Hurricane, was carried out with the device inside an obsolete frigate as the Admiralty felt it might be possible to smuggle bombs into ports concealed in the holds of ships. Britain had a very large fleet of strategic bombers at the end of the war, but one that was rapidly becoming obsolete with the arrival of the jet engine, and ill-suited to the task of dropping atomic weapons over a likely enemy. The Lancasters and their ilk were designed for distances no greater than the east coast of England to Berlin and back. They were slow and piston-engined, operating mainly by night. Their chance of survival against jet-powered interceptors operating under radar direction would be remote. The new American B29 far outclassed the Lancaster and its successor, the Lincoln, but piston-engined designs had effectively reached the limits of further development; the performance improvement opened up by the new gas turbine jet engines was very considerable.

An aircraft carrying an atomic weapon is a very high-value target for the air defences. During the war, Bomber Command had operated on exactly the opposite principle; in dropping a few kilotons of high explosive on the likes of Hamburg, up to 1,000 aircraft might have been used. Each of these aircraft was thus a low-value target. Losses of individual aircraft could be accepted. Further, although every effort was made to ensure accuracy, the aircraft of Bomber Command were at times notoriously inaccurate. Hence Bomber Command in 1945 had an operational capability which was the very antithesis of what was required for a nuclear delivery force. As a result, the Air Ministry put forward several operational requirements (ORs) for replacement bombers soon after the war ended.

Operational requirements were issued whenever there was a need for a new design of aircraft or other device and would specify performance figures such as speed, height, and range for an aircraft, as well as payload equipment that should be carried. OR229, issued in November 1946, was a specification for a jet-powered aircraft that should be 'capable of carrying one 10,000-lb bomb to a target 1500 NM from a base which may be anywhere in the world.' 'NM' stands for nautical miles (it may be assumed that, unless otherwise stated, 'miles' = 'nautical miles' throughout this book). The 10,000-lb bomb referred to was the first British atom bomb known as Blue Danube. Various euphemisms were often used for atomic weapons, such as 'special store', etc.

One of the problems for the new designs was the payload weight; early bomb designs were very heavy. Another unusual feature of the proposed aircraft was that no defensive armament was to be carried; they would rely on height and speed instead, and the lack of guns and turrets would improve the aerodynamics and reduce weight, thus improving performance. The wartime Mosquito aircraft had one of the lowest loss rates per mission flown; it carried no defensive weapons such as cannons, machine guns, or turrets, but instead used its height and speed to avoid interception.

Such an aircraft would be a completely new field for British aircraft designers, and it was recognised that its aerodynamics would be completely different from anything that had gone before. A deliberate attempt was made to produce as radical and modern designs as possible, but there were several rethinks before the final designs emerged.

The Air Staff recognised that the final and most ambitious designs would take several years to develop and so pursued less ambitious designs as well. Effectively, the Ministry was trying to skip a generation of aircraft in going from the Lancaster to the Vulcan and Victor. Hence an 'insurance policy' design was proposed—the Short Sperrin, which ironically was the only design built from the start in production jigs and was the only design not to be adopted by the RAF.

The Sperrin was a compromise design; compared with the likes of the Lancaster, it was very much 'cleaner' aerodynamically, but in other respects, the design was quite conventional and its resemblance to the heavy wartime bombers can easily be seen. The exception was the engine arrangement of two jet engines on each wing, mounted in a single nacelle, one above the other. The Sperrin first flew in August 1951 but was not ordered into production since a better interim design had appeared, one that could be built almost as quickly. This was the Vickers Valiant, a more advanced design than the Sperrin but not as ambitious as the Vulcan and the Victor.

The Valiant's performance figures looked better, and there was another important difference; being a more advanced design, there was a greater chance of developing it further. The Sperrin, while competent enough, did not offer much promise for future development.

The Valiant had been proposed as another 'insurance' design, or, at least, one produced to a less demanding specification than was originally required. Its development time was astonishingly short—twenty-seven months from the contract being issued to the first flight. The Sperrin first flew in August 1951, whereas the Valiant had already flown for the first time in the previous May. While the Sperrin might have made an excellent stopgap before the more advanced designs were available, the arrival of the Valiant ruled it out. Two Sperrins were produced, and use of them was made dropping the test bomb cases for Blue Danube. One was also used as a flying test bed for the Gyron jet engine.

Valiants first went into squadron service in 1955, and like all the V bombers, were to provide excellent service for the RAF. Britain's first airdrop nuclear test, as part of Operation Buffalo in Maralinga in 1955, was of a derated Blue Danube carried by a Valiant, and a Valiant of 49 Squadron tested the first British fusion bomb designs at Christmas Island. They also were pressed into service in the conventional role during Operation Musketeer, the Suez campaign, but there they were less than successful.

This pointed up one advantage of the nuclear-capable bomber—the capacity to use it in a conventional role. Indeed, one of the major justifications for the V bombers was that they would be as valuable in a conventional role as in a nuclear role. Thus, during Operation Corporate to retake the Falkland Islands in 1981, Vulcan bombers, then on the point of retirement, were used to bomb the runway at Port Stanley. The Victors had been converted into tankers, which had been essential to refuel the Vulcan on its flight to Port Stanley. The V bombers were the last long-range military aircraft produced by the UK.

The limit for all such designs is the speed of sound, around 580 knots at high altitude. The speed of an aircraft can also be described in terms of Mach number; this is the ratio of the speed of the aircraft to the local speed of sound. This was usually written in documents of the period as 'M =' followed by the relevant Mach number. Above about $M = 0.8$, a host of new aerodynamic effects become important in the control of aircraft. Aircraft flying close to or at the speed of sound ran into difficulties; in the 1950s, this was referred to as the 'sound barrier'.

Airspeed is not as important as altitude in evading the enemy air defences since interception by jet fighters at high altitude becomes increasingly difficult since rate of climb drops off with height. Ironically, by the time the V bombers came into full service, the threat was not from jet fighters but from surface-to-air missiles, which were far more effective at shooting down high-flying aircraft. To be fair, surface-to-air missiles were developments that came about long after the V bomber design and production began.

The Valiant was followed by first the Vulcan and then the Victor. Both these later designs turned out to be remarkably robust, particularly given that they spent a large part of their operational life in roles for which they were not designed. Their original function was to fly as fast and as high as possible, with no defensive armament whatsoever. They were also fitted with considerable electronic countermeasure devices (ECM) to enhance their survivability.

The Vulcan was built by Avro in Cheshire, the Victor by Handley Page at Radlett north of London, close to what is now the M25. They were very different in appearance, the Vulcan being almost a flying delta wing, whereas the Victor appeared much more slender and graceful. Both were to undergo considerable revisions in design as deployment progressed.

The Vulcan prototypes had a pure delta wing, but performance was found to be improved with a 'cranked' delta. The Victor was more graceful with its pointed nose and crescent wing. However, the Vulcan was more robust and fitted with more powerful engines. It was also a great deal more manoeuvrable. The sight—and sound—of a Vulcan in a low-level air display was very impressive! There is a video available on the internet showing a Vulcan performing a low-level barrel roll at the Farnborough Air Show in 1955.

Valiants began arriving at operational RAF units in the first few months of 1955. Although early production Vulcans were available in 1956, it was not until May 1957 that the first operational units began forming. The more sophisticated Victor went into service with No. 10 Squadron, beginning in April 1958. Various performance figures are quoted for the Vulcan and Victor, depending on mark, engine fit, modifications, and so on. Certainly, both aircraft were capable of Mach 0.9 at altitudes greater than 50,000 feet.

The RAF was first able to deploy a free-fall bomb capability from 1955 onwards. At this stage, the only atomic weapon available was the Blue Danube bomb with a yield of 10–20 kilotons. To eke out scarce supplies of plutonium, the yield was deliberately reduced. Around fifty-eight Blue Danube bombs were produced for the RAF. However, these in-service dates point up another contemporary defence problem. The V bombers would certainly have no problem with the air defences as experienced in the battles over Germany. They would have coped well enough against the relatively low thrust, low endurance jet fighters of the early '50s. The mid-1950s and onwards were a different matter. Air defences had improved very considerably on both sides.

Indeed, the UK had been aware of the 'mirror threat'; that is, the Russian equivalent of a V bomber attacking the UK and had several programmes running to counter this threat. These included the Saunders-Roe SR177, English Electric Lightning interceptors, and, most importantly, the Bloodhound missile, produced by Bristols.

The SR177 and the Lightning were optimised for acceleration and rate of climb rather than endurance. They carried airborne interception radar and missiles. Their sole purpose was to intercept high-flying bombers. The Bloodhound missile was the outcome of several years' research and development into guided weapons, using various Experimental Test Vehicles (XTV) flown at the rocket range at Woomera, Australia. Four solid-fuel rocket boosters accelerated the missile, and when they burned out, it carried on using two ramjet motors. It used a semi-active radar guidance: the transmitter was ground-based and the missile steered itself on to the reflection from the target. The Mark I missile had a range of only 20 miles, but the Mark II a range of up to 120 miles, depending on conditions. It was also exported to Australia, Sweden, Switzerland, and Singapore. A series of Bloodhound bases were built along the east coast of England in order to defend the V bomber bases. It entered service in December 1958 and continued in service in the UK until 1991.

Indeed, Bloodhound had looked so promising that in 1957 the SR177 was abandoned, and the Lightning was only spared because the development programme was so far advanced. This was the philosophy behind the notorious Sandys' White Paper on defence in 1957, and Sandys was quite right. The later Mark 2 Bloodhound would have had little problem intercepting the likes of the V bombers. The Air Ministry assumed that the Russians would have similar missiles coming into service at around the same time, which indeed they did.

Bloodhound achieved some excellent results during trials at Woomera:

> The first acceptance firings took place in February 1958 and the trials were completed by the end of 1959 ... In the Acceptance Programme, 85 homing missiles were fired, 56 (66%) were successful (i.e., within a miss distance of fewer than 100 feet), of which 15 were direct hits. Targets were engaged out to 52,000 yards and up to 52,000 feet, the highest altitude at which target aircraft currently can operate. Of the high altitude targets, many engagements were carried out of 50,000 feet and above, resulting in 5 direct hits on Canberras, 4 being destroyed. Of these, three were fully manoeuvring targets.[1]

However, it is often a mistake to assume that the same success rate will be achieved by the average missile in service as a trials missile. Given the cost of trials, every effort will be made beforehand to make sure that things are exactly as they should be. That might not be the case under wartime conditions and less experienced operators.

So, almost as soon as they were to come into service, the V bombers seemed to be becoming obsolete in their intended role. Carrying free-fall bombs, they were reckoned to be effective against the Moscow defences until around 1960. Given the in-service dates of the Vulcan and Victor as 1957 and 1958, this meant that their effectiveness in the nuclear strategic role was limited to a very short period. This was particularly ironic in view of the time, effort, and money that had been spent on them.

One way around the problem might be a different type of aircraft—perhaps a low-flying aircraft or a supersonic bomber. The Air Staff did look at both—a low altitude bomber, which turned out to be impossible with the technology of the day, and a supersonic bomber, which also would be vulnerable to guided weapons. A decade later, the TSR 2 would be, in effect, a low-altitude bomber, but its range was such that using it in the strategic role was not really possible. One of the problems with the TSR 2 is that it was a very complex and expensive aircraft with no clearly defined role.

This left one other option—the stand-off weapon, which would mean that the carrier aircraft would not have to penetrate the enemy defences, just as Fritz X had done with its attack on the *Warspite*. The first British attempt was a missile known as Blue Steel, which was over-engineered, far too late into service, and slow to deploy. It was also short ranged, and so more requirements (OR 1149 and 1159) were issued for longer-range missiles. At the same time, the RAF was in discussion with the US Air Force, who were considering another missile that would become known as Skybolt. This had an enormous advantage over all other air-launched missiles of the time, which were effectively cruise missiles. Skybolt was a ballistic missile, which meant that it soared out of the atmosphere on a ballistic path. A cruise missile was thought to be very vulnerable to enemy defences; a long-range ballistic missile was thought to be almost invulnerable, and even today, defending against ballistic missiles is extraordinarily difficult.

The story of Skybolt is a long and complicated one, one that has been told before, but the story has usually been told by historians with little or no technical knowledge and who have accepted the statements of politicians at face value (always a mistake). Instead, much of this account will consist of the plans which the RAF had for Skybolt and the events that followed the cancellation, particularly in terms of the panicked scramble for stopgaps which would be needed before Polaris came into service. It is also an interesting question as to what by the UK would have done if they have been refused Polaris on acceptable terms.

2

Britain's First Stand-Off Missile: Blue Steel

Group Captain Vielle joined the Air Staff in 1949 as part of the operational requirements team, and from his papers written during his time at the Ministry, he seems to have been something of an *enfant terrible*. On the other hand, he made various predictions that would prove to be extremely accurate. As early as 1950, he wrote a long paper to show that the V bombers would be obsolete before they left the drawing board, and he was right. His point was that, given the distances over enemy territory they would have to fly, they would be tracked long before they could reach their target, thus becoming easy targets for the defence. This was one of the most important point about Skybolt; its range was such that the carrier aircraft did not have to overfly enemy defences.

His other claim to fame is that he was the first in Britain to produce a working inertial navigation system. He then proposed a stand-off missile that would be guided inertially. The great advantage of inertial navigation is that the missile became 'fire and forget'. Information is fed to the missile—course, speed over the ground (measured with the new Doppler radar), and position at the moment of release—and the missile does the rest.

Such a system needs a stable system of gyroscopes, which control a platform on which accelerometers are mounted. From acceleration, velocity and thus displacement can be derived. This was a major challenge for the electronics of the 1950s, and also for gyro technology.

Vielle then proposed a new bomber that would fly at low altitude and carry a missile equipped with this new guidance technology. Such an aircraft would be extremely difficult to see on radar since radar coverage is limited by the curvature of the Earth and extremely difficult to intercept. Since it

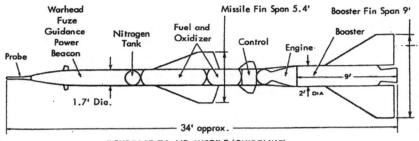

SURFACE-TO-AIR MISSILE (GUIDELINE)
SA-2–ESTIMATED MISSILE SYSTEM CHARACTERISTICS

Maximum Intercept Altitude	60,000 – 80,000 feet	Dependent on Target
Maximum Intercept Range	25 – 30 Nautical Miles	Type and Approach
Warhead Weight	500 Pounds	
Maximum Velocity	Mach 3	
Propulsion System		
Booster	Solid Propellant	
Sustainer	Liquid Propellant	
CEP	100 Feet	

SA-2 MISSILE SYSTEM (INCLUDING GUIDELINE MISSILE)

A view of the Soviet SA-2 Guideline surface-to-air missile as detailed in a CIA document of April 1961.

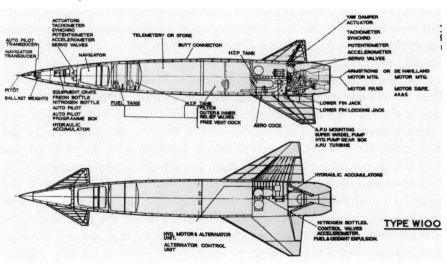

A cutaway view of the Blue Steel stand-off missile. Notice the large space in the centre of the missile marked 'TELEMETRY OR STORE'. 'Store' in this case refers to the warhead that the missile would carry. The design of the missile was finalised before warheads had become miniaturised. The original warhead, Green Grass, would have weighed 4,500 lb, whereas the Skybolt warhead weighed around 600 lb. The missile was finally fitted with the Red Snow warhead, weighing around 2,000 lb. Extra ballast had to be added to keep the centre of gravity in the correct place.

would not have to face the defences of the city it was attacking, as it had a stand-off missile, its chances of survival would be very much greater.

Both proved too much for the technology of the time, although much work was done on them, studying the problems and possible solutions. They were dropped, but the idea of a stand-off missile was carried forward to the V bombers. The aim was for a range of 100 miles (partly limited by the accuracy of gyros available at the time), which would avoid having to overfly the Moscow defences. It had to be in service by 1960, by which time the Russian defences would have been built up and be operational until about 1964, when ballistic rockets were expected to take over.

One of the major limitations on the design was the warhead weight. In 1954, when the operational requirement for Blue Steel was being issued, the UK had few ideas as to how to design megaton weapons. The warhead eventually chosen was extremely heavy at 4,500 lb and also physically large. It was a fairly primitive design and in the end was neither built nor tested. By comparison, the American warhead carried in Skybolt had a weight of 565 lb. Any missile that had to carry a weight of 2 tons over a distance of 100 miles would be correspondingly large.

The job of building the missile was given to Avro, who set up a special missile division staffed initially almost entirely by people from the RAE. The RAE tended to produce design solutions which had technical elegance but were often not the best from the practical engineering and servicing viewpoint. Two crucial design decisions were made at the outset, which would have major implications.

The first of these was to build the missile in stainless steel rather than light alloy. Light alloy is not useable at speeds more than around Mach 2 due to the high temperatures produced by air friction. The problem with stainless steel is that it is very difficult to bend in two planes; near the outset, AVRO was having such problems working with the material that they briefly considered a re-design with a much-simplified structure.

The second decision was to use a rocket motor burning kerosene and hydrogen peroxide: HTP (High-Test Peroxide). The use of HTP would produce considerable operational difficulties when the missile entered service with the RAF. Using a rocket motor rather than an air-breathing motor also meant a much bigger missile.

Almost all the tentative designs for stand-off missiles used turbojets or ramjets. The rationale behind the rocket motor was that, due to the large diameter of the warhead, there was no room for the air intake for the jet engines. On the other hand, it was simple enough to mount the jet engine above the main body or below, or to have two engines, one on each wing tip. A further advantage of an air-breathing missile is that it needs to carry fuel only.

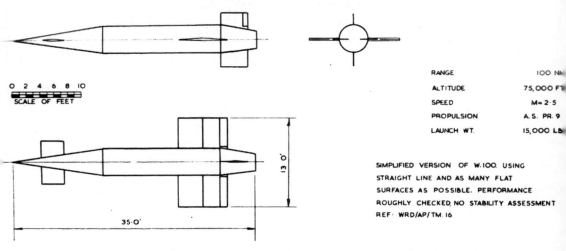

RANGE   100 NM
ALTITUDE   75,000 FT
SPEED   M= 2·5
PROPULSION   A.S. PR. 9
LAUNCH WT.   15,000 LB

SIMPLIFIED VERSION OF W.100 USING
STRAIGHT LINE AND AS MANY FLAT
SURFACES AS POSSIBLE. PERFORMANCE
ROUGHLY CHECKED, NO STABILITY ASSESSMENT
REF· WRD/AP/TM. 16

In the early days of Blue Steel (known to Avro as W.100), the firm experienced considerable difficulty bending stainless steel sheet in three dimensions. An alternative design was drawn up with much simplified lines, but eventually Avro managed to develop the technique successfully.

In addition, the new missile department at Avro, called the Weapons Research Department (WRD), headed by RV Francis, who had moved from the RAE, was to acquire a very poor reputation with the Ministry of Supply, the Ministry of Defence, and the Air Staff, who became increasingly exasperated at what they saw as the incompetence of the firm. The following is just one example:

> The programme proposed by A V Roe/Weapons indicate a steady deterioration in the situation with a more rapid slip as the time approaches for the commencement of trials. It is now difficult to establish what in fact constitutes a realistic programme.
>
> In parallel with slippages at AV Roe's there have been delays elsewhere. Elliott Brothers have not kept to their programme on the Inertia Navigator, but they have always been able to say that AV Roe have been unable to prepare an aircraft to carry the Navigator. De Havilland's are 12 months late in the supply of Spectre engines and this may have caused some delay to the W.103 light alloy programme, but again an aircraft has not been ready to start the trials. Armstrong Siddeley are two or three months late with the Stentor [rocket motor for the missile] but this is not holding up AV Roe and in fact the latest engine program shows that the Stentor is likely to be well in advance of the missiles.
>
> It is difficult to get A V Roe to appreciate the magnitude of the task and plan in detail to ensure that timescales are matched and that no component

part is overlooked. After much badgering a Planning Section was set up early this year and this section reduced the June 1958 plan referred to above. However, this is of very little value unless all concerned are convinced that it is a workable plan and that some one person or section has the power to insist that all sections play their part.

The weakness in WRD is in Project Management and in the lack of delegated responsibilities. There is no one under the Chief Engineer with power to coordinate the efforts of sections, and to insist on action to keep to programmes.... Again in my talk with Kay he tells me that they are considering creating such a post, but there may still remain the problem of effective coordination with other divisions of A V Roe, such as Production and Administration.

The situation is also unsatisfactory on the financial side. Estimates are slow to appear; details are lacking and would revisions are made without sufficient justification of additional expenditure, but no doubt with the indecision and lack of planning coordination within the firm, the difficulties of producing detailed estimates are considerable.

These criticisms reflect on the management of the firm as a whole and raise grave views as to the ability to handle a project of this magnitude. Much more effective management and control are required if the project as a whole is to be put on a satisfactory basis. The appointment of a coordinator for Blue Steel under Francis should help.

I must emphasise one point—we are still not convinced on present evidence and in the light of the firm's recent performance that even their revised programme discussed at the Production Meeting on 15 October is realistic and capable of being met.

With the slippage of 7 months before the programme even gets into its stride, the probability of snags in the missiles during firing trials (there have already been some) and with the optimistic firing program proposed by AV Roe's, it is our view ... that a full CA [Controller of Aircraft] release to the Service be difficult to achieve, even at the end of 1962. I believe AV Roe also do not disagree.[1]

Blue Steel was intended to be in service for the period 1960–64. In the event, it struggled to reach an operational capability by 1964, and even then, there were severe restrictions on its use. Preparing a missile from scratch could take several hours, which was not very desirable as a deterrent.

A range of 100 miles was all that was possible in the early 1950s, but as guidance technology advanced, the Air Staff began looking at longer range missiles. This led to another requirement, Operational Requirement 1149, for a missile with a range of 1,000 miles. A variety of proposals were

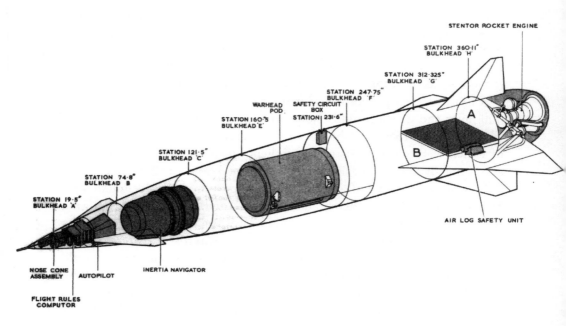

STENTOR ROCKET ENGINE

STATION 360·11"
BULKHEAD 'H'

STATION 312·325"
BULKHEAD 'G'

STATION 247·75"
BULKHEAD 'F'

WARHEAD
POD

SAFETY CIRCUIT
BOX

STATION 231·6"

STATION 160·5
BULKHEAD 'E'

STATION 121·5"
BULKHEAD 'C'

STATION 74·8"
BULKHEAD B

STATION 19·5"
BULKHEAD 'A'

A

B

AIR LOG SAFETY UNIT

NOSE CONE
ASSEMBLY

AUTOPILOT

INERTIA NAVIGATOR

FLIGHT RULES
COMPUTOR

A sectioned drawing of the Blue Steel missile showing the layout of the major components.

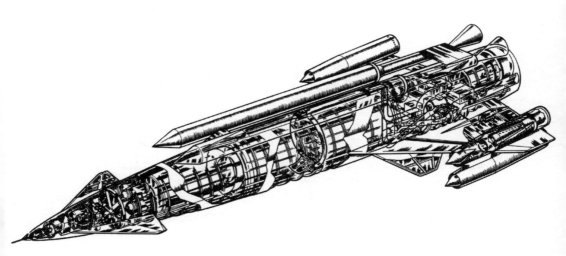

This shows the internal arrangement of the design for the OR 1159 missile. Although Avro produced a plethora of designs, this is the final version, though there may well have been further modifications as development proceeded. There were four turbojets mounted on the wing tips and two jettisonable boost rockets on top. These would have been in the Vulcan bomb bay, clear of the airflow.

received from the major aircraft manufacturers, including Handley Page, Vickers Armstrong, Shorts, and English Electric. Again, one of the major problems was the weight of the warhead, which meant that the missiles ended up being far larger and heavier than they needed to be. In the end, it was decided that the requirement was unrealistic, and it was dropped.

A more modest proposal was made for a missile with a range of only 600 miles and which could be adapted relatively easily to the V bombers. This was OR 1159. Avro had been producing design after design, some of which were more realistic than others. In the end, it was decided to adopt one of the Avro designs, which became known as Blue Steel Mark 2. However, the policy of 'interdependence' proposed by Macmillan after Sputnik meant that in theory, Britain and America would rely on each other in various defence projects. This was distinctly optimistic; the idea that the US would ever rely on British weapons was distinctly remote.

The US Air Force already had a long-range cruise missile, which would soon be in service—Hound Dog—but it was of no interest to the RAF since its geometry meant it could not be carried on the V bombers. Its performance was similar to that of Blue Steel Mark 2. But the US Air Force was also looking at the possibility of a ballistic stand-off missile. This was obviously of great interest to the RAF, and it rendered Blue Steel Mark 2 effectively obsolete. As a result, Blue Steel Mark 2 was cancelled as a result of the deliberations of the British Nuclear Deterrent (Study

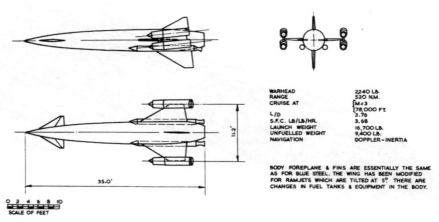

WARHEAD	2240 LB.
RANGE	520 N.M.
CRUISE AT	M=3
	78,000 FT
L/D	3.76
S.F.C. LB/LB/HR.	3.68
LAUNCH WEIGHT	16,700 LB.
UNFUELLED WEIGHT	9,400 LB.
NAVIGATION	DOPPLER—INERTIA

BODY FOREPLANE & FINS ARE ESSENTIALLY THE SAME AS FOR BLUE STEEL. THE WING HAS BEEN MODIFIED FOR RAMJETS WHICH ARE TILTED AT 5° THERE ARE CHANGES IN FUEL TANKS & EQUIPMENT IN THE BODY.

11·2'

35.0'

0 2 4 6 8 10
SCALE OF FEET

4 BRISTOL TYPE 822 (18" DIA) RAMJETS PLUS 2 GOSLING BOOSTERS.

O.R. 1159 MISSILE. (Z.44)

OR 1149 for a long-range stand-off missile had proved to be too ambitious, so a new requirement was issued, OR 1159, which was effectively written around what could be done with an extended Blue Steel; it was referred to as Blue Steel Mark 2. This is one of the many possible designs that AVRO produced.

ELLIOTT AUTOMATION
guides the BLUE STEEL STAND-OFF BOMB

Elliotts produced the inertial navigator and autopilot for Blue Steel. (*aviationancestry. co.uk*)

Group), also known as the Powell Report, which was also instrumental in the cancellation of Blue Streak and which effectively endorsed the purchase of Skybolt.

This did not stop Avro pushing more and more designs at the Ministry of Aviation and the Air Staff, in the forlorn hope that one of them might get adopted. However, the reputation of the Avro WRD had sunk so low that the chances of them being successful were remote. In addition, it was felt that putting any more work to Avro would mean increased delays in Blue Steel Mark 1. Blue Steel would be the first and the last British strategic missile to be deployed.

3

The Rise and Fall of Blue Streak

The ballistic missile has become the ultimate delivery system for nuclear weapons since no practical defence against it has yet been successful, although there have been many attempts (Britain worked on an ABM (anti-ballistic missile) system in the early 1960s and soon realized the difficulties). The ballistic missile is the ultimate stand-off weapon.

The first ever ballistic missile was the missile known to the Germans as the A4 and to the British as the V2. The A4 set the template for all future liquid-fuelled rockets; developments over the past eighty years have been incremental rather than revolutionary, but for military use, liquid-fuelled missiles have almost all been replaced by solid fuel rockets, which are far more robust and far easier to handle.

The payload of the V2 was only 1 ton of high explosive; in addition, the missile was designed to be streamlined so that it would descend through the atmosphere at high speed, and much of the damage was caused not by the high explosive warhead but by the kinetic energy of the descending rocket. Its range was not much more than 200 miles. Given the guidance of the day, accuracy was very poor, with a CEP of around 4 miles; a 4-mile CEP (circular error probability) meant that 50 per cent of the missiles fell within a 4-mile radius of the aiming point.

Early nuclear warheads were extremely heavy, and the ranges needed for nuclear missiles were measured in thousands rather than hundreds of miles. Hence little attention was paid in the 1940s to the idea of delivering nuclear warheads by missile, but as technology began to improve and warheads became lighter, the long-range nuclear-armed missile became increasingly possible. By the mid-1950s, Britain, America, and the Soviet Union were all looking at designs for such missiles.

The problem for Britain was that, apart from launching three V2s at Cuxhaven in Germany soon after the end of the war, it had little or no experience of ballistic missiles, but instead, it had concentrated on defensive surface-to-air missiles to defend the UK against attack from bombers—the Russian equivalent of the V bombers. Ironically, just as the Bloodhound weapon had been developed and deployed, the threat changed from bombers to ballistic missiles. Britain was also finding it difficult to produce a warhead that was light enough to fire over a distance of 2,000 miles since at that time, Britain had not yet exploded its first fusion device.

The answer was to license the technology for a long-range missile from the United States. The main rocket structure was to be built by de Havilland Propellers using welding machines bought from Convair. The rocket motors were to be built by Rolls-Royce using motors licensed from North American Aviation; although, to be fair, they were heavily re-engineered. Like its contemporary American and Russian counterparts, it would burn liquid oxygen and kerosene.

The missile, to be known as Blue Streak, was opposed by many in Whitehall—in particular, by the Treasury. The licensing fee for the body and the rocket motors had to be paid in dollars at a time when the currencies were not freely convertible. Special permission had to be obtained from the Treasury for this dollar payment, and the Chancellor of the Exchequer, Rab Butler, delayed the payment on the following grounds:

> Anything could happen in this field in the next 6 weeks. America might offer us the knowhow. Russia might agree to a halt in atomic tests. Everyone might agree that we should not make more fissile material. We might decide not to make a British missile.[1]

Even the Permanent Secretary of the Ministry of Supply, the Ministry that was responsible for the development of Blue Streak, Sir Cyril Musgrave, was against it, as one Treasury official noted:

> I explained that the Chancellor had felt it desirable to hold up his approval of this transaction until he had an opportunity of considering the future of the M.R.B.M. in relation to the rest of the air weapons programme. On this, I believed that the Ministry of Defence were on the point of producing a paper. I would certainly do what I could to accelerate both its appearance and consideration. Sir Cyril Musgrave turned out to be a bitter opponent of the M.R.B.M. and a passionate advocate of the supersonic bomber [the Avro 730, cancelled in 1957]. He evidently relished locking horns with the Ministry of Defence on this subject.[2]

Despite its unpopularity in Whitehall, work on Blue Streak continued, mainly because there was no alternative. Ballistic missiles were now the future. Yet one reason for its lack of support was the amount of money the project was threatening to swallow. Expenditure for 1957–59 amounted to about £20 million per year (by comparison, the United States Air Force had budgeted $1.335 billion (£480 million at the current exchange rate) for ballistic missiles in 1958 alone). The planned method of deployment in deep underground silos threatened to be even more expensive.

From the outset, it had been realised that a missile such as Blue Streak could not be deployed out in the open as it was extremely fragile. The skin was made of stainless steel so thin that the missile could not stand up under its own weight. The tanks had to be pressurised like a balloon to prevent the missile from crumpling into a heap. The intention was to deploy it from what was described as an 'underground launcher'. This is what today would be described as a missile silo. In 1955, the concept was entirely new, and a research project was begun at the Rocket Propulsion Establishment at Westcott, Buckinghamshire. This involved building a one-sixth scale model of the launcher and test firing rocket motors inside it to see what would happen. It is strange to think that some of the earliest work on that ultimate Cold War icon, the missile silo, was done in the English countryside.

The final design for the launcher was a reinforced concrete cylinder that was 66 feet in internal diameter and 134 feet deep, surrounded by a 0.75-inch mild steel liner, capped by a sliding lid that would weigh 400 tons. The cylinder was split in two vertically—one half containing seven stories of living accommodation and the other containing the missile. The missile was housed in one arm of a U-tube, so that when the rocket motors fired, the exhaust gases were passed down the U-tube and out the other end. Such a structure would be extremely expensive to build, and there were plans to build sixty such launchers. One snag was that finding locations for these launchers was proving extremely difficult. They had to be reasonably remote (which is not easy in the UK), preferably on the eastern side of England, and in suitable geological sites. One problem was that the water table in the UK is not that far down, which ruled out many potential sites.

In June 1959, the Prime Minister, Harold Macmillan, held a weekend meeting at his country house at Chequers, to which some of the most senior civil servants and the military chiefs of staff were invited. The purpose was to brainstorm future policy for the next ten years; defence spending—in particular, spending on the deterrent—was one of the topics involved. It was recommended that a study group be set up to look at the deterrent, but Duncan Sandys, the Minister of Defence, who was one of Blue Streak's major supporters, equivocated. Sandys, however, was moved from Defence after the October 1959 general election, to be replaced by Harold

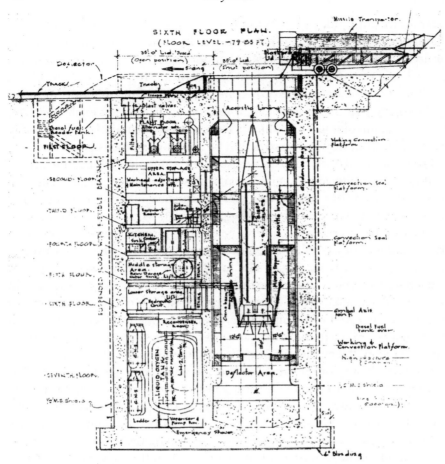

The 'underground launcher' or missile silo designed for Blue Streak. This is taken from the original architect's drawings of the launcher. Such a concept was extremely advanced for its time (1959), and features of the Blue Streak silo can be found in the design of the Titan II missile silo. Blue Streak was a first-generation ballistic missile, and the only available British warheads at the time were relatively heavy. This meant a large missile and a correspondingly large launcher. They would be extremely expensive, and finding suitable sites for these launchers would have been problematic. However, the idea that aircraft sitting in the open air on airfields are somehow less vulnerable than this deep underground launcher does seem fanciful. The launcher was designed to survive a 1-megaton blast half a mile away.

Watkinson. Thus, the British Nuclear Deterrent Study Group (BNDSG) was set up under the chairmanship of the Permanent Secretary at the Ministry of Defence, Sir Richard Powell. The study group was also known as the Powell Committee, and by extension, the report as the Powell Report.

Early drafts and minutes from the meeting of the study group are relatively bland. A review of the *status quo* was given, but deliberations were little further than that. Two events were to change this.

The first was a long and discursive paper from the Air Ministry Scientific Strategic Policy Committee, a little-known body that was chaired by Solly Zuckerman. Although the copy in the archives is unsigned, the style is unmistakably that of Zuckerman. It considers, among other things, the 'vulnerability' of the Blue Streak underground launchers, and in the words of Douglas Adams, it concludes that an 'infinitely improbable' event could also be considered as 'finitely probable'; in other words, if enough Russian missiles were launched at the UK in a first strike, then inevitably virtually all the silos would be destroyed. If this was the case, then the missiles would have to be fired before the first attack; in other words, Blue Streak was condemned as a 'fire-first' weapon, which was politically unacceptable. One of the crucial points about this analysis would be exactly how many Russian missiles would be needed.

The second event was the progress made in America on the Skybolt programme. When this became known to the committee, it changed things drastically. Before Skybolt, there had been no alternative to Blue Streak. Skybolt not only offered an alternative, but it also offered one that was far more attractive. Historian Richard Neustadt made a study of the effects of the cancellation of Skybolt for President Kennedy:

> Harold Watkinson, then Defence Minister, recalls late in 1959 when the British were deciding to abandon BLUE STREAK (their surface-to-surface missile) because of mounting costs combined with RAF distaste for 'sitting in silos', there came a 'bolt from the blue': reports of American enthusiasm for SKYBOLT.[3]

Skybolt was different from Blue Steel and all the other British air-launched missile proposals; Skybolt was a true ballistic missile. One argument against Blue Steel and the others is that they had to fly within the atmosphere, and so they were vulnerable to missile defences. Intercepting re-entry vehicles from ballistic missiles fired from 1,000 miles away was a good deal more difficult.

From almost every point of view, Skybolt fitted Britain's requirements perfectly. It was to be developed by the Americans, with Britain contributing little or nothing towards the development costs. All it needed to do was to buy the finished product. The US Air Force would guarantee that the final

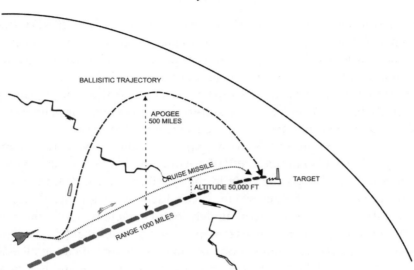

This illustrates the difference between a ballistic missile and a cruise missile. The ballistic missile soars out of the atmosphere and re-enters 1,000 miles later. The cruise missile travels at a height of around 50,000 feet and is very much more vulnerable to missile defences.

design would be fully compatible with the V bombers, and Skybolt would give them a new lease of life. Blue Streak with its cryogenic fuel seemed to be obsolescent, and the silos seemed to be an open-ended cheque. Cancellation of Blue Streak would solve many problems. Whitehall was delighted. The Services were equally delighted since less money being spent on nuclear weapons might mean that more would be spent on conventional weapons. One of the last champions of Blue Streak, the RAF, was equally delighted since as Watkinson observed, they would no longer be sitting in holes in the ground but instead doing what a proper air force should do: fly aircraft.

Yet if Blue Streak was to be dropped in favour of Skybolt, some pretext had to be found. A great deal of money had already been spent on the project, and simply to cancel it without some form of adequate excuse was politically unacceptable. The opposition would have had a field day in Parliament. The whole point of Blue Streak was that it would be deployed in underground launchers and if these launchers could survive a nuclear attack, then such issues as how long it took to fuel the missile became irrelevant. Indeed, the operational requirement for the underground launcher had specified that not only should it be able to withstand a nuclear attack, but that it should be capable of launching the missiles for a period of up to twenty-four hours after any attack.

The question was: what scale of attack would be necessary? The answer the Powell Committee came up with was an attack by 300 to 400 missiles carrying 3-MT warheads. The crucial paragraphs in the report of the study group read:

> Before deciding to mount a pre-emptive attack, the Soviet government would need to be confident that they could neutralise the bulk of the 60 BLUE STREAK sites with one swift blow, in order to prevent any substantial weight of counterattack. If we assume that the Soviet attack would be made of ballistic missiles of an accuracy equal to that which we expect to achieve ourselves (0.55 NM) and that a warhead of at least 3 MT would be available, 95 per cent of the underground BLUE STREAK sites could be destroyed by between 300-400 Soviet missiles ... we have no doubt that the Soviet stockpile by 1967 would be sufficient to provide these warheads for attack on the United Kingdom ...
>
> This analysis shows that unless the political decision were delegated, the Soviet Union could carry out a successful pre-emptive attack on the BLUE STREAK sites, whether these were underground or on the surface; and that even if the political decision were delegated, the Soviet Union could still make a successful pre-emptive attack on the United Kingdom alone ... Because BLUE STREAK missiles could only be successfully fired before a Soviet nuclear attack on this country, an underground deployment is not strictly necessary ...[4]

An attack on this scale would not only have destroyed the Blue Streak sites; since they would have been ground bursts, they would have produced enough fallout that, given a good westerly wind, the whole of Western Europe and probably western Russia would have been rendered uninhabitable. It is not much point attacking a small deterrent in a country such as the UK if at the same time you destroy your own cities with the resultant fallout.

The conclusion of the study group was even more surprising given the minutes of a meeting of the study group held a month earlier to discuss the draft report:

> ... the calculations show that, in order to neutralise 95% of the planned Blue Streak sites in this country, the Soviet Union would have to deliver some 400 × 3 MT warheads, i.e. the explosive yield from the attack would be equivalent to 1,200,000 tons of TNT. Such an attack would not only obliterate this country, but would also inevitably result in a serious radioactive fallout hazard in large parts of Western Europe and the Soviet Union. In such circumstances the United States would be bound to act. For these reasons, it was surely unrealistic to assume that the Soviet leaders would contemplate an attack of this magnitude on the United Kingdom alone.[5]

This does seem to be a remarkable turnaround in a very short period of time. Within the space of a month, a scenario condemned as 'surely unrealistic' has suddenly been elevated to the status of being completely feasible.

An obvious point was raised by the dissenters. No doubt, 400 Russian missiles would take out the Blue Streak silos, but, equally, they would be able to take out the airfields and the V bombers just as effectively. Even if some aircraft were on Quick Reaction Alert (QRA), they would still need time to take off and clear the runway. Given that there was a maximum of thirty-six airfields in the UK that the V bombers could use, the Russians could devote a dozen 3-MT warheads to each one, and the chances of any V bombers escaping would be remote. This was a point glossed over in the Powell Report. The only way in which it could be guaranteed for the bombers to escape a Russian attack would be if the RAF mounted standing patrols—that is, keeping some aircraft in the air twenty-four hours a day. With the existing bomber force, that would not be possible.

What is equally surprising is that the Government's expert on missiles, the CGWL at the Ministry of Aviation, Sir Steuart Mitchell, was obviously kept out of the loop:

> I have now seen the Interim Report of the B.N.D. Study Group ... Adequate opportunities did not occur during the drafting of their report by the Study Group for my Controllerate to brief you properly on the technical issues as they arose, nor to discuss with you the conclusions and recommendations of the report.
>
> I write this to say that now that I have seen the report I am seriously disturbed at the picture it presents in so far as the technical issues are involved, and. that I disagree with some of the conclusions.

It is an interesting question as to why the study group did not consult one of the Government's chief technical specialists on technical matters. Sir Steuart closes his memorandum with the sentence, 'In my view the plan proposed in the report is dangerously unsound'. The phrase 'dangerously unsound' when used by a civil servant in an official memorandum is a polite way of saying the idea is barking mad.

Sir Steuart went on to discuss which of the two systems—Blue Streak or bombers with Skybolt—would be the more vulnerable.

> Blue Streak is condemned because of alleged inability to withstand 300 3-MT rockets directed against 60 sites. It is therefore fair to consider what 300 3-MT bursts could do to our V bomber force.
>
> The Air Ministry claim that they can get '4 bombers airborne from an airfield in 4 minutes', presumably four minutes from the local order to scramble.

The distance travelled by a typical V bomber from the point of take-off (i.e. from point where airborne) is

After 1 minute airborne flight ... 6 n. miles.

After 2 minute airborne flight ... 13 n. miles.

After 3 minute airborne flight ... 20 n. miles.

The disabling radius of a 3-MT airburst against a V bomber is approximately as follows:

V bomber on ground ... 14-15 miles (not tethered since it is about to take off).

V bomber airborne between zero height and 12,000 ft ... 12 miles.

One 3-MT burst over the airfield ... would therefore disable not only all aircraft still on the airfield but also all airborne bombers within 12 miles of the burst.

Further, it would be reasonable to suppose that the Russians, in addition to the airburst directly over the airfield would at the same time lay on two additional airbursts along the direction of the bomber flight path...

It will be seen that the combination of one airburst over the airfield and two airbursts about 14 miles away and about 30 degrees to the axis of the runway would disable not only all aircraft still on the runway but also all aircraft that had become airborne during the preceding 3 minutes. If these rocket bursts occurred at any time within the period up to 6 (not just 4) minutes before the order to scramble, it is difficult to see how any significant number of the bombers could escape.

I do not know the number of airfields which the V bomber force would use under dispersal conditions. But if one supposes the number to be, say, 50 at the most, then to carry out the attack outlined above would require a total of $3 \times 50 = 150$ missiles.

If the Russians were in any doubt as to the direction of take-off of the bombers, they could remove the ambiguity by placing two other airbursts 14 miles at 30° from the other end of the runway to cover the reverse direction of take-off. Thus, for 50 airfields, would require a further 100 missiles, thus bringing the total missiles up to 250, which is still below the 300 postulated for the knocking out of Blue Streak.

Further, a number of the dispersal airfields are understood to be sufficiently near each other for the damage radius of a burst on one airfield to overlap on to the neighbouring airfield, thus reducing the weight of attack required.

Finally, it should be realised that the bomber bases in East Anglia would only get 2½-3 (not 4 minutes as commonly stated) warning by BMEWS of the Russian 1,000-mile rocket if fired on a low trajectory from satellite territory.

It should also be added that it is unlikely that, 'on the night' and for the first time ever, a delay of less than 1-2 minutes would occur between the first radar reception at BMEWS and the local order to Scramble on a bomber airfield.

The S. of S's claim is therefore more correctly stated as being four bombers airborne in 5-6 minutes after first radar reception. The rocket however could burst in less than 4 minutes from first radar reception, and indeed a pattern of bursts an shown in the sketch could burst as late as 7-9 minutes after first radar reception and still catch all or nearly all the bombers.

Bomber Command are well aware of the problem of getting away from bursts directly over an airfield, and are known to have studied optimum escape flight plans. It would be interesting, however, to know how they would cope with a pattern of bursts as outlined in the sketch.[6]

As a description of the vulnerability of bombers on airfields, that is an excellent summing up. Sir Steuart concluded:

The Air Ministry, as far as I know, have never made any external statement on the logistics of maintaining a constant airborne alert. I suggest they should be asked to do so.

In particular, they should be asked what C-in-C Bomber Command does, in a period of tension, if the Russians start jamming BMEWS [Ballistic Missile Early Warning System]. Does he fly off, or does he not?

If he does not fly off, why have BMEWS? If, on the other hand he does fly off, then presumably he would re-land his force in shifts and shake them out on to a constant airborne shift basis. He should then be invited to say how he would handle the subsequent logistics if the jamming of BMEWS continued for, say, six hours, or twenty-four hours, or a week, or a month. It would, I think, be difficult not to be run ragged.

(NOTE. BMEWS would not be difficult to jam sufficiently for this purpose, i.e. to raise doubts in C-in-C Bomber Commands mind, with one or possibly two aircraft jamming from about 200 miles range.)[7]

Duncan Sandys, now sidelined as Minister of Aviation, was the last, probably the only, supporter of Blue Streak left in the government. He produced a memorandum which was circulated around to other ministers, making the same basic points:

The military case for the adoption of SKYBOLT rests primarily on the claim that the 'V' bomber is less vulnerable to a preventive attack than the BLUE STREAK rocket, and that it has not the disadvantage of being a 'fire-first weapon'.

All the expert advice I have received suggests that this is incorrect, for the reasons set out below. The calculations in this paper, which have been made by the Royal Aircraft Establishment at Farnborough, based on the assumptions:—

(a) that the Russians would launch 3-MT rockets on a low trajectory from East Germany, so as to minimise the length of warning we should receive;

(b) that 25 seconds should elapse between the first detection of the rocket attack by the B.M.E.W. Station at Fylingdales and the receipt of the air crews of the order to scramble; and

(c) that 80% of the Russian missiles fired burst within 2 miles of the aiming point, which is well within our assessment of the accuracy and reliability.

Our operational plans provide for the dispersal of the 'V' bomber force on 36 airfields in times of crisis. But it requires from 24 to 48 hours to complete this redeployment. Thus in the event of a surprise attack, out of the blue, our 'V' bombers would be caught on the six main bases. These are sited so close together that the Russians would need to fire at only three aiming points. With six 3-MT rockets (two aimed at each of these points), they would certainly wipe out the whole 'V' bomber force.

In order to destroy our bombers, once they have been alerted and dispersed, the Russians would have to burst a sufficient number of rockets to render it lethal not only the airfields, but also an area around them, up to such distance as the aircraft could fly during the warning period available. The number of rockets needed to do this would vary according to our state of readiness.

Assuming that the bombers had been dispersed, but that the air crews were not kept continuously in the background, the Russians could, with about 50 rockets, destroyed virtually the whole bomber force on its dispersal airfields, many of which are close to one another.

On the other hand, if air crews were sitting in the aircraft in relays day and night, and if the engines were continuously running, it might be possible to reduce to 15 seconds (from the receipt of the order to scramble) the time needed to get wheels rolling. But even if this very high state of readiness can be achieved, it would still be possible for the Russians to eliminate 80% of our 'V' bomber force with about 250 rockets.

That would leave us only about 20 aircraft. With the Russian defences concentrated on them very few would get through, and the threat on this extremely reduced scale would not constitute any appreciable deterrent.

Moreover, it would be unrealistic to imagine that even if the spare crews needed were available, are bomber force could be Poised in the state of extreme alert for more than a short time, on the other hand, experience shows that acute international crises are quite liable to continue for several months on end.

It must also be remembered that this whole system depends upon a single warning station at Fylingdales, which could be jammed by a small number of aircraft flying 100 miles or more away over the North Sea. If that were to occur we should be obliged either to go out and shoot them down and thereby risk provoking war, or alternatively to resort to the ineffective expedient of trying to keep our bombers in the air. We could hope to keep only a small proportion airborne, and that for a very limited period.

It will thus be seen that the calculations in this paper lead clearly to the following conclusions:—

(a) if dispersed, our 'V' bombers are just as vulnerable as BLUE STREAK.

(b) if caught without warning, they are incomparably more vulnerable.

(c) therefore SKYBOLT is just as much a 'fire-first weapon' as BLUE STREAK.[8]

The idea that the entire V force could be scrambled within twenty-five seconds of receiving the first radar reports does seem distinctly fanciful, but this was the logic on which the RAF was working. The paper did arouse some anxiety in the Air Ministry, since if both Skybolt and Blue Streak were 'fire-first' weapons, then the best option would be to go for Polaris. No one attempted to refute the logic in Sandys' paper; indeed, it would be very difficult to so. The simpler technique was merely to ignore it. The decision had been taken on political grounds, not on military grounds.

Even the Navy, which had been vociferously opposed to Blue Streak, was privately dubious about the conclusions of the report:

> I must say it seems hard to believe that the Russians would be prepared to allocate 250 or 300 3-megaton rockets to an attack on this country. Much smaller numbers (45) have been quoted as being sufficient to destroy, by blast, every V bomber.
>
> The conclusion reached by the first paper, that SKYBOLT is just as much a 'fire first' weapon as BLUE STREAK is one which I do not think the Admiralty would wish to disagree. The First Lord will probably not wish to intervene in any controversy which the papers may cause at the Defence Board meeting. Our prime objective must be to ensure that BLUE STREAK is removed from the programme.[9]

A Treasury memorandum made exactly the same point:

> If we say we are going to adopt SKYBOLT, people will at once ask how we meet the argument about the vulnerability of the airfields. The airfields would of course be a great deal more vulnerable than BLUE STREAK's underground installations. The argument is of course that we should keep a due proportion of the V-bombers in the air. But this is tremendously expensive, for it really means keeping them at a war-time state of readiness. The Americans find this too expensive, and when we thought about it earlier the cost was prohibitive. We should therefore have to accept great risks of a surprise attack. Again, it seems to us a tremendous mistake for the Government to announce a decision on the matter of this kind without having worked it out.[10]

When, in 1958, the Air Staff began evaluating the Russian medium-range ballistic missiles that were sited in Germany, the issue of the vulnerability of airfields and missile sites was raised. It was thought that the CEP of the missile was around 1.5 miles; a member of the Air Staff commented:

> This firm information on the accuracy of the 650nm ballistic missile means that we now know that only one megaton weapon has to be delivered on a V base to destroy all the aircraft on that base.[11]

Even the Americans seemed dubious about the proposal to change from Blue Streak to bombers on airfields. An article in the *Observer* newspaper in April 1960 quoted an anonymous United States Air Force general:

> He and other senior officers contend that if a fixed-based missile, like the Blue Streak, is too vulnerable to missile attack, the airfields from which the V-bombers would take off are even more vulnerable.
>
> If the bombers can be destroyed on the ground in a surprise attack it makes little sense to buy the American Skybolt for them. Even with the ballistic missile early-warning station at Fylingdales Moor, Britain would only have a three-minute warning against rockets from East German bases 600 miles away.
>
> Russia already has hundreds of these medium-range rockets and it takes a minimum of 15 minutes to get United States bombers airborne... To avoid having her bombers destroyed on the ground, Britain would have to maintain an airborne alert.
>
> And we don't seem to be able to afford that.

Despite these objections, the report was accepted, mainly because it said what its audience wanted to hear. In his statement to Parliament, Watkinson said: 'The vulnerability of missiles launched from static sites, and the practicability of launching missiles of considerable range from mobile platforms, has now been established'. Since the Powell Report and the debates that followed were kept secret for very many years, most historians have concentrated on the vulnerability issue, and it was assumed that 'vulnerability' referred to such issues as using liquid oxygen, or to the relatively fragile nature of the missile. Both of these were irrelevant; if the silos could survive an attack—and there is no reason to suppose they would not, despite the Powell Report—then the time it would take to prepare and launch the missile was irrelevant. However, it is an idea that has taken deep roots into academic writing and popular histories, which concentrate on the issue of vulnerability without taking into account the proposal to house the missile in silos. Equally unfortunately, these writers were looking at the vulnerability of the Blue Streak silos but not at the vulnerability of aircraft on runways.

In retrospect, it might be said that the debate was rigged; while the Blue Streak silos might have been vulnerable to an attack of enormous proportions, the bomber force was vulnerable to a far smaller attack.

Yet Skybolt was far too attractive a proposition. Although the cancellation of Blue Streak would cause some political embarrassment, it also avoided the political embarrassment of trying to find sites for sixty silos. The pilots of the RAF kept their flying pay rather than being consigned to a hole in the ground. The Treasury could save hundreds of millions of pounds. The Army and Navy were grateful that there might be more money to spare for conventional weapons. The only supporter of Blue Streak was the Ministry of Aviation, and they were easily overruled.

To reduce the political embarrassment of the cancellation, Watkinson announced that the project would be continued in a civilian role as a satellite launcher. Even this would prove to be too expensive for the UK, so partners were sought in Europe, leading to the formation of the European Launcher Development Organisation (ELDO). ELDO began in a blaze of enthusiasm, and Blue Streak was a great technical success. Unfortunately, the same could not be said of the other stages of the launcher, provided by France, Germany, and Italy, and the project died amid a good deal of acrimonious squabbling in 1971.

Yet Blue Streak as a missile had now gone, and the Skybolt story begins.

4

Setting the Scene for Skybolt

One of the major issues with any missile is its accuracy, which in turn depends on its guidance system. Ground-based missiles know their starting point very accurately. This is not the case with an air-launched missile. In this case, the missile has to know its exact position, height, speed, and bearing at the moment of release. Furthermore, most guidance systems are based on gyroscopes. These gyroscopes tend to wander as time goes by, and so the accuracy of any missile becomes less and less at the time of flight becomes longer and longer. A cruise-type missile might travel at 500 knots over a distance of 1,000 miles, which implies a flight time of two hours; during that time, considerable errors can creep into the guidance system, particularly with the fairly primitive guidance systems available in 1950s electronics. In addition, high-flying cruise-type missiles were becoming increasingly vulnerable to defensive surface-to-air missiles.

The first strategic stand-off missile deployed by the US Air Force was Hound Dog, which used a jet engine for propulsion. It had a range of over 700 miles; it flew at a height of 56,000 feet and a speed of Mach 2.1. It could also fly at low level, but this reduced the range. The jet engine was fitted in a pod underneath the missile, but since it was to be carried by the B-52, ground clearance was not an issue. The missile featured small canard foreplanes, rear delta wings with ailerons, and a small fin and rudder. Deployment in the US Air Force began in December 1959. It remained in service for around thirteen years. In very many ways, it was similar to all the air-launched missile proposals for OR1149 and 1159, as well as the later OR 1182.

However, a ballistic missile was always going to be a better option than a cruise missile, and, partly spurred on by the success of the Navy's Polaris programme, the USAF decided to investigate the feasibility of using air-launched ballistic missiles. The RAE was well aware of the work is being carried out, as they had had representatives at the presentations:

> The study requirement SR 168, in response to which fourteen contractors have submitted proposals, asked for consideration of warheads weighing 500 lb, 1000 lb and 1500 lb, and it had become clear that for the smallest of these warheads, a missile with launch weight acceptable to the USAF and capable of 1000 n.m range was feasible. Interest has therefore shifted from the original requirement of 300 n.m to the longer range, and even 1500 n.m. was being considered. It was further apparent that for the smallest warhead 1000 n.m range could be achieved by rocket-propelled missiles, either winged or ballistic. The speeds and heights attained by such vehicles would appear to render them far less vulnerable than missiles propelled by air-swallowing engines, and these latter were therefore no longer of any great interest and had practically faded out of the picture.
>
> The results of the individual studies to SR 168 were not accessible to the UK members of the Task Group, and the information obtained was partly from a USAF presentation, partly by an appraisal by ARDC of the firm's proposals. This appraisal, of which four copies were lent to us for the duration of the discussions, should be available in the UK after the necessary formalities have been completed, but this may take some months. The data quoted here are from these mixed sources and their [*sic.*] appear to be some inconsistencies, probably because the missiles are intended for use on three aircraft (B-52, B-58 and B-70) giving widely ranging launch conditions and it was not always clear during the verbal presentation which aircraft was associated with the missile weights and dimensions quoted. Furthermore, a warhead weight of 600 lb, as for Polaris, was mentioned and it is therefore likely that the missiles described in the USAF presentation were modified somewhat from the SR 168 proposals. The figures of weights and dimensions of most interest to us are those for missiles launched from the B-52, at a nominal speed and height of M = 0.8 and 35,000 feet.[1]

The report went on to describe the test vehicles and the launch programme:

> Some experimental vehicles, sketched in figure 4, had been made and were being fired, by three firms, Martin, Convair and McDonnell. The programme was initially being run at firm's expense, but funding is now via WADC and they are therefore in a better position to control the work. As far as possible, components of missiles already being developed were being used. All the vehicles had Sergeant motors as the main boost, the XM 12 for the Martin and XM 24 for the Convair and McDonnell ... The Martin missile, which had

made a successful flight of about 220 m, launched from a B 47 at M = 0.6, 37,000 feet, is shown in figure 4 (a), and has four rear fins for roll control with four forward fins, indexed at 45 degrees to the rear ones, for pitch and yaw control. Originally, only a flared skirt at the rear had been fitted to stabilise the vehicle, but it had proved unsatisfactory at launch. The missile was released in a horizontal attitude, the motor being ignited 4 secs after launch; the pull-out occurred very shortly afterwards and the climb appeared to be established at about 12 secs, with burn out at M = 7 at 115,000 feet. There was some talk of fitting a Vanguard second stage to the missile in future trials.

The Convair missile, about the same size as the Martin one, has all its controls at the back. The estimated range is 240 m for a M = 2 launch. A launch has been made at M = 0.995 presumably from a B 58, which should have given 175 m range, but it did not result in a successful flight. Apparently the controls were saturated by the attempt to cope with some unexpected demands soon after launch, and failed to re-establish stability. A remark was made, with some pride, that no tunnel-testing had been necessary on this vehicle; this pride seems somewhat unjustified.

The McDonnell missile, described as aero-ballistic, is a shell-shaped body, spinning slowly (about 20-40 rpm) about its long axis, in order, it was said, to even out the temperature distribution. It is designed to fly at incidence, using body lift, and a lift-drag ratio of 2½–3 was estimated. Consideration of the difficulties of estimating (a) the aerodynamic forces that arise in any given attitude (b) the moments necessary to establish the desired attitude, as well as the other problems that would arise in engineering such a missile explain the question mark put against this vehicle by ARDC in the table of 'estimated times to first flight' above. Nevertheless, a ground-launched vehicle is scheduled for firing in January 1959. A Sergeant XM 20 will be used to boost it to 38,000 feet from a ground launcher at 75°. It will coast to 75,000 feet and then the missile motor proper, a Nike-Hercules XM 30, will boost it to M = 6.5. Peak altitude will be 120,000 feet and the glide will be to M = 3 at about 80,000 feet.

The Martin missile was given the name Bold Orion, the Convair missile High Virgo, and the McDonnell missile Alpha Draco.

The Martin Company was awarded the contract for Bold Orion in March 1958, to be launched from a B-47 aircraft. It used a Thiokol Sergeant solid-fuel rocket motor with a nose cone, which held flight control, electronics, and guidance systems. Four missile launches between June and October 1958 revealed a succession of problems in the flight control system, but following a major modification, the fifth missile was launched successfully on 17 November 1958 with a range of about 250 nautical miles.

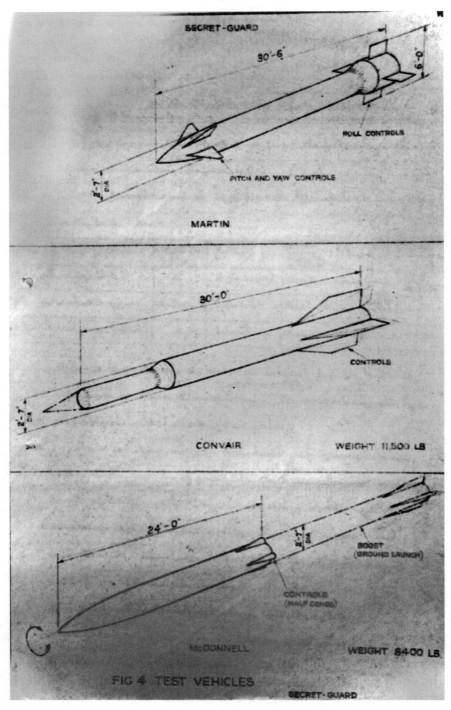

The drawings attached to the RAE report show the three missiles that would become Bold Orion, High Virgo, and Alpha Draco.

Given this success, the USAF was interested in seeing whether the range could be extended, and so a spin stabilised second stage, the Altair, was added. On the first test of the two-stage version, the first stage motor failed to ignite. On the second attempt, the second stage radar beacon signal was lost, but predictions indicated a range of around 930 miles. The last launch, in October 1959, was an attempt to demonstrate that an anti-satellite weapon was possible, and was aimed at the Explorer VI satellite at an altitude of 156 miles. It passed within 4 miles of the satellite.

Project 199C, High Virgo, was to use a supersonic B-58 to launch the missile. Lockheed and Convair produced a proposal which was accepted by the Air Force, which was 31 feet long, using a XM-20 solid propellant rocket motor. The first launch was a failure since the missile went out of control a few seconds after launch. The second launch on 19 December reached a range of 185 nautical miles with an apogee of about 44 miles. The third missile flew successfully on 4 June 1959, following a Mach 1.46 launch at 40,000 feet. The missile was steered with four movable fins, and the first two flights used a pre-programmed flight profile, as did the early Skybolt test missiles. The third flight used an inertial navigation system, derived partly from the Hound Dog missile, and was completely successful. The fourth and final flight was also intended as a satellite interception, but about thirty seconds after launch, contact was lost with the vehicle.

Project 199D, named Alpha Draco, was built by McDonnell Aircraft. Again, it was boosted by Thiokol Sergeant rockets. This was not a ballistic missile but what was described as a boost-glide. It was launched to a height of nearly 100,000 feet before the gliding re-entry vehicle separated and steered itself to a pre-programmed destination. Again, this was a success, but a boost-glide vehicle is more vulnerable to missile defences than a purely ballistic missile.

From the results of these launches, it was clear that launching a ballistic missile from an aircraft in flight was perfectly feasible. Thus, the way ahead to Skybolt was now clear.

5

The Origins of Skybolt

The Air Ministry commented:

> Following the Interdependence meeting between the Heads of Government of the U.K., the U.S.A. and Canada in September 1957, a Tripartite Technical Committee met in Washington in December 1957 and established a number of sub-committees to cover specified areas, one of which was strategic air-to-surface weapon systems. Sub-committee D decided that an examination of the field should be undertaken by a joint RAF/USAF Task Group which met in Washington in April and November 1958.[1]

The RAF already had the Blue Steel stand-off missile in development at the time, but Blue Steel had limitations in terms of range and was not a true ballistic missile. While there were British contenders for the new requirement, OR 1159, the proposed joint missile might also fit the bill.

Having the UK on board was no doubt useful for the USAF since they could claim that costs would be reduced as a consequence of the British contribution, and it is likely that they thought the credibility of the system would be increased by British participation. Sir Frederick Brundrett, Chief Scientist at the Ministry, noted to Sir Richard Powell (Permanent Secretary at the MOD) in January 1959:

> They are anxious this should be a joint project, in the sense that we should agree to go ahead with them. To this end they are prepared to give a guarantee that the weapon they develop will be compatible with the V bombers. They do not expect to do this for four months, but are anxious

that we be associated fully with their thinking and would welcome United Kingdom representation in their Project Office.[2]

However, although this might nominally be a joint project, there was no doubt at all that the US Air Force was the driving force and that the UK was very much along for the free ride. Whereas the US could hedge its bets by deploying as many different systems as they could irrespective of cost, effectively, the UK was looking for the single cheapest system it could find.

The Task Group then issued a requirement for an air-launched missile, which would be known initially in the US as WS138A. The requirement was circulated to American aerospace companies; a meeting was held to begin to evaluate their proposals. To the astonishment of the British representatives present, proposals were produced from more than 100 American firms. The meeting narrowed this down to a mere fifteen, who then gave brief presentations.

> There was a bidders' presentation from the 18th to 20 March 1959, at which British representatives are present. Each bidder was given about 40 minutes to present his case and 15 firms took part. These 15 had been weeded out of over 100 firms who were originally in the competition. These included Martin, Republic, Fairchild, Convair, Temco, North American, McDonnell, Raytheon, R.C.A., Lockheed, Douglas, Boeing, Hughes, Northrop, Bell/ Ramo Wooldridge. All but Temco, Raytheon and R.C.A. proposed two-stage solid-fuelled ballistic missiles.[3]

One of the conditions of the meeting was that there should be no personal approaches from any of the bidders to the working party. The British delegation had been instructed that if such an approach was attempted, it should be met with a firm refusal to discuss anything. In addition, the bidders have been instructed that they must not communicate directly with the V bomber firms. One of the British team who was present remarked:

> Of the original 100 possible contenders for this contract, 25 made firm bids and during the dates of the presentation a total of 15 remained in the competition. I gained the impression, and this was largely confirmed by the Working Party, that almost any one of these 15 potential contractors could produce a weapon system in all ways superior to Blue Steel at varying dates between mid-1961 and mid-1963.[4]

Considering that Blue Steel had already been under development for two years by March 1959 and would not be operational until 1963, that is quite a revealing comment.

The British observers made brief notes of the various proposals, listed here in a slightly edited form:

Martin Aircraft

This proposal embraced pure inertial linked to a star tracker and embodying terminal guidance in the form of map matching. The missile will be of plastic body construction and ballistic form incorporating two-stage solid propellant motors. The missile weight would be 9,800 lb and the total cost for an order of 500 missiles is claimed to be $410M.

Confidence—good.

Republic Aircraft

This proposal embraces a two-stage solid ballistic missile weighing 9,800 lb with a range of 1,200 miles. The guidance system is Stellar Inertial which would probably be mounted in the aircraft pylon with a slave in the missile. Only one such missile could be accommodated on the V aircraft and, in this case, the CEP would be approximately 12,000 feet at 1,200 miles. Estimated cost for 500 missiles—310M.

Confidence—not very good

Fairchild Corporation

The proposal is for a boost-glide liquid-propelled rocket embracing pre-packaged fuel and weighing 8900 lb. The length is approximately 26 feet long but in this form, they may be some C of G difficulties. Guidance is Stellar Inertial and only one missile could be carried by a V bomber. Estimated cost for 500 missiles—$310M.

Convair

This proposal embraces a boost-glide single- or double-stage solid propellant missile with an inertial midcourse guidance system linked to map matching for the final stage. The missile has a range of 1,200 miles and would weigh 9,900 lb.

Confidence—very good.

Temco Corporation

This proposal embraces a boost-glide two-stage liquid-propelled missile embodying pre-packaged fuel. An inertial guidance system is included in the missile with Stellar monitoring from the parent aircraft which is claimed to give a range of 1,500 miles from a subsonic launch. The missile weighs 5,700 lb and the claim is that the first missile could fly in 14 months and the first squadron could be equipped in 40 months. Estimated cost for 500 missiles—$296M.

Confidence—good.

North American

This proposal embraces a ballistic missile with two solid propellant stages, the guidance of which is based on Stellar Inertial with map matching for the final stage. Accuracy on the V force would be very low because of the need for the missile to have Stellar guidance before launch.

Confidence—very good.

McDonnell

This proposal embraces an aero-ballistic missile with inertia guidance in mid-course and map matching for final stages. It includes two stages of solid propellant the missile is 39-foot long and weighs 8,100 lb but assumes a warhead weight of less than 600 lb.

Confidence—highly imaginative.

Raytheon

The proposal is for a Skip rocket embracing single stage solid propulsion and relying on inertial navigation coupled with map matching. Weight 4,000 lb. The missile could have provision for three or four alternate target possibilities and provision can be made for coding the missile progress up to the point of impact.

Confidence—questionable.

RCA

This proposal embraces a two-stage storable liquid-propelled ballistic missile of less than 7,000 lb all-up weight with provision for a re-entry head of 1,000 lb. Inertial guidance is proposed linked to data transfer from the parent aircraft. The length of the missile is 20 feet with an overall diameter of 30 inches.

Confidence—not very good.

Lockheed Aircraft

The proposal embraces a two-stage solid propelled ballistic missile weighing 10,000 lb.

Confidence—good.

Douglas

This proposal embraces a two-stage solid propellant all-inertial missile with star tracker facilities required in the parent aircraft. The all up weight is under 8,000 lb for a length of 26 feet. A CEP of 3 nautical miles at a range of 1,150 miles is claimed for the V bombers.

Confidence—most encouraging

Boeing aircraft

This proposal embraces a ballistic two-stage solid propellant rocket, relying on inertial mid-course guidance and map matching for terminal guidance all up weight is 9,700 lb and a range of 1,500 miles.

Confidence—questionable.

Hughes Aircraft

This proposal embraces a rather complex system of Stellar inertial infrared and possibly map matching two-stage solid ballistic missile. The all-up weight is 9,000 lb and it is 25 feet long. The missile will be housed in a pod carried on a pylon and the pod would be stripped prior to release. A CEP in the V bombers of worse than 4 miles is likely because of lack of Stellar information.

Confidence—questionable if the fully complex system is maintained.

Northrop Aviation

This proposal embraces a two-stage solid propelled ballistic missile with Stellar inertial guidance. The all up weight is 11,000 lb and length 39 feet. CEP for the V force is 3.02 miles at a range of 1,400 miles.

Confidence—good.

Bell

This is a two-stage solid ballistic missile weighing 9,100 lb with a length of 26 feet. The missile relies on Stellar inertial guidance prior to launch but pure inertial after launch. The missile system allows up to 100 target selection possibilities and provides for re-targeting less than 10 seconds. Encouraging growth potential. Pylon attachment to V bombers considered essential.

Confidence—good.

The author went on to say:

It is possible that the final selection will be made from one of the proposals presented by Martin, Convair, McDonnell, or Lockheed. These four presented the most acceptable technical proposals but it does not necessarily follow that the best management and technical proposal will receive the contract. The Source Selection Board indicated that politics would play a not inconsiderable part. Hughes Aircraft Corporation proposed a very acceptable solution but the current workload on that Corporation may well reduce their chances of being selected contractor.[4]

PUBLISHED WEEKLY

Airview News

VOLUME 22   MONDAY, JANUARY 18, 1960   **NO. 23**

Gen. White Praises Sky Bolt

Special Airview Picture Page for AID Next Week

Airview News will carry a special one-page layout in its regular edition next Monday to help launch Douglas AID-United Givers week beginning January 25.

In addition to informing n o n - participating employes how they may join the Douglas AID chapter, the AID layout will contain features and stories detailing the way AID funds work for the underprivileged in various communities.

President Donald W. Douglas, Jr. will prepare a special AID message.

Credit Union Holds Annual Meet Jan. 26

The annual shareholders' meeting of the Douglas Aircraft Federal Credit Union will be held in the dining room of the Globemaster Grill, 2907 Ocean Park Blvd., Santa Monica, at 4:15 p.m., January 26, 1960.

The board of directors will report to the shareholders on the accomplishments of the Credit Union for t h e year 1959. Other

DOUGLAS STUDY WORK PROCEEDS ON POTENT AF AIR-LAUNCH MISSILE

General Thomas D. White, Chief of Staff, United States Air Force, publicly lauded the Sky Bolt, an air-to-ground missile for which Douglas is the prime contractor, in a speech last week at the National Press Club in Washington.

Work on the Air Force's Sky Bolt missile system, also known as GAM-87, is proceeding now at Douglas' Santa Monica division on funds allotted in a study contract.

In lauding the Sky Bolt, General White said:

"For the present, the advent of long-range air-to-surface weapons launched from aircraft presents us with a whole new realm of possibilities. Early this year, the first of these weapons will be operational with Strategic Air Command units.

"One of them, the Hound Dog, is a supersonic air - to - surface weapon with a nuclear warhead. It will enable t h e bomber to launch attacks while still several hundred miles from its designated target.

"**We also have under study an air-launched ballistic missile. This missile, which I have nicknamed the Sky Bolt, will, of course, be hypersonic. It is being designed to attain ranges of approximately one thou-** sand miles. We have already proved in prototype tests of this new weapon that it can be launched from aircraft at both subsonic and supersonic speeds.

"You can well imagine t h e potential of such weapons when carried by o u r current longrange b o m b e r aircraft — a n d eventually by nuclear propelled aircraft with practically unlimited endurance. This combination of aircraft and missile will provide our country with the most mobile striking power ever achieved.

"Sky Bolt aircraft would possess true global mobility. They could operate over the high seas, friendly land masses, or areas inaccessible by other means — with the capability of attacking within minutes. In addition, they would be essentially invulnerable to surprise attack."

From these fifteen bids, Douglas—not a bid regarded as being in the top four by the British observers—was chosen to produce the final design. In view of the saga that would follow as to the design of the missile, this was not perhaps the best choice.

One of the principal motives behind the US Air Force requirement was the desire not to be left out of the scramble among the US armed services for nuclear weapons systems. There was a considerable amount of inter-service rivalry (just as in the UK), and the Air Force considered that if the Navy could launch a ballistic missile from a submarine, then the Air Force could launch one from a bomber.

A system such as the new proposed missile would significantly enhance Strategic Air Command's capability and credibility. However, it was not envisaged so much as a strategic weapon, a 'city buster', but rather more as a tactical device. SAC's long-range bombers would take several hours to reach the heart of the USSR and would have to overfly a good deal of hostile territory. The new missile was intended to be fired as the aircraft approached the Russian borders, and the relatively low yield warhead (1 MT and 400 kT were the initial choices for the warhead) was designed to suppress Russian air defences so that the aircraft would be able to deliver their multi-megaton bomb load to Russian cities unmolested.

> The USAF has consistently maintained that Skybolt is a secondary weapon to be used to allow the bombers to penetrate the defences and drop the gravity bomb on those targets requiring accuracy.[5]

It would not be a major weapon in the US arsenal, which would soon contain Atlas, Titan, and Minuteman ICBMs, plus Polaris and the bombers of SAC. Instead, SAC saw it as a way of enhancing its credibility, so it would not be elbowed out by these other systems. However, in 1959, only Atlas was ready to be deployed; all other systems were still under development and had not been deployed. Skybolt joined the list as one of the many possible weapons systems. Although the US Air Force was great advocates of the system, others in the Department of Defense were less enthusiastic.

So, in effect, the UK wanted to be able to purchase a highly sophisticated weapon that they would not have to have the expense of designing and developing. In addition, rather than deploy various different delivery systems, as America was doing, with its emphasis on land-, sea-, and air-based systems, they wished to concentrate on just the one; despite the limited requirement in terms of numbers (the RAF would take perhaps 100 missiles, the USAF 1,000), the British still wished to have a say in the design of the weapon so that it would be usable by British aircraft, such as the V bombers.

The UK also wanted to exert influence over US policymaking—a much more difficult process, as Wing Commander Bunting of the BJSM (British joint services mission) noted in October 1959:

> I have discussed with Col. Low the question of the validity of the USAF action in changing their policy without consulting us. Although he is sympathetic he has adopted the line that they are taking our interests into account and so far they have not changed their policy and might not do so. I cannot help feeling however that if they consider that an advanced Hound Dog is the thing to go for, they will do so regardless of us. Having been working and living intimately with the USAF for a year I believe that most of the officers at the lower levels consider us to be a hindrance rather than a worthwhile ally.

Hound Dog was not ballistic and could not be fitted to the V bombers.

Such motives would lie behind very many of the UK actions with regard to nuclear weapons. The archetype was, of course, the strenuous, almost desperate, efforts to resume Anglo-American co-operation on nuclear weapons, almost regardless of the other distortions of policy that were implied. Thus, not only with Skybolt, but with Polaris and Trident, the UK wanted to buy a weapons system already developed and up and running, expect to be able to operate it independently, and yet offer little in exchange.

Indeed, regarding financial liability, in a memorandum dated May 1959, the Ministry of Supply wanted confirmation from America of the following:

(a) UK should not contribute to the basic development costs.
(b) missile and associated aircraft and ground equipment will be developed for V bomber application.
(c) UK will pay only extra development costs involved in making missile compatible with V bomber.
(d) range and trials facilities needed in US provided free of charge.
(e) development missiles and experimental hardware provided at UK cost unless US will provide free.
(f) supply of production equipment on government to government basis.
(g) free and full user rights will be awarded to UK.[7]

This implicit policy was to become much more explicit in the 1960s. After the cancellation of Blue Streak in 1960, there was never again an attempt to develop an indigenous strategic delivery system with the possible exception of the Polaris improvement system, Chevaline (although this was still dependent on American missiles). Instead, the 'buy American' policy was to become much more overt, to the anger of many in British industry.

A report on the progress to date of WS138A, as the project was then known, was prepared by Group Captain Bonser of the Air Staff in July 1959 after a visit to the USA. The initial requirement issued in January had been for a joint USAF/RAF missile with a range of 1,000 nautical miles, a weight of 10,000 lb and a circular error probability of 3,000 feet (meaning that 50 per cent of the missiles should fall within a radius of 3,000 feet from the target.) The warhead would either be a lightweight one of 600 lb and a yield of 0.4 MT (400 kT), or a heavier 1-MT warhead, which would cut the range to 600 miles.

The weight of the warhead was important for two reasons—firstly, the British would have problems producing an indigenous warhead of

only 700 lb in weight and, secondly, because there was a crucial pay off
between weight of warhead and range. Any increase in weight of the
warhead would cut the range considerably.

In all other respects, it fitted British requirements perfectly. The range
was such that strikes against almost any part of the Soviet Union could be
launched without having to fly over hostile territory. Each Vulcan bomber
would be able to carry two missiles comfortably. Given that the US was
to pay the development costs, it would be an extremely cheap deal, which
offered the possibility of extending the useful life of the V bombers by
several years.

In the meantime, the Department of Defense had not been impressed
with the work Douglas had done. Unfortunately, Skybolt was to become
a victim of American internal politics, particularly between the USAF and
the Department of Defense (DoD) in the Pentagon; the extent of this was
not fully appreciated by British officials. Skybolt was very much a project
put forward by the USAF, and there were many in the DoD who opposed
it. Even from the outset, Skybolt was to be the victim of turf warfare
between the Air Force and the DoD.

As part of the reorganisation of defence after the launch of Sputnik,
which had had a galvanising effect on the American Defense Department,
a new position was created in the DoD, the Director of Defense Research
and Engineering (DDR&E). The first DDR&E was Herbert York, who
had been the first director of Lawrence Livermore National Laboratory.
The director was responsible for 'supervising all research and engineering
in the Defense Establishment'.

John Rubel, who was then working for Hughes Aircraft, was invited
to become assistant director. After the Kennedy Administration took
over, Rubel was asked to stay on by McNamara as Assistant Secretary
of Defense for Research and Engineering. Rubel was a constant and
consistent opponent of Skybolt, describing it rather extravagantly as 'a
proposal of enormous complexity and dubious feasibility'. Fortunately for
historians, Rubel has written extensively about his time in the Pentagon
and, in particular, about Skybolt. From his writings, he comes over as a
forceful individual who would not suffer fools lightly, but his is, to put it
mildly, not an altogether unbiased account.

Prior to the establishment of the Defense Research and Engineering
Department in the Pentagon, the Air Force ran its own research and
development without any supervision from the DoD. The point of
the new department was that it would oversee all defence research and
development. Skybolt fell between the two. The Air Force had started the
project independently of the DoD, and now found themselves no longer
masters in their own house. Soon after Rubel was appointed, he was given

a briefing by the USAF on Skybolt, which he found distinctly patronising. He described it thus:

> The top chart identified the briefing subject: the ALBM. The second chart was a cartoon-like sketch showing a mushroom cloud above the inscription: Atomic bombs are powerful. The rest of the briefing was almost equally empty of content, an emptiness that conveyed an air of arrogance, as if the mighty Air Force could simply start a major development by making a pro-forma, ill-conceived presentation to me and then expect to have a multi-million dollar undertaking approved. Approved in the name of what? One more weapon, or one more ballistic missile, doing something that hadn't been done before, with the flimsiest of operational justifications? I was not impressed.[8]

As a consequence, he withheld approval for the project, asking for more detailed work to be carried out by Douglas. This did not make him popular with the Air Force. Soon after that briefing, he had a meeting with General Curtis LeMay, who might also be described as a rather forceful personality. He wrote up the conversation in his autobiography, and part of it refers to Skybolt:

> I turned to the ALBM matter. *You say I am holding up the ALBM. What I have done is to show how ill-prepared the contractor is to be given the go-ahead*. I asked him if he knew how much had already been spent on the ALBM for nothing more than some basic studies critical to any successful project. He said he didn't.
>
> About $10 million, I said. And do you know what you've got for your money? I asked. He said he didn't. I pointed to some papers on his desk. See those papers on your desk? You have ALBM reports from Douglas about as thick as that thin pile. Do you know what they are worth? He looked quizzical. About as much as the paper they are printed on, I said [Emphasis as original].[9]

Rubel consulted with Herbert York, the Director of Defense Research and Engineering, and they both considered that the technical difficulties—particularly regarding propulsion, guidance and control, and the airborne selection of the multiplicity of targets—had been treated by Douglas with undue optimism. Before they would release more money, they wanted a critical reappraisal of the project.

Douglas had initially prepared a design designated Able 1, with seven nozzles and a bulbous first stage. In this design, the missile was to be controlled by fins on the front of the missile—that is, a canard configuration. The firm stated this was necessary in order to fit the missile into the V class bomb bays. The firm estimated the cost of developing and producing a 1,000-missile programme at $389.4 million, and the estimated cost to the RAF of equipping 135 aircraft at £34.75 million. At that time, the exchange rate was fixed at £1 to $2.80. However, the overall cost of the programme to the RAF was thought to range from £42–48.5 million, exclusive of development costs of some £2.5 million.

In June 1959, representatives of Avro and Handley Page, as well as officials from the Ministry of Supply, visited Douglas to give them further details of the V bomber designs. One of the other problems was ground clearance. This version of the missile would have to be carried semi-recessed in the bomb bay, like Blue Steel, and the Victor, with its low undercarriage, gave particular problems. Even with the underwing carriage, there was still very little clearance, and despite the superior performance of the Victor, it was decided that the Vulcan would become the main carrier. The Valiant, an older aircraft of more modest performance, was ruled out from the start.

The bulbous first stage gave considerable drag and control effects when mounted on the B-58 aircraft. Douglas' response was that the design had been dictated by the requirement that the missile should fit the V bombers. There was another problem in the early designs: an important part of the guidance system was a star seeker. Mounting the missile in the bomb bay would then be more difficult, requiring some form of periscope, and so an underwing location was thought to be preferable, one where the star seeker would have an uninterrupted view of the sky.

As a consequence, the missile had to be redesigned, and matters had got to the stage where there were four different versions of the missile:

Able 1—this was the original type as detailed in the brochure. It had seven nozzles and a large-diameter first stage to permit carriage in the bomb bay of the V-bombers but has to be carried semi-submerged the case of the Vulcan.

Able 2—this was 32 inches longer than Able 1. The missile diameter was reduced but there are larger stabilising fins and now four nozzles per engine. It could be carried in the bomb bay of Victor, but clearance with the ground was marginal if it were mounted underneath the wing. It could be mounted semi-submerged in the bomb bay of Victor or underneath the wing.

Able 3—this had similar dimensions to that of Able 2 but the star tracker was placed much further forward to avoid data transfer problems. The star tracker was mounted on the upper surface of the wing with a 50-inch-long data transfer distance in the case of the B-58 aircraft. If it were carried in a V bomber bomb bay, the data transfer link would be about 9 feet long. However, the reduction of interference drag compared with Able 1 was about 25–30 per cent.

Charlie 1—6 feet longer than Able 1, this version also had the capability to carry smaller or larger warheads. The range with a small head was 920 miles and with the larger warhead 550 miles.

It could not be mounted in the Victor bomb bay without expensive and unacceptable modifications. Mounted underneath the wing, it fouled the ground. It could be carried by the Vulcan.

As a consequence of all this muddle, a technical committee was set up under the chairmanship of Dr J. C. Fletcher, then President of the Space Electronics Corporation. The Fletcher Committee was charged with scrutinising all aspects of Douglas's latest design proposal, Able III, which was broadly similar to the vehicle proposed to the evaluation group at Dayton in March 1959.

Although the Able III missile had some attractive features, its canard control systems had never appealed to the GAM-87A Weapon System Project Office at the Wright Air Development Center (WADC). With a 1,650-pound warhead, it had a serious problem with the centre of gravity position. As first-stage burnout approached, the centre of gravity shifted forward of the canard centre of pressure, causing a reversal of the longitudinal and directional control, which was not a desirable situation.

When the span of the fins on the after body had grown to a span of 96 inches, the Project Office decided it was time to start again. They produced an entirely new proposal, which dispensed with the canard controls in favour of a combination of relatively small after body control surfaces and swivelling second-stage nozzles. In other respects, it was very similar to Douglas's design.

The WADC proposal was not welcomed by Douglas; however, when it became apparent that the Fletcher Committee had serious reservations about Able III, Douglas decided to accept WADC's suggestions as a basis for a new submission, which was presented to the Fletcher Committee at its final meeting in January 1960.

The new missile, known as Delta II, was longer and slimmer than Able III but appeared to be readily compatible with the B-52, the Victor 2, and the Vulcan 2. It retained the stellar-inertial guidance system but with the star tracker now positioned in the body of the missile instead of in the underwing pylon, and made provision for two alternative payloads to ranges of 600 and 1,000 nautical miles respectively. Impact accuracy was to be within a 50 per cent CEP of 1.5 nautical miles at a range of 600 miles with provision for almost infinite target flexibility.

The Fletcher Committee reported to HQ USAF and Doctor York later in January, saying that the Delta II proposal, which would become known as 'SKYBOLT', was technically feasible, though they considered that its

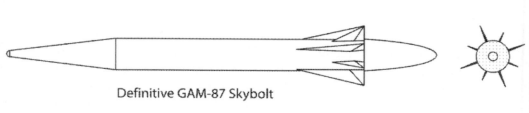

WS-138A - Able 1

WS-138A - Able 2 and 3

WS-138A Charlie 1

WS-138A Delta 2 Phase B

WS-138 Delta 2 Phase H (Lightweight Warhead)

WS-138 Delta 2 Phase H (Heavyweight Warhead)

Definitive GAM-87 Skybolt

0   Ft   10

0   Mtr   3

This graphic shows the evolution of the Skybolt design. The final version, prompted by the work of the Fletcher Committee, is very different from the original Douglas design. (*Graphic by courtesy of C. J. Gibson*)

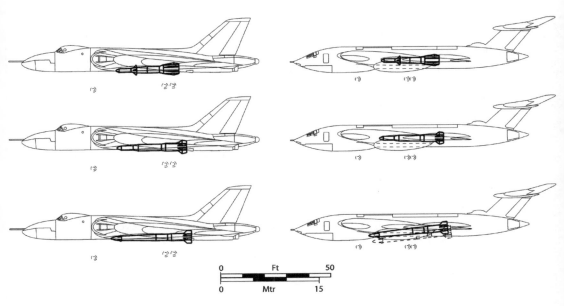

The different variants of the Skybolt missile mounted on the V bombers. Most of them had problems with ground clearance. (*Graphic by courtesy of C. J. Gibson*)

cost had been underestimated and that it would take longer to develop than had been forecast. They also thought that if the Department of Defense decided to continue with the project, it would need a strong USAF management team that was well-versed in inertial guidance principles to support Douglas.

When the Fletcher Committee produced its final report, the main proposals were as follows:

> (i) the development of a propellant with a specific impulse of 255 seemed unnecessary in view of the range achievable for the Delta II missile based on a specific impulse of 245;
> (ii) development of the guidance system was considered to be the most difficult problem;
> (iii) unless considerable effort was applied on detailed design and specification and on testing of components the overall reliability would be so low as to make the system of questionable value as an operational weapon;
> (iv) the USAF would require as strong a supervisory team as can be assembled.[10]

The committee also predicted that the schedule would slip by at least one year, so that the operational date of the first squadron would probably be during the summer of 1964. It was also thought that the total R&D cost estimated in the present development plan was too low by a factor of about three.

The Deputy Secretary of Defense, James Douglas, received the report from the committee on 30 January 1960; two days later, he approved the GAM-87A programme. His letter of approval contained the following reservations:

> Changes to technical specifications (other than necessary design changes and embodiment of improved techniques) must not be made without approval of the Office of the Secretary of Defense;
>
> The Air Force must provide increased funding out of their own resources;
>
> Management such as that used successfully in ballistic missile development was to be used;
>
> The Director of Defense Research and Engineering (DDR&E, Dr. York) would review the program every four months for at least two years.[11]

Another report produced for the DDR&E made it clear that in many respects, Skybolt was breaking new ground, which made direct oversight by the USAF all the more important. There were many 'firsts' to the project:

> a ballistic air-to-surface missile;
>
> a 1,000-mile air-to-surface missile;
>
> the application of automatic celestial navigation for in-flight position fixing and missile guidance;
>
> the development of a celestial navigation system of proven high reliability;
>
> the development of an airborne digital computer of high capacity and speed.

The report went on to say that close oversight of the project was necessary:

> In the past, many development programs have suffered from the distracting effect of model development. The effect of this has been to increase cost, extend schedules, divert key technical people from the fundamental objectives, and finally, to fail to provide operationally suitable equipment in the hands of the fighting forces at the time when such equipment is most needed to ensure the capability to carry out their assigned tasks. We recognise, of course, that growth does have a place in any development programme. It is, however, a basic responsibility of management to ensure that growth does not interfere with the meeting of initial goals but rather is handled in an orderly fashion and introduced only after initial success is demonstrated. In this weapon system the introduction of model improvements or growth advances must only be after specific approval of the Director of Defense Research & Engineering, for in the initial phases of the program the

contractor's effort must be directed entirely to the achievement of the present technical specifications. This restriction, however, is not to be construed as preventing the introduction of necessary design changes of the introduction of improved techniques and materials should such become available on a timescale consistent with the development schedule of the ALBM. On the other hand, the development of such techniques and materials is not to be conducted as part of this program.[13]

The new design was now a uniform 36 inches in diameter, although this meant that the missile would be 27 inches longer. Even this design caused problems with ground clearance on the V bombers, owing to the size of the fins carried at the rear of the missile. For several months, the issue of whether the missile would have four or eight fins was undecided. This was unfortunate, because the result affected carriage on the V bombers—in particular, the Victor. The final version would have eight fins, four of which were used to guide the missile in the early part of its flight. The other four fins were fixed. The second stage would be controlled by swivelling the single nozzle of the rocket motor; the Delta II approved by the Fletcher Committee had four nozzles, but this was changed to a single nozzle in April 1960, after approval had been granted by the DoD.

The B-58 Hustler aircraft had been intended to be the prime carrier of Skybolt, but the development of the aircraft was cancelled in July 1959. Instead, the B-52 would now be the prime carrier. It would be fitted with two twin Skybolt pylons under each inner wing. In this configuration, each aircraft could carry a total of eight missiles in addition to its multi-megaton free-fall bombs.

The new design also simplified carriage by the Vulcan. Handley Page wrote to the Ministry of Aviation that in order to fit the revised version of the missile on the Victor, there would need to be major modifications to the fins and strakes of the missile. This was passed on to the United States, but no reply was received. The firm had second thoughts and told the Ministry of Aviation that the problem of ground clearance could be overcome by mounting the missile 18 inches further forward and that the new position would be satisfactory structurally and aerodynamically. The Ministry was not impressed and decided to stick to their original decision that the Vulcan should be the sole carrier.

Douglas was not the sole constructor; much of the work was subcontracted out, particularly the propulsion and guidance. The rocket motors were to be made by Aerojet, who had started building solid-fuel rocket motors soon after the end of the war. They also supplied the rocket motors for the Minuteman missile for the Air Force and the Polaris missile for the Navy. Guidance was subcontracted to Nortronics.

The following description of the final version of the missile is based on a report written by Group Captain Bonser in May 1960:

Skybolt is a two-stage solid rocket ballistic missile designed for launch from B-52 and the Vulcan. As the design exists at the moment, it will not fit on the Victor aircraft.

The overall length of the missile, including tail fairing, is 38 foot 3 inches, and the diameter over the major portion is 36 inches. The tail fairing is 6 feet long weighing approximately 45 lb. It is separated from the missile by the firing of explosive bolts just prior to the ignition of the first stage. If the missile is to be released in the free-fall role then the fairing remains attached to the weapon.

The first stage motor, including the rocket nozzle, is approximately 12 feet 6 inches long and, including the four fixed fins and the four all moving control fins which are mounted on the rear, weighs 6,435 lb, of which 5,425 lb is propellant. The propellant is an aluminised polyurethane, which is used for Minuteman with a design level specific impulse of 245 ('specific impulse' is a measure of how energetic a rocket fuel is—one way of looking at it is that it gives the thrust produced per unit weight of fuel per second). Figures of 245/6 have been achieved on Minuteman.

The motor case, which also forms part of the structure, is 0.067-inch thick steel, and this will be coated in phenolic Refrasil-nylon to give some protection to the case from corrosion handling, stones thrown up from the runway, and also serve as insulation. The nozzle of the first-stage motor is fixed and the missile is controlled by the four movable fins during the forty-second burning period.

The second stage motor including rocket nozzle is approximately 7 feet long and weighs 3,320 lb including the actuator mechanism for controlling the movement of the single nozzle, and a small roll limiting motor. The propellant weight is 2,735 lb. The motor has four ports or thrust reversers at the head end of the case, which are vented by bursting covering disks when the velocity has been achieved for the designed target range. The general case construction will be similar to that of the first stage motor.

Ahead of the second stage motor is the guidance bay weighing some 400 lb inclusive of structure. This bay contains the stellar inertial navigator and power supplies and is approximately 3 feet long. Information from this bay is taken to the first and second stage controls down a strake on the outside of the motor case.

The re-entry vehicle is attached to the guidance bay and separates shortly after second stage burn-out.

Generally, the position of maintenance joints coincide with the five major components of the missile; there are a number of access ports located alongside the main sub-components such as actuators, hydraulic power units and roll motor. The maintenance joints are not always on the separation plane owing to the complexities that arise due to the explosive bolts.

The weapon is suspended from the aircraft at three points—two side-by-side at the forward end and a single one to the rear. The three release slips are operated simultaneously through a fixed linkage, which is actuated by firing a cartridge. The firing circuit and cartridge are duplicated. The suspension unit is housed on a pylon mounted on the aircraft wing and all the missiles services pass from the aircraft through this unit.

The existing navigation equipment such as radar, doppler, and bomb/navigation systems are used to provide information on the aircraft's position, velocity, heading, and altitude to a pre-launch computer mounted in a position which need not be accessible. The control unit for the Astro tracker and the converter assembly for converting analogue bomb/navigation information into a digital form for the computer can also be mounted in positions which do not need to be accessible during flight. The launch panel (one per missile) and the target panel, which serves both missiles, together with a warhead control panel and sidereal clock, must be accessible to the crew. Individual missiles can be aligned on different targets and launched within a short time of each other.

The USAF has stated two conditions of use for the Skybolt missile system. The first is one of ground alert, where the aircraft is ready and in normal circumstances remains adjacent to the end of the runway over a period of seven days and at the end of this period takes off for a flight of approximately eleven hours. During the seven-day period, the missile will only receive the normal daily inspection and the missile will be checked out as far as is possible by the associated airborne equipment.

The second condition of flight is air alert. This is a scheduled flight lasting some 24 hours but planned sufficiently far ahead as to allow a reasonable time for full preparation of the aircraft and missiles.

In order to provide the pre-launch computer with the appropriate data on the general ecliptic values of the stars and their position relative to each other, it is necessary to upgrade the information twice a month. The information, together with target data, is produced at SAC HQ Omaha. This is then read off by a ground-based unit called the Computer Fill Unit, which in turn transfers the information to the airborne computer. The Computer Fill Unit is also used to check the calibration of the gyros and accelerometers of each individual missile against a tape, which will be produced as each table is calibrated. Thus each guidance set will be unique and have its own calibration tape and require checking once a month.

Missile trajectory: the missile on release is allowed to free fall for two seconds until it is approximately 50 feet below the aircraft. The tail fairing is then separated by firing a series of explosive bolts and simultaneously the first stage rocket motor is ignited. When released at Mach 0.8 and 40,000 feet, the missile is pitched up to its flight path of 40 degrees in about twenty-three seconds. First stage burnout occurs after 40 forty seconds, and then the missile is allowed to coast for a few seconds before the ignition of the second stage. The coasting period depends on the altitude of burnout of the first stage and will be longer for the lower altitudes. The second stage has a maximum burning time of forty seconds but this can be terminated at any time after the minimum time for the guidance stage which is ten seconds. When the correct velocity relative to target range has been achieved the thrust reversers are operated and the re-entry vehicle separated from the guidance bay and second stage motor. The re-entry vehicle will be spun to around 10 rpm.

Once or twice a year, the motors should be returned to a central depot where ultrasonic, x-ray, leak detection, etc. tests should be carried out. This series of tests should take approximately three days. In practice, the life of the propellant is likely to be about three years and then it will probably be cheaper to buy a new rocket motor, rather than attempt to remove the grain and refill. During the majority of this time, the missile is in a relatively quiet environment as the worst cases are during take-off, landing, and low-speed dash.

The report concluded by noting that it was proposed to build three different types of re-entry vehicle; a dummy for ground handling only, a training RV for training flights housing telemetry, and the operational heads.

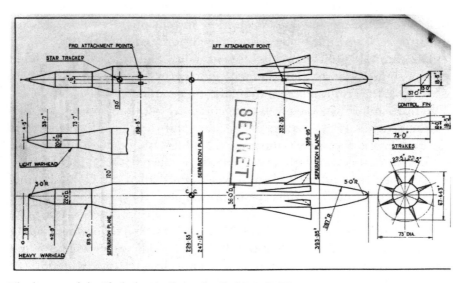

The layout of the Skybolt missile as detailed in a RAE report.

It should be possible to change from a training role to an operational role within thirty minutes, including arming the first and second stage motors.[14]

One issue that would give rise to some controversy was the guidance system, which was undeniably complex. It was an inertial system, with stellar alignment by the star seeker prior to launch. While the missiles were attached to the pylon, the guidance system depended upon the carrier aircraft for information to align the system and stabilise its computations. The bomb navigation system provided trim, heading, drift angle, range north of fix-point, range east of fix-point, altitude above sea level, and ground speed. These signals were fed to the analogue-to-digital converter assembly, then to the pre-launch computer. Using a star seeker guidance system would prove controversial, the more so since many of the principal opponents of Skybolt had little technical knowledge or understanding of the system. In fact, a star seeker system had been used on the Snark missile, which had been deployed briefly between 1958 and 1961. Hound Dog used an almost identical system, so there was little that was new about it. On the other hand, given the high velocity of the Skybolt missile and its long range, the system needed to be a great deal more accurate and so more complex than those in previous missiles. The star seeker system was first tested in a C-131 aircraft in April 1962. The system acquired the first star that was programmed into the pre-launch computer approximately halfway through a twelve-minute search period. Three different stars were acquired with a total of thirty detections on a planned flight path from Hawthorne California, to Phoenix, Arizona, and back.

When all elements of the guidance subsystem reached their respective operating temperatures, the system was started up. Gyros came up to speed, the platform gimbal control servos were activated, and the platform was slewed to approximately a vertical position.

The position and velocity data could be transferred directly to the missile from the aircraft, but not the azimuth or heading. Since it was exposed to the high-speed airstream, the missile was not fixed rigid to the aircraft as it was subject to buffeting and vibration. This meant that the azimuth reference could not be transferred directly from the aircraft navigation system, so the star tracker had to be mounted in the missile.

The star tracker operated in association with the pre-launch computer which was carried in the aircraft and which stored a star catalogue with the stars listed in descending order of visible magnitude. The position and heading of the aircraft determined the stellar region visible within the total field of view of the star tracker which was +/-20 degrees in azimuth and +55 degrees to +82 degrees in elevation for the B-52. The field of view for the B-52 was obscured somewhat by the wing; this was less in the V-bombers, which increased the upper band of the elevation.

The computer ran through the catalogue stopping at the first star (i.e. that of greatest magnitude), which lay within the field of view. The star tracker was then put into a search mode about the bearing of the star using an approximate bearing reference transmitted from the aircraft, and the system searched, using an expanding rectangular search, until the start was located or until an area about 2 degrees in azimuth by 0.5 degrees in elevation had been scanned.

When the star was discovered, the tracker adopted an acquisition search mode, consisting of a thirteen-point star shaped search area over an area two arcseconds in diameter, and the style bearing was located by an averaging process. On completion of this stage, the star tracker repeated the whole cycle for the subsequent acceptable star in the catalogue, and when that was located, the system, using a much-reduced scan, alternated between the two stars and generated current bearing information throughout the period of alignment of the missile's stable platform and then monitored platform drift until launch.

The average time to acquire a star in average background conditions was about five minutes, increasing to about fifteen minutes for a high probability of acquisition, implying a complete single search. This depended upon a fairly accurate bearing reference being available for aligning the star tracker in a search.

As the carrier aircraft came within range of the target, the launch sequence was initiated. The pre-launch computer calculated a predicted time-zero position by extrapolation from its present position and velocity. The time of flight and range angle to the target were then fixed, the trajectory plan and target bearing at time-zero computed. The initial velocity-to-be-gained vector was computed from range angle, time of flight, latitude, and target bearing. Targeting parameters were transferred to the ballistic computer in the missile and data transfer verified. The actual launch occurred soon after time zero. At the time of launch, the ballistic computer began a continuous computation of velocities to be gained in the ballistic trajectory coordinate system.

After launching at Mach 0.8 at 40,000 feet, there would be a two-second delay before the first stage motor was ignited. The ballistic computer would generate commands to the flight control system for a programmed pitch-up steering manoeuvre. The control fins were used to pull the missile up to a maximum incidence of 15 degrees and then the missile would be held at that angle until it had turned up to a thrust angle of 40.5 degrees, which was maintained throughout the remainder of powered flight until second stage cut-off. Sixteen seconds after launch, the missile had regained the launch altitude after its initial drop and pull up. At twenty-five seconds, the pull-up was complete and, at this time, the dynamic pressure reached its peak value.

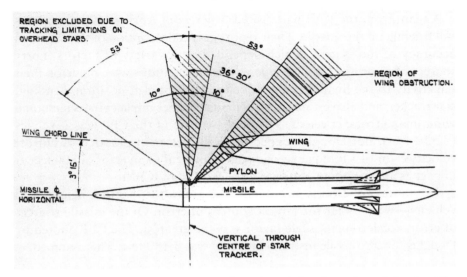

The star tracker was located in the missile and needed a clear view of the sky. The wing of the Vulcan obscured a small part of the field of view, but otherwise, most of the sky was visible.

First stage burning continued for forty seconds; that is until forty-two seconds after launch. The velocity reached was around 5,000 feet/sec., and the altitude was 87,000 feet. During second-stage operation, commands to the control system were based on computed velocities to be gained.

The dynamic pressure was then too high for satisfactory control of the second stage on its own, so a coast period was introduced between first stage burnout and second stage separation. The coasting period varied from ten to twenty seconds for high- and low-altitude launching respectively, although the auxiliary power system for the first stage controls had allowance for up to forty seconds of coasting. The range penalty for coasting time was 2.1 miles for each second. Second-stage burning lasted for about forty seconds, unless cut-out was commanded earlier by the guidance system. For a range of about 1,000 miles, the apogee was 250 miles and impact occurred 680 seconds after launch.

The missile also had to be robust enough to be carried on the aircraft for hours at a time, day after day. The design criteria were for the missile to withstand 18,000 flying hours of carried flight, including 750 take-offs and landings, as well as 288 loadings on and off the aircraft. 'Ground alert' operations were included. Within the total hours, twenty flying hours a year were to be at low altitude, and forty hours at maximum take-off power. Some eight years was the total life expectancy required, but at that time, the life of the propellants was only between three and four years.

A team from the RAE had visited America in April 1960 to receive a full briefing on the missile. Their report gave a description of the expected accuracy of the system, which depended on a variety of factors. Forty sources of error had been considered and calculations were made on their sensitivity to the final burnout velocity, e.g. Doppler, position, heading, star tracker, and also estimates were made of other impact errors including wind, map errors, et cetera. The final estimate of the CEP was 1.5 miles (7,920 feet), but Douglas expected to do better in practice. A cut-off velocity error of 1 foot per second was equivalent to an error of 800 feet at impact as against about a mile (5,280 feet) for an ICBM.

The initial conditions at launch—the aircraft's position, height, and velocity—were by far the largest sources of error. Of the missile sources of error, accelerometer scale factor was the greatest. The CEP quoted by Douglas for the missile instrument errors was 3,180 feet. This assumed:

one hour settling time;
ground radar position fix prior to launch;
optimum flight conditions;
European theatre (600-mile range);
expected *g* component;
bomb-navigation system achieving specified performance.

The effect on CEP of failure of various navigation instruments in the aircraft was shown below compared with a nominal value of 3,000 feet for everything working:—

nominal CEP:	3,000 feet;
without radar fix:	4,000 feet;
without Doppler:	4,250 feet;
without astrocompass:	4,500 feet;
without radar fix and Doppler:	5,250 feet;
without Doppler and astrocompass:	5,500 feet;
without radar fix an astrocompass:	6,500 feet;
without radar fix, Doppler, and astrocompass:	7,000 feet.

The system was complex but appeared to work well on all the flight testing. A greater concern was that of reliability. An early version of the launch computer contained a total of 1,562 transistors, 9,020 diodes, 1,419 carbon resistors, 3,311 film resistors, 985 tantalum capacitors, and 1,385 ceramic capacitors. Based on the computer used for the Snark missile, Nortronics estimated that the mean time to failure was six hours. WADD, using USAF data on component reliability, estimated this at thirteen hours. Thus, the chances of a successful launch after a two-hour alignment period and a five-hour flight were between 50 and 80 per cent. This was not impressive.

Apparently, however, the system proved more reliable than had at first been thought—at least, according to a memo from Thorneycroft, when he was Minister of Defence:

> Doubts about the reliability of the system are not borne out by trials to date. On the contrary, the reliability of certain critical components such as the pre-launch computer in the aircraft and astro-navigation systems have exceeded expectations.

Even John Rubel, who would be such a bitter opponent of the missile, had reassuring words. LTD Williams, Director-General, Defence Research Staff, wrote to Sir Robert Cockburn, describing a meeting with Rubel:

> Most of the time was taken up with GAM.87A, Skybolt, on which we had a good exposition from Dr. John Rubel, who has since been nominated to replace Doctor Wilcox as Deputy Director, Defense Research and Engineering,

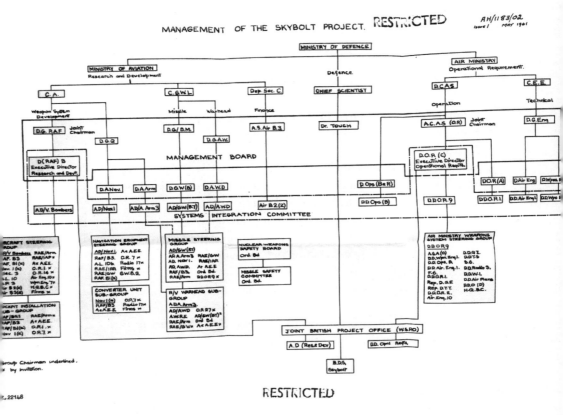

A chart of the organisation of the British part of the Skybolt programme.

consequent upon the latter taking up the job of directing General Motors' newly-created Defense Research Division. Rubel, who was at one time extremely critical of several aspects of WS.138A, as the project was known in its earlier days, made very clear the extremely thorough going-over the project has had. He asserted firmly that all the dubious aspects had been squeezed out, and ... there was no doubt that the whole exercise could be carried through within the existing state of the art, and without having to depend on some new technical breakthrough. Indeed, it is thought that better accuracy than 1½ mile will be realized; this would validate the user [*sic.*] of the lighter warhead, and in turn enable the range of 1,000 miles to be obtained.[15]

As far as the RAE and RAF were concerned, the way ahead seemed clear. The Victor had been ruled out for Skybolt since ground clearance still remained problematic, and the ministry was aiming for flight clearance for the Vulcan version from the Controller of Aircraft by June 1964.

It would be necessary to carry out trials on the missile in America, but before this could be done, the Vulcan had to be adapted to carry the missile with pylons fitted underneath the wings. Once the modifications had been made, then trial drops could be made with dummy missiles. These were carried out in the UK, but at the same time, teams were being prepared to send out to Eglin Air Force base in Florida for live trials.

Target dates for the programme had been set out:

February 1960	programme approval given
February 1961	first inert release
August 1961	first powered launch
January 1962	first guided round
March 1962	production to be authorised after two guidance flights
October 1962	start Category II tests
August 1963	start Category III tests (RAF Service Trial equivalent)
August 1963	first operational squadron beginning to be equipped
March 1964	first Squadron operational
September 1964	first RAF squadron
March 1966	twenty squadrons equipped

The first guided launch occurred in November 1962, ten months later than had been planned. Given the slippages that occur in any advanced project, this was really quite satisfactory progress, and given the delays produced by budget cuts, it was excellent progress. There was little chance of the first RAF squadron being operational by September 1964, but a good chance of achieving this by 1965. This would have fulfilled the UK's requirement satisfactorily.

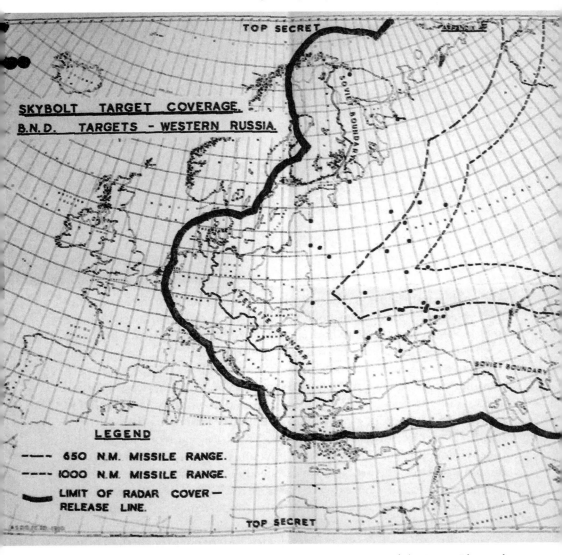

The thick line on the chart marks the limit of radar coverage of the Soviet Bloc and Warsaw Pact. The dotted lines show the coverage obtainable by the two versions of the Skybolt missile.

The Warhead

Although Britain had collaborated with the United States in the Manhattan Project during the war, this collaboration was terminated by the United States as soon as the war had ended. However, the returning British scientists were familiar with the design of the bomb, and a programme began to build a British atom bomb. The bottleneck was the production of plutonium, and, as a result, it was not until 1952 that a device was tested successfully. Unfortunately for Britain, America had moved on and had now tested a fusion device—what is popularly known as the hydrogen bomb. Therefore, British scientists had to start again from scratch, this time without any real knowledge of how a fusion device worked. Despite limited resources, the problem was cracked in a relatively short time; two partially successful devices were tested in 1957, with a fully successful test later in the year. As a result of this, Anglo-American co-operation was resumed.

Since Britain had developed its device independently of the United States, it had developed various techniques which American scientists were extremely interested in. In September 1958, Sir William Cook, at that time the deputy director of AWRE, had long discussions with his counterparts in America. He reported:

> No doubt that our technical achievements in thermonuclear warheads, invulnerability, and in component techniques have considerably impressed United States delegates and has been the reason for more forthcoming attitude than formal procedure would dictate. [General] Starbird has been very co-operative and is genuinely anxious that exchange should be increased ...

Discussions on specific thermonuclear warheads were broadened by me to show ideas on which we have had no time to work. Teller, in particular, and all United States representatives, expressed admiration of technical basis of our designs. Teller anxious for United States procedure to permit frank discussions on general physics problems in thermonuclear weapons and on specific features not yet calculable by either side. Los Alamos, Livermore interested in EDC3 explosive which appears somewhat better than their best, and in OCTOPUS multi-point initiation of implosion which was new to them. Sandia extremely anxious for closest collaboration of electronic and electrical components including neutron sources. We have solved some problems which they are now meeting and they have cleared difficulties which we have not anticipated. Livermore interested in our delayed initiator work for possible application to United States 155 mm. shell. Above gives you some idea of range of interest in our work.[1]

As a result of the discussions, Britain was given the blueprints for two American weapons—the Mark 28 and the Mark 47. The Mark 47 was a much lighter warhead than the Mark 28, weighing 630 lb and having a yield of 400 kT. Its drawback was that it used 40 kg of highly enriched uranium 235.[2] Using this warhead for Skybolt would have its problems, as Sir Frederick Brundrett remarked:

I am, however, extremely worried over the warhead question. Admittedly, York is not quite the man to talk to on the subject, even though he was some time ago Head of Livermore and therefore knows the ins and outs of the American atomic field very thoroughly. The difficulty about York's approach to the problem is that he cannot conceive the situation of shortage of fissile material. He merely thinks I am being silly on this issue. The fact is, of course, as everybody here knows, that it is an absolutely critical issue.[3]

Brundrett, somewhat to the annoyance of the Chiefs of Staff, had persuaded the minister that the Mark 47 should not be produced in the UK. At that time, there was little need for a lightweight warhead. The Mark 28 was Anglicised and built in the UK under the name 'Red Snow'. It had a yield of just over 1 MT and weighed approximately 1 ton. It was used in the free-fall Yellow Sun bomb, replacing the highly unsafe Green Grass warhead, which had been used as a temporary measure. It also replaced the Green Bamboo warhead that was to be deployed in Blue Steel (Green Bamboo also had some very dubious safety issues) and the Orange Herald warhead intended for Blue Streak. The US was considering the use of the Mark 28 as the heavy warhead for Skybolt. This was certainly acceptable to the UK, apart from the loss in range, which was significant.

There was one problem with Red Snow:

> As regards the heavy warhead, they [the Americans] were planning to use Red Snow in a slightly lighter case than we were adopting. Arrangements were in hand to ascertain whether the US would construct the re-entry head so as to carry our slightly heavier warhead. This was highly desirable to provide interchangeability between Skybolt and other British weapons. If, however, the Americans were unable to accept the range penalty involved, the Air Ministry would forego interchangeability and we would, therefore, have to purchase thinner cases from the US or manufacture them. No difficulties were envisaged on this score.[4]

At the same meeting, lightweight warheads were discussed. There were three possibilities, which were referred to as Steven, Fife, and Acorn.

> Steven and Acorn weighed about 700 lb, although the latter was still in an early design stage and no firm weight can yet be given. Fife was also in the design stage and a weight of about 600 lb was forecast. Both Fife and Acorn give a substantially higher yield than Steven.[5]

Fissile material was still an issue; Steven contained about four times as much U235 as Red Snow and nearly twice as much plutonium, which would mean an overall cost per warhead of about £0.5 million more.

The other lightweight design available to the UK was the Mark 43, which again used considerable amounts of fissile material and which had been vetoed by Brundrett. However, the preferred American design was different—the J-21, which was renamed the W-59. Therefore, the prohibition could be quietly evaded.

There was a problem with the W-59. Its primary, called Tsetse in the US, used a high explosive which was considered too sensitive by the British Ordnance Board, and for the British version, a less sensitive but less effective explosive had been substituted.

> R.O. 106 (to be used in Blue Water and Seaslug Mk. II). This is a British version of the US Tsetse, which has been tested successfully. It differs from the American device in that it uses the British explosive EDC.11, and not the US PBX9404, which has high graze-sensitive and which, when once initiated, almost always proceeds to detonation. R.O. 106 is one point safe, and its yield is estimated at 8½ +/- ¾ kT. R.O. 16 has been considered as the primary for the Skybolt warhead, but it has been concluded that its yield is not adequate to ensure reliable functioning of the secondary.[6]

In the end, RO 106 was never put into service; both Blue Water, a short-range surface-to-surface missile for the British Army in Germany, and Seaslug Mark II, a surface-to-air missile for the Royal Navy, were cancelled in the early '60s. There was an alternative primary:

> Cleo. This important AWRE device represents an innovation in that it uses a new principle known as the Octopus system. This principle has been tested in the British firing in Nevada in March 1962 (Pampas), and the Americans have expressed keen interest in it. In the form tested in the Pampas firing, it is compatible to R.O. 106 in yield, but it is more compact and has greater development potential. It is also more robust and less critical as regards tolerances in manufacture and assembly ... The Octopus system is also well adapted for use as the primary in the Skybolt warhead.
>
> RE179 (Jehu, Klaxon) (to be used as the warhead for Skybolt; variants of it are proposed for the higher-yield successors to Red Beard for the Royal Air Force). This warhead is a British version of the American XW.59, which is now being tested successfully. However, XW.59 employs Tsetse as the primary, and, as noted above, British version of this device, RO 106, has a somewhat smaller yield (owing to the use of a safer British explosive) which will be inadequate to ensure reliable functioning in this particular role. The most attractive solution would involve a development of the Octopus principle (Cleo) using a rather larger supercharge than the device tested at Pampas; it is highly probable this can be done successfully, but it must be recognised that the necessary changes to the device used in Pampas have to be kept within the limits imposed by the size of the warhead case, and by the requirements of single point safety.[7]

Information on Octopus is still highly classified; there is a file in the Public Record Office entitled 'OCTOPUS: possible implosion system to replace baratol and air lenses', but it is a closed file, not available to read. All fission devices up to this point had used an explosive lens (the British system used an explosive known as baratol). It has been suggested that the new principle was a form of multi-point ignition implosion device, which fits with William Cook's comment above: 'OCTOPUS multi-point initiation of implosion'. The explosive used to implode the fissile core was contained within an aluminium sphere. Grooves were cut into the outside of the sphere; these grooves terminated in a hole drilled through to the explosive. The grooves of the hole were also filled with explosive. Thus, one detonator could be used to fire the explosive on the outside, and the shockwave would explode in succession the explosive in the grooves, the explosive in the holes through the aluminium, and finally, the explosive used to implode the plutonium core. However, this is a very much a speculative interpretation.

Apparently, 'The principle was tested by the UK in 1958 [presumably as part of the Grapple tests in the Pacific] and attracted particular interest in the US'.[8] A subsequent paragraph suggests that the device would form the primary for the Skybolt warhead. The device was tested in the American underground test site in Nevada under the codename of 'Pampas' in March to be used as the Skybolt primary if modified. This could be done either by increasing the fissile material content (in which case, it would be necessary to incorporate a mechanical safeing arrangement with some loss of reliability and ease of handling) or by increasing the chemical explosive content (in which case, it would be necessary to test the device again). The latter solution was technically preferable; arrangements were made for the necessary test to be carried out in the course of a further programme of tests in Nevada in October–November 1962.

So the British version of the warhead would have the same secondary or fusion arrangement, but an entirely different primary. It could have other uses as well:

AWRE believe it is possible to produce by 1963/64 a British warhead of approximately 400 kt yield for about 700 lb weight and dimensions to suit current proposals for the configuration of WS.138A. Any engineering improvement between now and that date is expected to produce a yield growth factor without any corresponding weight growth, and the value of that growth might be about 25 per cent. It is believed that such a warhead would use approximately half the quantity of fissile material to be used in the US Mk.47 head, but nevertheless, it would produce a comparable yield. Such a warhead might have other applications such as a depth charge or tactical weapon should it prove necessary to replace RED BEARD. If stipulated early enough warhead might be so designed to be capable of giving variable yields by predetermined derating from the maximum value of which the final design is potentially capable.[9]

Any warhead would need to be carried in a re-entry vehicle which would contain the ancillary services such as power supply and fusing. The warhead and the re-entry vehicle had to be robust enough to stand the high temperatures and rapid deceleration on re-entry into the Earth's atmosphere. The job of designing and producing the re-entry vehicle was given to General Electric (GE).

Design of the vehicle depended very much on the selection of warhead, particularly the diameter of the warhead. One possibility was to use the Minuteman vehicle, but this was still under development, so it was considered too high a risk.

The final selection of the lightweight warhead, and the cancellation of the requirement for a heavier warhead, meant that the design of the re-entry vehicle could be changed: the sphere-cone-cylinder-flare configuration gave way to a sphere-cone shape (the increased aerodynamic efficiency gave an increased range of 20 to 30 miles). The change in design gave some other advantages; the elimination of the step from sphere to cone to cylinder reduced the erosion of the ablative material covering the re-entry vehicle and reduced the shockwave that had been affecting the star tracker. The frontal radar cross section area was also reduced, which would mean that it would be more difficult to detect by enemy radar. For planning purposes, the maximum parameters of the warhead were weight 675 lb, diameter 18 inches, and length 48 inches. Any change in warhead parameters would cause considerable slippage in the Skybolt programme schedule. This new version was officially known as the Mark 7.

Consideration was also given to what was described as CLAW (CLustered Atomic Warhead), using two warheads for greater effect, but studies showed that there would be no significant increase in on-target effectiveness while such an undertaking would incur additional complexity, system unreliability, programme costs, and possible delays in the development schedule. A single warhead with effectiveness and payload advantages equivalent to the CLAW concept would be less expensive and less complex.

Under consideration for a time was the Mark 7A re-entry vehicle, which provided simple decoys, increased separation between the second stage and re-entry vehicle on re-entry, and a reduced radar cross section while maintaining the range of 950 nautical miles.

On a longer-term basis, the British were not entirely happy with just a simple re-entry vehicle with no decoys, since it seemed increasingly likely that the Russians would begin to deploy an anti-ballistic missile (ABM) system towards the end of the 1960s. If Skybolt was to form the basis of the deterrent in the 1970s, then it was looking vulnerable to the new defences:

> Although some steps have been taken in the design of Skybolt to reduce its potential vulnerability it is still a 'simple' warhead to any defence system. The Technical Sub-Committee concluded that both Skybolt and Polaris may require the introduction of new features such as decoys for the 1970 era to counter possible simple defence systems. I am not sure how much of the intelligence situation was available on Russian activities in the field of ballistic missile defence was before the committee when it reached this judgment. If, as I suspect, there has been a considerable recent accumulation of information which was not then available, then perhaps the Technical

Sub-Committee should reconsider, in the light of this information, its advice about whether Skybolt, as it is now conceived, will remain credible as deterrent until the end of the life of the Vulcans.

If there is any substantial doubt about this then presumably there should be a proper technical investigation of the possibilities and consequences of improving the Skybolt system. What I have in mind is a study of the possibility of replacing, in due course, the Skybolt re-entry vehicle at present being developed by a more sophisticated version carrying decoys. One would clearly hope for a solution which have little or no effect on Skybolt performance, required only a minimal modification to the rest of the missile, but how far these hopes could be realised could only be determined as a result of detailed studies. I should emphasise that I feel strongly that such studies, where they undertaken, should in no way be allowed to interfere with the current development programme of Skybolt or with its present re-entry vehicle. Any interference could only result in delaying the entry of Skybolt into service with the RAF.

Considerable thought has, I understand, already been given to the improvement of Skybolt in this way in the United States, but so far as I know, there are not at the moment any concrete development plans. Incidentally, the whole field of design of low vulnerability re-entry heads and matched decoys is one that that was pioneered in the UK in our work on Blue Streak, and even though Skybolt is an American vehicle the UK would have the most valuable contribution to make in the sort of studies I have outlined. [10]

As it happened, Polaris was the deterrent in the 1970s, and similar arguments were applied. In fact, the problem was more acute with Polaris since the probability was that only one submarine would be on patrol at a time. Each submarine carried sixteen missiles with three warheads each. The idea of targeting forty or more cities had gone, to be replaced with what would be described as the Moscow criterion. As a consequence, at least £1 billion was spent removing one of the three warheads and replacing it with a highly complex system of decoys as part of a project named Chevaline. One of the reasons for the increased cost of the system was the delay imposed by Treasury equivocation. One of the techniques used was to put the project on a three-monthly approval; in other words, after three months, the Ministry of Defence would have to apply for more funding. This had several implications—firstly, many private companies were reluctant to take part; secondly, the morale of those working on the projects was considerably affected; and, thirdly, it was very difficult to order long-term lead items. Cost overruns and delays on defence projects are not always the fault of the contractors or of the Ministry of Defence.

No Fight More Bitter

Inter-service rivalry is nothing new, and in many ways, it was increased by the advent of nuclear weapons, not only in the United States but in the UK. Not even the US Navy wanted to be left out of the field, and although the US Navy was interested in getting their share of the deterrent, early experiments with liquid-fuelled missiles were discouraging. Launching any long-range ballistic missile from a surface ship in any degree of seaway was also problematic. Even the largest surface ships roll and pitch in any sort of a sea state; in the early 1950s, the only long-range missiles that were feasible were large, fragile, and liquid-fuelled. Tests to see what would happen if such a missile were to explode on deck rapidly discouraged any such plans, although the Admiralty briefly toyed with the idea as early as 1953:

> A ship-launched Ballistic Weapon might well be half the size of a land-based weapon for the same warhead weight, if the range to the target could be halved by taking the launching platform halfway to that target.[1]

In other words, if a ship could carry the missile closer to enemy territory, then the missile could be smaller, which is a reasonable assertion. There was an underlying agenda, however, as the note went to say:

> ... the suggestion for using a submersible launching platform is probably in the realms of fantasy, even beyond the next 20 years, but furtherance of this project with a Naval application may well imply the preservation of the K.G.V hulls for many years to come.[2]

The 'K.G.V hulls' is a reference to the four remaining King George V battleships, which were then in reserve and scrapped in the late 1950s, and since battleships were still dear to the naval heart, any way in which they might be preserved would be very welcome.

The problem was solved by the appearance of three new technologies—the nuclear-powered submarine, more effective solid-fuel rocket motors, and lightweight warheads. Polaris was instigated before these technologies became fully mature, in the anticipation that they would become available as development continued. The initial designs simply took the hunter-killer submarine and cut it in two just aft of the sail or conning tower. A new hull section with space for up to sixteen missiles was inserted.

The Royal Navy had also seen the possibilities of nuclear power for submarines; indeed, the Admiralty had assigned an engineer to the nascent nuclear programme even before the war had ended. A reactor design for a submarine had been drawn up and a report presented at the Harwell Power Conference of 1951.[3] The reactor would be gas-cooled and graphite-moderated, using slightly enriched uranium. As a design for a submarine, it was totally impracticable. The large thermal capacity of the graphite would mean that it could take hours for the reactor to reach full power, there was no suitable design of fuel rod to operate under those conditions, and the system would be far too fragile to install in a submarine which might be depth charged. The idea was dropped in favour either of a pressurised water reactor (PWR) or a liquid-metal-cooled reactor. The idea of the liquid metal cooled reactor was soon dropped, although one example was built in the United States and various designs were also used in Russian submarines.

There were many problems associated with fitting a reactor into a submarine which have no land-based counterpart. One of the major problems was that of shielding; in a land-based reactor, weight is no problem and a biological shield of several feet of concrete can be used. This is not an option in a submarine, and in 1954, Harwell suggested to the Navy that a 'swimming pool' reactor be built to test out different materials for shielding. This is a type of reactor that has a core immersed in an open pool of water, with the water acting as neutron moderator, cooling agent and radiation shield all in one. The reactor was named LIDO by Harwell (a pun, as in England, a lido is an open-air swimming bath) and would need a few kilograms of enriched U235, but by 1955, that was no longer a problem.

A naval section was set up at Harwell, and by 1957, around 160 professional staff were working on the development of a PWR for submarine use. The project was making good progress despite the occasional setback, when an agreement was reached in July 1958 between the British and American Governments on co-operation in the use of atomic energy.[4]

Mountbatten, that charismatic figure of the Navy, was able to work his charm on Rickover, responsible for the first American nuclear submarine, the *Nautilus*. As a result, an amendment of the US Atomic Energy Act was passed, which allowed details of the reactor design to be passed to the UK. The first UK nuclear-powered submarine was HMS *Dreadnought*, launched in 1960. The *Dreadnought* design evolved into what were described as 'hunter-killer' submarines, whose job it was to intercept and destroy Russian nuclear submarines.

The *Nautilus* had gone to sea in 1954. By 1956, Polaris was in development. To save time, the George Washington, already under construction, was cut in half and sixteen missile tubes installed. The submarine was commissioned in December 1959. The first model of the missile—A1—had a range of 1,200 miles. This was increased to 1,500 miles with the A2 missile in 1962 and 2,500 miles with the A3 missile in 1963. The later models could be fitted into the tube designed for the A1 missile.

Needless to say, the Admiralty was also very interested in Polaris and its progress, and almost from the outset, a RN liaison officer was appointed to the American project. Just as with Rickover, there was a close personal relationship between Mountbatten, soon to become Chief of the Defence Staff, and Arleigh Burke, the American admiral in charge of the Polaris programme. Yet Naval interest was accompanied by an almost paranoid view of the Minister of Defence, Sandys, and of the possession by the RAF of Britain's nuclear forces. Sandys was a hard-working and effective politician, although he could be extremely abrasive.

Sandys was not in favour of Polaris, as this note to the First Sea Lord in January 1959 shows:

> I heard in the House of Commons that the Minister of Defence, when asked whether a submarine equipped with POLARIS would not be a useful deterrent replied that he thought it would soon be just as easy to pinpoint the position of a submarine as to pinpoint the position of a land-based rocket. Do you know what grounds he had for saying this?[5]

To this, the reply came: 'In fact the Minister of Defence was wide of the mark in suggesting it was easy to pin-point a submarine. Indeed, if he were right, we should very much like to know how to set about it'.

In fact, it was the Admiralty, rather than Sandys, who was correct, which is why such submarines still form the basis of our deterrent today. Yet the Admiralty was also aware that there would be no chance of acquiring Polaris if Blue Streak was given the go ahead. As a consequence, the Admiralty was determined to do all it could to hinder and delay the development of Blue Streak, in the hope of eventual cancellation. The tone of Admiralty papers of the period gives some flavour of this.

Thus Selkirk, First Lord of the Admiralty, wrote in a memo of 1959:

> My aim last year was not only to make the Prime Minister, Minister of Defence, and other members of the Defence Committee aware of the possibilities of Polaris, but also to check, as far as this was possible, the Blue Streak programme before it gathered momentum. We have had some success ...
>
> Blue Streak has become more firmly established and it looks at the moment as if the 60/61 Estimate discussions this autumn may strengthen it further. If this should be so, its formidable cost, as shown in the draft paper you attached, will become a most serious threat to our hopes of increasing the size of our conventional naval forces—even of the total defence vote were to be fairly substantially enlarged.[6]

This would imply that the Admiralty was lobbying hard in Whitehall and Westminster. Further papers indicate similar lobbying. In a note on a possible European IRBM from the First Sea Lord in February 1959, he comments:

> Nevertheless, mainly thanks to the Treasury, it was possible to secure a chance to refer this point to Ministers on the grounds that, in the highly unlikely event of our NATO partners taking up the offer, HMG would be committed to the completion of Blue Streak with all that entails.

Later on in the note, commenting with reference to problems with solid-fuel motors, he says, 'unless we can effectively answer them the chances of upsetting BLUE STREAK may be considerably weakened'.[7]

Yet one of the most striking pieces of lobbying, relating to this idea of Blue Streak becoming a European missile, comes in a handwritten note to the First Sea Lord from Admiral Sir Charles Lambe:

> I have discussed with the Treasury the idea that First Lord should send a minute to the Chancellor about Blue Streak. They welcomed it.
>
> I have accordingly prepared the attached draft. The First Lord will of course be aware that strictly speaking he would be acting unconstitutionally in by-passing the Minister of Defence—not that any good could be done by approaching him at this stage. The First Lord may therefore feel that it would be safer to cast the minute into the form of a letter to the Chancellor, to be marked 'Private'.[8]

The attached draft began:

I gather that when this subject was discussed at the Ministry of Defence yesterday both your representative and mine expressed the fear that we might become irretrievably committed to BLUE STREAK as a result of offering it once more to European countries.[9]

This goes beyond lobbying; it was a deliberate attempt to undermine Government policy as agreed by the Prime Minister, Chancellor, and Minister of Defence. It also illustrates the Mountbatten hubris; someone else without his ego, self-confidence, and family connections might well have thought twice before going behind his minister's back in this way. Field Marshal Sir Gerald Templer reputedly said to him, 'Dickie, you're so crooked that if you swallowed a nail you'd shit a corkscrew!' Although there were second thoughts about the memo, the fact that it was even considered is revealing enough in itself.

Indeed, any project of any kind relating to Blue Streak caused alarm in the Admiralty. In April 1959, a Cabinet decision was taken to initiate design studies for a possible satellite launcher, which would have been based on the Blue Streak and Black Knight rockets. The Cabinet had authorised a budget for this of £100,000–200,000. As far as the Admiralty was concerned, the consequence of this decision had these implications:

a) Blue Streak more firmly established
b) conflict in money and resources between the R&D and military R&D
c) possibility that because of military possibilities some of the expenditure would be passed to defence vote.[10]

The Admiralty pushed hard to set up the study group that was to lead to Blue Streak's cancellation, the BNDSG, although the most active opposition in the study group to Blue Streak came from the Treasury. Nevertheless, the BNDSG recommended Skybolt, and, other than the vulnerability argument, the Skybolt/V bomber concept had a lot going for it.

Even so, there was considerable support for Polaris in Westminster and Whitehall generally, so much so that the Air Ministry became alarmed:

The Minister of Aviation's minute of the 25th February to the Prime Minister casting doubt on the immunity of the V-force to attack, ought to be refuted at once.

His line of argument leads straight to the conclusion that we should mount the deterrent in a submarine rather than equip the V-force with SKYBOLT, and in due course replace the V-bombers with a new airborne platform for SKYBOLT. We would be very foolish to discount the gathering momentum behind the submarine-based deterrent. Judging from the report of the Defence Debate there appears to be a substantial bias in political circles in favour of the submarine. It is probably true to say that the majority of Whitehall Departments are similarly mesmerised by the difficulty of detecting and destroying the submarine and by the fact that POLARIS tends to be regarded as an existing option; outside the Air Ministry the V-bomber successor is still widely regarded as a pious aspiration. The arithmetic in the Powell Committee's report can be used (and was used by the Minister of Aviation) to suggest that the submarine deterrent is not merely the most effective but also the cheapest. I am sure we cannot afford to lose a trick from now on in this game.[11]

The position of the Admiralty after the Blue Streak cancellation is summed up in a very revealing letter from the vice chief of the naval staff to Vice Admiral Sir Geoffrey Thistleton, currently serving in Washington as part of the British Joint Service Mission. The letter was dated April 1960:

After Dermot Boyle left as CAS [Chief of Air Staff], the Chiefs of Staff agreed unanimously that BLUE STREAK was a nonsense in view of Russian missile accuracy. In making a brave political decision to drop it, our Minister had to find something to show opinion here as an improvement. SKYBOLT lay ready to hand (he thinks) as a blood transfusion to keep the V bombers effective from 1965–70. We have the Bombers and obviously it is sense to exploit them to their limit before buying POLARIS submarines at £50M apiece. This argument might be different if we had NO V bombers, but as we have, the different dates of readiness of POLARIS and SKYBOLT are immaterial for our present purpose (1965–70). The Minister has assured us however that the Committee re-examining the relative merits of SKYBOLT and POLARIS for 1970 onwards will not be prejudiced by using SKYBOLT temporarily.

Our trouble is that the Minister has been advised by interested parties, in very optimistic terms, about SKYBOLT's state and prospects. I would almost say he has been led up the garden path. I would warn you that some of the advisers he will bring to you with him are bitterly anti-Navy and anti-Polaris, and if you see a chance you might warn [Arleigh] Burke in guarded terms of this tendency.

The Minister however is extremely shrewd and we are confident that when the facts relating to SKYBOLT and POLARIS respectively come to light, he is quite capable of discerning that SKYBOLT in 1966 or '67 may be not only invalid (in terms of its aircraft vulnerability), but also nearly as expensive as a modest POLARIS programme. He will then draw his own conclusions about spending millions on a very expensive short duration stopgap, and going straight to POLARIS.

In this situation, no-one here is going to throw away the V bomber force in 1965 after the millions spent on it, and it is useless for us to 'plug' POLARIS by high-level presentations at the moment—which would be interpreted as an attempt to jump the Committee's findings.

The Admiralty line (very successful too under Charles Lambe) is to be completely objective and national in all these problems, in contrast to the incessant and often foolish Air Ministry intrigue and false presentation of the facts which I'm ashamed to say still goes on.[12]

This latter paragraph seems to be written with no sense of irony whatsoever, which in view of the earlier comments is astounding. The letter goes on:

My own feelings are frankly of some doubt whether POLARIS (or any native British deterrent) will follow the V bomber force. It seems to me curious to expect the Pentagon to supply us with the weapons for an independent British deterrent whose purpose, quite frankly, is more to influence State Department policy than to frighten the Russians. If they do so, it will surely be more from the motive of getting the UK to share with them the odium of world opinion for having the thing at all! Their reasons, however, are their business.[13]

There were also attempts to involve the United States Navy. Prior to the visit of Watkinson and Macmillan to America, a letter, marked 'PERSONAL', to Admiral Arleigh Burke asked for help:

Our Minister of Defence will be visiting you about 27th May to spend five days each on POLARIS and SKYBOLT and anything you can do to make sure his facts are right on POLARIS, will be gratefully acknowledged ... Thanks to you, our knowledge of POLARIS is now up to date, but we are not in the same position regarding SKYBOLT. It might be very important to the Admiralty to have your detailed case against SKYBOLT and its general system, to check on the information obtained by the Royal Air Force, beyond what you sent with your letter of 12th March, 1960.[14]

Watkinson was certainly aware of the lobbying going on. Before his visit, he wrote a two-page memorandum to the Prime Minister, in which he noted that 'There are powerful forces in the POLARIS lobby which would like to see this project [that is, Skybolt] cancelled'.

So, from 1960 until 1962, the Admiralty conducted a low-level campaign on behalf of Polaris, but it seemed that the chances of success were becoming less and less likely. Notes still appear in the files such as one headed: 'Another Nail in the Skybolt Coffin?', concerning an article about Skybolt in an American magazine, *Missiles and Rockets*. It was clear that at a meeting in the Treasury in 1961, there was still obvious resentment that Skybolt had been chosen over Polaris:

> My clear impression was that, at all events at the level represented at this meeting, the only impartial minds were those of the Treasury. The Ministry of Defence and the Ministry of Aviation representatives quite clearly were there to back the Skybolt solution as against the Polaris solution, to the extent that they were prepared to keep quiet about the likely drawbacks of Skybolt unless they were quite strongly pressed, and, on the other hand, they played down even the merits of the Polaris system as far as possible.[15]

Meanwhile, in Whitehall, the controversy regarding the effectiveness of the bomber force compared with a submarine rumbled on, which was not helped by the uncertainties surrounding Skybolt. This reached such a pitch that a paper was circulated to the Air Staff entitled 'The Deterrent— the Weakness of Our Position'. It began by saying:

> There has been a powerful and almost universal resurgence of the Polaris lobby in Whitehall. This will merely receive added impetus from the latest news about Skybolt.
>
> The indications are that the choice of our long-term deterrent system will turn entirely upon arguments about vulnerability to pre-emptive attack.
>
> Polaris is widely credited with being wholly invulnerable to pre-emptive attack, and with being the only deterrent weapons system which has this quality. It is also operational now.[16]

It then went on to make the political argument:

(a) Both the Admiralty and the War Office (and a fortiori the soldiers and the sailors in the Ministry of Defence) would like to deprive the RAF of the deterrent, which they believe is prejudicial to their own financial interests.

(b) The Admiralty is divided in its views as to whether it would wish to maintain the deterrent in Polaris, but the odds are that in due course they would press for a few Polaris submarines.

(c) The civilian officials of the Ministry of Defence appear to be impressed with the representations made to them, e.g. by the DCNS [Deputy Chief of Naval Staff] and Sir Solly Zuckerman about the vulnerability of bombers to pre-emptive attack. They do not appear to appreciate or attach much importance to explanations that if Polaris submarines are not vulnerable, their communications are so vulnerable as to make them virtually fire first weapons or weapons which must be fired on delegated authority.[17]

It is certainly true that the Polaris missiles effectively had to be fired on delegated authority since they were intended as a retaliatory weapon. If the UK Government had been wiped out in a Soviet first strike, there would be no one left in a position of authority who could communicate with the submarines; all means of communication would almost certainly have been destroyed in the attack. It is interesting to see Zuckerman's name mentioned here since he was to be given the task of chairing a technical subcommittee of the British Nuclear Deterrent Study Group (BNDSG), which was to look at possibilities for the deterrent in the 1970s. The BNDSG had originally been set up to consider the viability of Blue Streak and was instrumental in its cancellation of the missile in favour of Skybolt. Having delivered its report, it lingered on in a quiet half-life for a few more years. Now, a technical subcommittee was to be set up to decide the nature of the deterrent in the 1970s. There were, in effect, only two options—Polaris or Skybolt—and the bitterness between the advocates of the two systems reached new depths during its meetings. In attempts to act as an advocate for one side or the other, some remarkably bizarre statements were made.

The terms of reference for the subcommittee were as follows:

(a) to consider the broad categories of weapons systems (e.g. ballistic missile and submarine, ballistic missile and an aircraft) that might be used by the United Kingdom for maintaining a nuclear deterrent in the period 1970–1980.
(b) to assess the vulnerability of each category of weapons systems to enemy countermeasures in that period taking into account of the possible results of the application of existing knowledge and the possible developments which could arise out of knowledge not at present available.
(c) to draw attention to technical considerations favouring the choice of one category of system rather than another.[18]

The Air Staff paper went on to say:

Since the British Nuclear Deterrent Study Group have remitted the initial examination of the problem of long-term deterrence to a panel of Scientists [*sic.*], S.A.A.M. should be present at their meetings to discuss these problems and should be given the clearest possible directions regarding the line he should take.[19]

'S.A.A.M.' stood for Scientific Adviser, Air Ministry, who at that time was Hayne Constant, who had been an early pioneer in the field of jet engines. Constant had been the director of the National Gas Turbine Establishment, which was part of the RAE, from 1948 to 1960, and was awarded the Gold Medal of the Royal Aeronautical Society in 1963 for his outstanding contribution to gas turbine development.

The subcommittee did indeed consist of scientists, all of whom were eminent in their fields. The chairman was Sir Solly Zuckerman; the members were Dr F. P. Bowden, Prof. R. Hanbury Brown (professor of radio astronomy at the University of Manchester), Sir Edward Bullard, Prof. D. G. Christopherson, Sir John Carroll (Chief Scientist, Royal Navy), Sir Robert Cockburn (Chief Scientist, Ministry of Aviation), Mr H. Constant (Scientific Advisor, Air Ministry), Sir William Cook (at that time, the member for production at the Atomic Energy Authority), Prof. W. R. Hawthorne, and Mr M. J. Lighthill (Director of the RAE).

Constant reported details of each of the meetings to the Deputy Chief of Air Staff (DCAS). His reports were not written in the usual official manner but in a much more idiomatic style. They give some fascinating insights, and he obviously felt that he was very much in the minority in this company:

> It is quite clear to me that everyone came to the first meeting convinced that the submarine was the answer and everyone except Lighthill has succeeded in preventing his mind being changed. That this should be so in spite of the facts and arguments that have been presented makes me feel that there must be some strong psychological appeal in the submarine. On the other hand, if the bomb is air-launched, every time an aircraft goes overhead they will be reminded of it.[20]

It must be said that Constant, who was representing the Air Staff and reporting to DCAS, may not have been entirely objective himself. Yet it must be said that if Hayne's reports were accurate, the quality of debate did not seem to be that high:

> The discussion then switched to the effectiveness of the weapon and a long argument about defence against low-level missiles developed. Cook said local defence of cities against low-level attack by aircraft or stand-off weapons could be cheaply accomplished by towers and balloons carrying nuclear warheads. Cockburn said that TSR 2 was no good because it could be jammed if under automatic terrain clearance control and the pilot could be blinded by searchlight if under manual control. Cook thought low-level attack absolute nonsense; Hanbury Brown thought one TSR 2 would be enough, so as to force Russians into the expense of building defences.[21]

It is difficult to jam the radar of an aircraft flying just above ground level; all radars are limited by the horizon. The suggestion that the pilot would be blinded by a searchlight also seems distinctly far-fetched. The idea of defending your city against low-level attacks by putting nuclear weapons on towers and balloons does seem rather absurd. Preventing an attack by nuclear weapons by detonating a nuclear device at low altitude above your own city seemed somewhat self-defeating. This was not the first time that Cook had made this suggestion; at an earlier meeting of the BNDSG, he had made a similar assertion. At the time, an Air Ministry official noted:

> The level of prejudice which seems likely to inform this study is revealed by Sir William Cook's suggestion that the TSR 2 would be vulnerable to Russian S.A.G.W., because the Russians would fire kiloton weapons at it while it was flying at altitudes of 200 feet or so over their own countryside.[24]

On another occasion, the idea of airborne patrols was being discussed. Constant relates the following:

> ... it was possible to conceive of more economical ways of putting on an air alert. For example, by the use of six missiles for aircraft instead of four. Solly Zuckerman burst in with glee that this would result in over hitting, since the aircraft would get schizophrenia if it tried to direct missiles to more than one target. In this he was supported by Cockburn and Hanbury-Brown, with Lighthill and Christopherson making affirmative noises.[25]

This was not the case; each of the missiles on the aircraft could be targeted separately. Lighthill should have been aware of that since he was the Director of the RAE. However, Zuckerman had to back down on this one. It fell to the secretary of the sub-committee, Dr Touch, to correct him:

> At the meeting of the BND Technical Sub-Committee on February 28th, if I understood you correctly you said you could not accept the statement made by Constant that an aircraft fitted with six missiles could attack six targets. The argument revolved around the possible cost of keeping the aircraft on the alert in the air.
>
>   As you probably know, with SKYBOLT the pre-launch computer in the aircraft can perform the necessary computations to permit simultaneous operation of two missiles against <u>different</u> targets. If three computers are installed, six missiles could be sent to six targets. The system is capable of attacking targets at least 45° off the aircraft heading, with slight loss in range.

It therefore seems to me that a system could be developed which would allow targets to be attacked with n missiles, without undue operational difficulty or limitations. But maybe I have missed your point?[26]

Constant had other many clashes with Zuckerman, the chairman. The two obviously did not get on, as one of Constant's comments on Zuckerman illustrates: 'I am afraid that he had no compunction in resorting to verbal sniping and clever dialectics whenever convenient'.

There was also the issue as to which system was the more secure—aircraft or submarines. Constant describes it:

A study of our draft report opened with a long and remarkable discussion about the likelihood of a commander in the air or at sea taking the law into his own hands or going mad and firing without orders. Bullard said and Cockburn agreed that there was danger of this happening in both cases but the danger was worse with the aeroplane. Although Zuckerman try [*sic.*] to prevent me, I finally succeeded in saying if they really believed that such a thing could happen, it could be prevented by fitting a ground-operated arming device so that the weapon could not be fired until a signal had been given, if necessary, by the P.M. himself. It was then decided that there was no advantage either way so far as unauthorised firing was concerned.[27]

There followed an even more bizarre episode:

The meeting concluded by a vote being taken from everyone in the room—the waitress serving tea had left and was unable to vote—and everyone except Lighthill and myself voted for Polaris. After the meeting, the chairman took another vote on whether there should be a deterrent at all. Everyone voted for no deterrent except Hawthorne, who thought they should be one, and the waitress and myself who didn't vote.

I have a feeling this is not the way the Queen's business should be conducted.[28]

The debate centred around the two potential options—either Skybolt or Polaris. The Air Staff had produced a report that showed how a fleet of VC 10 aircraft, which were equipped with six missiles each, could maintain a system of standing patrols. The capital cost would be of the order of £300 million. In one of the meetings, there was an interesting comment:

Lighthill [Director of the RAE] gave Skybolt a clean bill of health, saying that it was going well and that there were no obvious snags ahead. Solly Zuckerman commented, at considerable length, that it would not be completed on time, but agreed when I pressed him that it would certainly be done by the date we were discussing, namely 1970. Everyone except Lighthill expressed doubts as to whether the Americans would in fact press this development through to completion.[29]

The subsequent report was written by Zuckerman, and not surprisingly, Constant objected to its conclusions, as did Lighthill. Constant wrote:

> On a balanced view of the available evidence (including a great deal of evidence which is reflected in the report) we believe that the airborne deterrent in terms of credibility, vulnerability, relative cost, and other factors offers substantial advantages over the submarine deterrent during the period which we are studying. We do not consider that the report reflects the evidence given to the Committee accurately or in full, and we believe that the conclusions suggested in the covering letter are not in accordance with the evidence provided.[30]

It was clear that no agreement could be reached that would satisfy all the members of the committee, and so it was suggested that the secretary of the committee, Dr Touch from the Ministry of Defence, who was a neutral observer might be of some help. Touch noted:

> After a long discussion, the chairman expressed the hope I could rewrite the conclusions of the report. I said I could not, since I did not know what conclusion the committee had reached. No one had changed their views; no new detail of argument had been advanced. It was left that committee members disagreeing with the conclusion of the draft report should submit their versions to the secretary for consideration at the next meeting. Of course, this could result in members of committing themselves on paper to positions from which they may not be able to withdraw; I have no hope that it will produce any new material, though it may bring into focus more clearly the points of disagreement.[31]

He also felt that 'The majority report is also distasteful and unconvincing'. Constant threatened to produce a minority report, which led to one final meeting of the subcommittee and a new amended report. Constant had had the support of Lighthill, who had obviously been upset by the partisan nature of Zuckerman's chairmanship. Lighthill expressed his dissatisfaction in a fairly forthright letter:

Dear Solly,
    Until the last meeting of the B.N.D.S.G. Technical Sub-Committee, I had thought that its report was going to be a properly dispassionate one, reviewing

the respective technical advantages of the different possible solutions. Indeed, the main body of report, paragraphs 1 to 41, still sets out fairly satisfactorily the technical facts which were uncovered by the Sub-Committee.

At its last meeting, however, on your return from the US, you urged the sub-committee to go beyond its terms of reference and make something like a specific proposal, essentially on subjective grounds, by sharpening the Conclusions in paragraphs 42–51, beyond what was justified by the facts previously uncovered …

May I voice my opinion that the distinction between carefully sifted U.K. technical judgment on the one hand and hunches based on slanted U.S. tittle-tattle on the other is being blurred in M.O.D., under a Chairman of the Defence Research Policy Committee [Zuckerman] who since his appointment has never even visited R.A.E. (for one thing) to get a feel for the complexity and quality of actual U.K. Defence Research?

For example, you influenced the sub-committee subjectively at its last meeting by telling an American story about an air accident with a megaton weapon. I inquired about this of D.G./D.R.S. (Washington), who states categorically that the story is known to be false, as well as that the facts are in M.O.D. hands. He and I regard some of your remarks about the status of Skybolt as equally unfounded, or founded on information deliberately slanted for propagandist purposes. Only an impartial assessment of information from all available US sources by those in the Scientific Civil Service whose job it is to make such assessments can obtain trustworthy results.

You ruled discussion out of order to such an extent at the last meeting of the Sub-Committee, and proposed modification to the Conclusions in such a piecemeal manner, that I observe only now how much, when taken as a whole, they distort the balanced picture given in the penultimate draft of the paper. I cannot accept these Conclusions … and I am arranging with Constant to table a joint Minority Report.

… Although I don't consider the Sub-Committee competent to venture beyond the technical field into the political field and suggest a combined techno-political conclusion, nevertheless, when you asked me to do this, I did not 'decline your invitation' (as Constant, perhaps rightly, did). I said that from a technical point of view the Skybolt and Polaris solutions are rather evenly matched, as shown in the body of the report, but that the political point that <u>no one can be sure</u> if the U.K. government of the 1970s will retain a deterrent policy makes me greatly prefer the 'multi-role VC 10' solution. I did not say that I believed the deterrent would be abandoned, only that we cannot be sure; so let us not sink a large amount of capital in duplicating on a small scale the massive, inflexible, U.S. Fleet of nuclear missile-carrying submarines.[32]

The letter shows the depth of feeling that had arisen on both sides of the argument and shows the degree of frustration reached by advocates of one particular system or the other. It does seem obvious from this and similar correspondence that there was little common ground between the two sides, but given the composition of the committee, that was predictable almost from the outset.

Both sides had also made some rather exaggerated claims about the costs of each of the two systems, and the secretary of the committee was able to find more about the comparative costs from statements made by McNamara, the American Secretary of Defense.

In view of our arguments over the relative costs of an air patrol system and a nuclear powered submarine system, it is interesting to read in 'Missiles and Rockets', dated June 26th, page 9, that Defense Secretary, McNamara testified before the Mahon committee in June as follows:

About $1 billion is required it to 1) buy 40 B-58s and operate them with tankers for 5 years, 2) buy 45 B-52s with tankers and operate them for 5 years 3) buy 150 Minutemen in silos and maintain them for 5 years, 4) buy 6 Polaris submarines and operate them for 5 years.

There is a striking resemblance to the conclusions we reached regarding relative costs, and actual costs. The American figures would result in an estimated cost of $3 million per POLARIS missile per year on station, whereas the Admiralty estimates given to BND is £1 million [At the time, the exchange rate was £1 = $2.80]. As the B-52 carries four missiles only, the cost per missile per year is estimated at $3.3 million, compared with the Air Ministry's estimate of £1 M for the VC-10 proposal. Presumably the American basis of calculation does not allow for continuous patrol, so the running costs should be increased for comparison with Air Ministry's estimates. This increase would be counterbalanced by the cheaper operating costs of the VC-10 compared with the B-52.[33]

He also noted the cheapest option was Minuteman—in other words, land-based missiles in a silo.

The whole rather sad episode illustrates the deep divisions within the defence community. However, whether or not any attention would be given to the deliberations of the committee became irrelevant with the subsequent cancellation of Skybolt eighteen months later. With the demise of Skybolt, the debate collapsed, since the only other viable option was Polaris. If Polaris had not been available, the government would have been faced with some very expensive alternatives.

The VC 10 Airliner as a Skybolt Carrier

In the 1950s, BOAC (British Overseas Airways Corporation, then state-owned) had ordered Boeing 707s as their long-range airliner. However, the Boeings were underpowered for the short runways of the Empire routes, which were often at a relatively high altitude, and where the aircraft had to operate at tropical temperatures (conditions referred to as 'hot and high'). Various British aircraft manufacturers offered alternatives, and BOAC selected the Vickers design, which would become the VC 10. The most noticeable feature of the aircraft was the four jet engines mounted on the end of the fuselage, which resulted in a clean and efficient wing and reduced cabin noise. The first prototype flew in June 1962.

The Air Staff were interested in the VC 10 as a transport, but they took a very early interest in the idea of using the airliner as a Skybolt carrier, as a note from DCAS (Deputy Chief of Air Staff) in March 1960 shows:

We have been discussing the V.C.10 as a Skybolt carrier with MOA [Ministry of Aviation] for some weeks. A large number of variants have been proposed but it is not until we come to what is currently termed 'first stage development VC 10' that we come to one which meets the requirements we have in mind. This version which the M.O.A. believes would be available in 1966 would carry four Skybolts with an endurance of 11.5 hours, can operate from existing Class 1 airfields, has engines of 26,000 lb thrust, and an all up weight of 380,000 lb.[1]

Using an airliner as a missile carrier might seem a bizarre idea, but in this case, it made sense. Skybolt had a range of up to 1,000 miles, so it was possible for the carrier aircraft to release the missile well outside enemy territory. Hence the aircraft does not need any special defensive equipment. In addition, part of the concept was to use standing patrols if need be, something that the RAF had never attempted before. One of the points of a commercial airliner was to be able to fly as many hours as possible with a short turnaround time and relatively low maintenance—exactly what was needed for a Skybolt carrier on a standing patrol. The modifications that would need to be made to the airframe were minimal, although radar and other navigational equipment (Doppler, etc.) would be needed. In order to increase its attractiveness to the RAF, Vickers proposed a version of the aircraft that could be used either as a transport or as a missile carrier and could be quickly and easily changed from one role to the other.

Design changes to the basic VC 10 were to be kept to a minimum as a missile launcher. The nose section, forward of the flight deck, would be modified to allow for the fitting of an H2S radar scanner, which together with a dual Doppler aerial would enable the aircraft to be 'fixed' for missile launching. To provide for the necessary computers, display equipment, and instruments, a completely removable navigator's station was proposed. When the basic aircraft was required to be converted to the ALBM role, this complete console

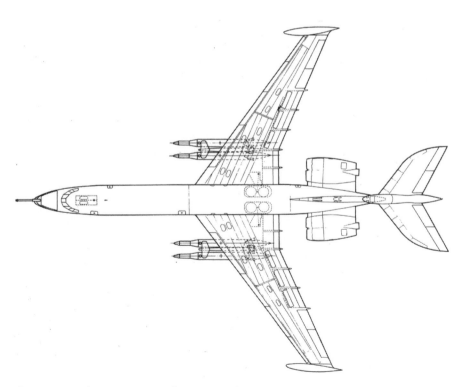

The VC 10 airliner in a new role as a missile carrier.

could be checked externally then loaded into the aircraft through the normal side door and secured into position. This reduced to a minimum the amount of specialist equipment required to be carried when the aircraft is used as a normal transport aircraft. Extra fuel tankage could be carried in removable cylindrical tanks in the fuselage when used in the missile launching role.

Indeed, it was not only the RAF that was thinking along these lines. The USAF had also looked at the possibility of using various transport aircraft, including the C-135 and C-141 aircraft, in the same role.

There was no intention at that time to use standing patrols; indeed, the idea was dismissed in the Air Ministry:

> I believe it will be equally fatal to suggest that we must resort to standing patrols. The Air Staff may retort that it is nevertheless true. In that case I believe that the choice of future deterrent will fall on POLARIS.[2]

The same memorandum contained an interesting final paragraph: 'Lastly, I think it would be a bad tactical mistake to drag the issue of whether or not we have an independent deterrent into this paper. We are the only department in Whitehall which wants one.' An Air Ministry report concluded:

> 36 VC 10s could initially provide on average a ground alert force of about 20 aircraft. This force has the capability of inflicting either:
> (i) 50% damage on the BNDSG cities, and the same degree of damage on 15 additional cities of population 100,000 or more, or
> (ii) 60% damage on the 40 BNDSG cities
> … 36 VC 10s could maintain an airborne patrol force of about 15 aircraft for the period of a little over a week. This airborne force could inflict either:—
> (i) 50% damage on 26 BNDSG cities including Moscow and Leningrad, or
> (ii) 50% damage on 30 BNDSG cities, excluding Moscow and Leningrad, or
> (iii) 30% damage on the 40 BNDSG cities.[3]

'BNDSG cities' refers to the forty cities listed by the British Nuclear Deterrent Study Group as targets for Bomber Command.

The Air Staff's interest in the idea did not quite square with Watkinson's statement to Cabinet in June, 'that no need was foreseen at the present time to order additional replacement aircraft of this or another type, such as the VC-10, that would add to the cost of the programme'.[4]

Vickers produced brochures describing how the aircraft might be used not only as a carrier of missiles, but also in the transport, tanker, and marine reconnaissance roles. As a missile carrier, endurance was obviously an important factor, and extra fuel could be carried in the otherwise empty fuselage. In addition, wingtip tanks could be added. The company quoted an endurance of eleven hours while carrying four missiles or fifteen hours with two missiles. The aircraft would be operating at its maximum all up weight of 380,000 lb. There were also proposals to replace the Conway engines with the Rolls-Royce Olympus since a more heavily laden aircraft would need more power on take-off. Some structural modifications would be needed if the wings were to carry the weight of four or six missiles. Vickers quoted a price of £2.75 million per aircraft for a transport version of the VC 10, and the Ministry of Aviation estimated that after various modifications, the price would work out to be £3–3.25 million. For a missile carrier, the unit cost would be nearer £4 million.[5] A fleet of forty-two would then come in at the not inconsiderable price of £168 million. The creation of the Technical Subcommittee of the BNDSG in 1962 meant that the Air Staff had to produce a fully costed operational plan for the use of the aircraft:

The operational force envisaged is 42 VC 10s, equipped with six Skybolts, operating at an annual rate of 3,200 hours per aircraft, with 15 aircraft permanently airborne. In conjunction with the Air Staff, we have made a series of planning assumptions namely:—

no dispersal of the aircraft is needed;

no overseas deployment is envisaged;

the force would have a single role only, i.e. as a Skybolt carrier;

the 4 Vulcan/Skybolt bases are available for the VC 10 force;

there is no requirement for short runway or emergency overload take-offs and the nature of the operational flying can be regarded as comparable with the VC 10 civil counterpart;

the first squadron is required to be in service by 1971;

a tanker force of 24 Victors would be available and would be used solely for VC 10 refuelling.

A flight refuelled sortie would last for nine hours.[6]

The size of the force needed was worked out on the basis:

(a) that there will be a period of tension before any war, which will allow the aircraft force to be brought to a state of maximum readiness (in the air alert role only, force aircraft would then be launched sufficient in number to achieve the task).

(b) that in the air alert role aircraft will patrol near the UK because of the certainty of VHF communications and because of the security from attack in that area.

(c) that in the European context four main launch areas will be used with the following mean distances from the UK

Central Norway   820 nm

Skagerrak	530 nm
Adriatic Sea	820 nm
Aegean Sea	1,600 nm

(d) that the aircraft turnaround time will be five hours.[7]

Carrying six missiles would mean a considerable redesign of the aircraft. The engines in the VC 10 were mounted at the rear of the fuselage, and the wings were free from encumbrances. To take the weight of the missiles, they would need to be strengthened quite considerably, and adding fuel tanks on the wing tips would mean strengthening the wings still further. This would also increase the take-off weight of the aircraft. Vickers' brochure for the design shows that it would need to be refuelled at least once during a twelve-hour patrol.

This was the scheme put forward to carry the deterrent in the 1970s when the V bombers would be reaching the end of their fatigue life. As part of the scheme, standing patrols were envisaged, which could be stepped up in what were referred to as times of tension. The Air Staff estimated that a force of thirty-six VC 10s could maintain an airborne patrol force of about fifteen aircraft for a period of a little over a week.

The alternative to the VC 10/Skybolt combination would have been Polaris. It is difficult to compare costs, although attempts were made. The VC 10 scheme would have the great advantage that the missiles which had been carried on the V bombers could simply be transferred to the new aircraft. With the cancellation of Skybolt, the whole scheme became moot, although it remains as an interesting concept.

The VC 10 was not the only aircraft to be considered as a Skybolt carrier. Short Brothers, based in Northern Ireland, were producing a heavy transport aircraft for the RAF. This was powered by four turboprop engines, which limited its speed and altitude. It was not a particularly successful aircraft (only ten were built) and its length of time in RAF service was fairly short. The suggestion was fairly rapidly dismissed:

You asked for our views on the potential of the Belfast strategic transport in the role of deterrent missile carrier.

Using as a basis the performance estimates given in the firm's brochure—'The "Belfast" as a Skybolt Missile Carrier'—I have the following comments:–

The launch height is given variously as 23,000–31,000 feet, depending on the number of missiles carried and the particular version of the aircraft considered, in each case referring to the aircraft weight at half-range point. This limitation in launch height and in particular the cruising speed of the Belfast could be serious. I understand that, in its present configuration, the missile is designed for launch speeds between 0.8 and 0.85M and heights between 40,000 and 50,000 feet. If the missile had been launched at considerably lower heights

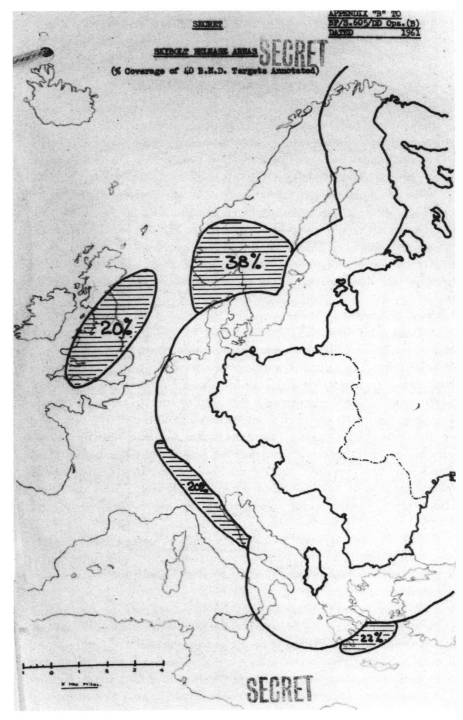

SECRET

APPENDIX "B" TO
BF/S.605/DD Ops.(B)
DATED 1961

SKYBOLT RELEASE AREAS
SECRET

(% Coverage of 40 B.N.D. Targets Annotated)

38%

20%

20%

22%

SECRET

Launch areas for VC 10 Skybolt carriers on patrol.

at very much lower speeds, a considerable amount of development work and testing would be necessary to establish the feasibility. There is also the obvious limitation that at 23,000–31,000 feet aircraft would on many missions be in cloud and star acquisition would be impossible.

The range of the Skybolt missile is certainly reduced by the effect of launching at lower height and speed. I understand that the reduction quoted (range of the order of 850n.m.) is approximately correct. The need to penetrate closer to enemy defences in an aircraft of such poor performance is reason enough for rejecting the Belfast as a successor to the Vulcan, unless very long-range missiles also succeed Skybolt.

The maximum weapon carriage offered is four Skybolt missiles, which reduces the cost effectiveness when compared with aircraft capable of lifting greater numbers. An aircraft of this type has little or no development potential in the role of carrier of future missile systems.

If the Vulcan replacement is to have a limited war capability also, the Belfast would be ruled out, excepting conditions of negligible air opposition.[8]

However, there was another aircraft that was briefly proposed as a possible Skybolt carrier: the TSR 2. Fitting the missile to the aircraft would be extremely difficult. If it were carried underneath, it would block the doppler radar. The only alternative was to mount it on top of the aircraft, which given their relative sizes, would make life rather difficult. The result would no doubt greatly increase the drag of the aircraft and blank the airflow to the fin. In addition, in addition, there would also be the problem of how to launch the missile. Firing the rocket motor *in situ* would not be a very good idea; apart from anything else, it would blow the aircraft fin off. The answer was that the aircraft would have to turn upside down and then release the missile. This does not seem an entirely satisfactory way of going about things. Various scenarios were considered:

Skybolt, if launched from TSR 2 at low altitude, is unlikely to have a range of more than 300 or 400 nautical miles, making, with the aircraft flying at high subsonic speed at low altitude, a total of about 1,000 nautical miles radius of action.

Flying at medium altitude (about 25,000 feet). During the early part of the journey from this country and to the enemy radar is reached would only add about 100 nautical miles to the radius, making a total of 1,100 nautical miles, i.e. about 500 nautical miles less than is needed to allow the aircraft to start from and return to this country. If, in spite of the resulting increase in vulnerability, to the region of 40,000 feet could be made before releasing the weapon, the range of Skybolt, would be increased to about 800 nautical miles and, with a medium altitude early flight for the aircraft,, followed by a

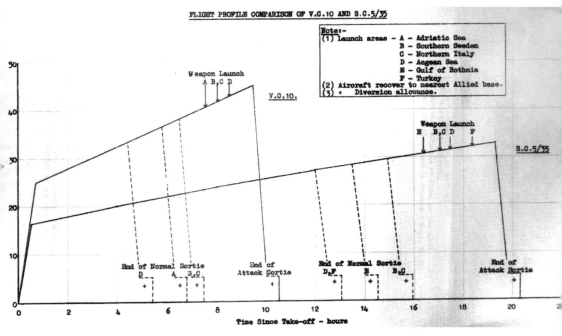

Comparison of the mission profiles of the VC 10 versus the Belfast (S.C5/35). The superiority of the VC 10 is very apparent.

descent to low altitude to avoid enemy radar, the total radius of action to be about 1600 miles; sufficient to allow the aircraft to start from and return to this country. Since the climb to 40,000 feet would only occupy two or three minutes, the increase in vulnerability might not be significant.

In this employment Skybolt would be modified so as not to use a star tracker, because at low altitude it could not depend on seeing the stars. In these circumstances, and with Skybolt having an assumed range of 800 nautical miles, the accuracy is unlikely to be better than 4 miles CEP. Development of this modified Skybolt would require trials, not only of the aircraft installation, but also of missile functioning and accuracy.[9]

However, it did seem rather pointless to adapt a highly expensive and versatile military aircraft to carry only one missile, and that with difficulty.

Given that each VC 10 would cost nearly £4 million each, and that the Air Staff wanted forty-two of them, that would give a bill well in excess of £150 million. In addition, there would also be the need for training, new ground equipment and other ancillary services, which would probably put the bill closer to £200 million. As we shall see later, Handley Page made a proposal to convert thirty-six existing Victor aircraft to carry six Skybolt each at a total cost of £3 million. Even if Handley Page's estimates had been out by a factor of ten, they would still have been a complete bargain.

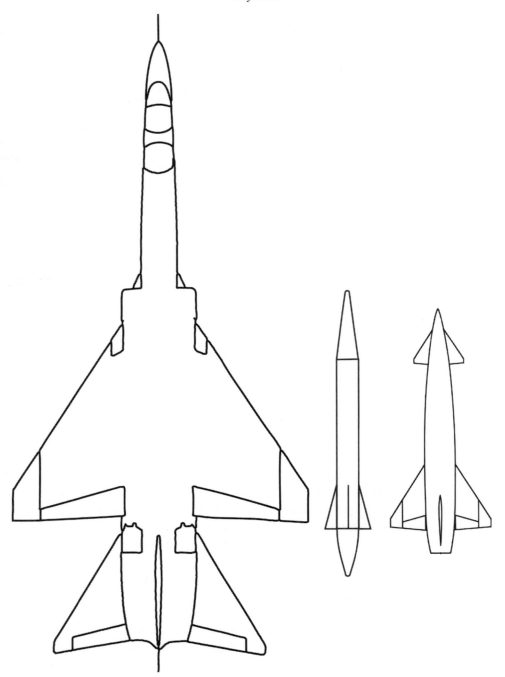

The TSR 2, Blue Steel, and Skybolt to approximately the same scale. Both missiles were far too large to be carried by the aircraft. Putting Blue Steel onto TSR 2 made no sense at all, and the only place on the aircraft where Skybolt would fit was on top, blanking the fin and forcing the aircraft to fly upside down to release the missile.

An Insurance Policy: OR 1182: The Last Attempt at an All-British Deterrent

Bristol Aircraft had been working on ramjets since the early 1950's—in particular, on the surface-to-air missile Bloodhound, which was boosted to supersonic speed by four solid-fuel rocket motors and which then continued on to its target under the power of two ramjets. Ramjets have a major advantage over rockets in that they take their oxygen from the atmosphere and do not need to carry their own oxidant. They are also simpler than conventional jet engines since they do not need turbines. Instead, air is forced into the engine ('rammed in'), which means it needs to be travelling at speed before the engine can be started, hence the need for solid-fuel rocket boosters.

Aircraft manufacturers were always looking for new opportunities for their wares, and so Bristol put forward a proposal to the Air Staff for a long-range stand-off missile powered by a ramjet. As it happened, the Air Staff were indeed interested in this proposal, as they saw this new missile as a possible insurance policy against the failure of Skybolt. As time went on, though, it seemed as though Skybolt was more secure and that no insurance policy would be needed. Indeed, in June 1961, an Air Ministry official wrote: 'The weapon could be regarded as ... an insurance against the SKYBOLT programme falling through. I hope we can now dismiss this from the realm of practical politics.'[1]

He was wrong, and as a result, there was no insurance. To be fair, the new Administration in the United States seemed to have accepted Skybolt as part of the defence programme, and spending large sums of money on a weapon, which would have been inferior to Skybolt would seem distinctly wasteful.

The initial proposal was for a ramjet missile capable of being released at a speed of Mach 0.87 at 50,000 feet from V-bombers at ranges from the target of up to 1,300 miles. The missile would fall freely for three seconds, before being boosted by four Gosling solid-propellant rocket motors to a speed of Mach 2.7 in a further three seconds, after which it would climb and accelerate under the ramjet alone to a cruising speed of Mach 3 at an altitude of around 57,000 feet. After a high-level cruise to about 67,000 feet, the final approach to the target would be made at Mach 2.2 at low altitude, about 200 feet, over a distance of about 50 miles. Greater sea level distances could be achieved at the expense of overall range; for example, if the entire trajectory was carried out at a low altitude, the weapon would have a range of 300 miles. The missile would carry a forward-looking terrain clearance radar, inertial guidance equipment and a nuclear warhead. Without the boosters, it would be just over 31 feet long and 28 inches in fuselage diameter with an overall height of 4 feet and 9 inches. Its weight would be 7,800 lb, and four missiles could be carried on a Vulcan B Mark 2.

The Air Staff were obviously impressed by the proposal, but one of the snags was that under the cumbersome and bureaucratic procurement procedures of the time, the Air Staff would have to write an operational requirement, have it approved by the Defence Research and Policy Committee, submit it to the Ministry of Aviation, who would then send round the requirement to various selected aircraft companies, receive their designs, evaluate them, and then choose what they thought was the most suitable for the requirement. Not for the first time and not for the last time, the Air Staff felt frustrated by this procedure. The Deputy Chief of Air Staff (DCAS) wrote:

> I am quite sure that the Ministry of Aviation will waste a good deal of time and energy examining whether we ought to have a weapon of this kind unless it is made clear from the start that the need for the weapon has been endorsed by Ministers and that their task is to see how the need can be met within the comparatively short time available.[2]

Julian Amery, the Secretary of State for Air, wrote to Harold Watkinson:

> In drafting the requirement we have had very much in mind the ideas of the guided weapons division of the Bristol Aircraft Ltd ... You may agree with me that in view of the stringent timescale we should take a chance and give the firm an immediate contract for a detailed design study.[3]

Thorneycroft, then Minister of Aviation, was not impressed by this attempt to short-circuit the procurement process:

> This is a proposal for a major project. Its cost might be in the region of £100 million. We cannot afford to make a major error, in view of past history in this field. Before we place a design study contract, we ought to have the best

advice we can get in on the broad outline of the missile system to be studied and the resources likely to be needed to develop and use it. This is most necessary if we are to save valuable time and money in the long-run.

I have, therefore, asked for a report by 18th December on the technical possibilities and operational value of developing a long-range cruise type weapon ...

Secondly, it would be a mistake to think only in terms of AVRoe or Bristols to undertake work of this type. They are members of the Hawker Siddeley Group and of the British Aircraft Corporation respectively. It is for instance most important that effort should not be diverted from introducing Blue Steel Mk.1 into service at the earliest possible moment. It is going to be a major undertaking to get a missile of the type you propose in to service by 1966. It may not indeed be practicable. In order to give us the best possible chance of succeeding, we must take a little time now to decide how the work can best be undertaken without detriment to existing projects. Here again, I have asked for an urgent report on the resources which are likely to be needed.

Before the end of the year we should be able to take an informed decision about the nature of the design study contract or contracts which we should place and with whom we should place them.[4]

Thus the Air Staff had to write out a full operational requirement (OR1182) for the new missile, which was issued in November 1960. The Air Staff were rather irritated by this demand, with a comment that was indicative of the poor relations between the Air Staff and the Ministry of Aviation:

The M.O.A. [Ministry of Aviation] undoubtedly was seriously put out by Bristol's attempt to secure a contract for an air-to-ground missile, the O.R. for which had not at that stage been through the lengthy but normal M.O.A. processes and the M.O.A. interim report reflected general antagonism. I think we must now try to quickly isolate this parochial opposition from the real issue which is whether this country as a policy first, requires, and secondly, has the ability within a reasonable timescale, to develop a viable long-range cruise type deterrent missile.[5]

There was the usual frustration at having to deal with another ministry that did not want to provide the weapons the Air Force thought it needed, as the record of a conversation between a senior member of the Air Staff and the Chief Scientist at the Ministry of Aviation, Sir Robert Cockburn, illustrates:

Following the DRPC meeting yesterday, I had about forty minutes good-natured but serious argument with Sir Robert Cockburn and the views he expressed throws some light on events of the last few days ...

Sir Robert firmly believes that the time taken to produce a sophisticated weapons system in this country is not more than 8–10% greater than the equivalent project time in the USA. As you heard it in the DRPC meeting yesterday he fixes a period in the UK at 8–10 years. When I confronted him with the American claims that Thor was produced in two years, Polaris in four, Hound Dog in three and Skybolt (God willing) in four, he contended that these periods of time did not meet with his definition which takes account of the period elapsing from first conception of the project to initial operational capability. He argues, for instance, that considerable work and therefore time had been devoted to the components of most of the projects I named long before the equivalent of the OR was issued to the contractors.

This seems to be the root of the present trouble with MOA and the Bristol's idea of X12. The Bristol project, as with Skybolt, is based on the use of proven components and techniques were not dependent on new ideas. The timescale is to be the predominant aim, but it is my understanding the MOA still persists in saying that at least 7–10 years of development will be required.

It seems that we must reconcile this issue with them and have the MOA pinpoint precisely which components are new and will require such a long period of development. I am confident that there will not be many, and if there are any at all which justify their pessimism, the solution is to buy that particular component of off-the-shelf from America. The aim in producing X12 is after all to produce a weapon in five years, not to create a weapon which we called in all honesty say is entirely conceived and made in Britain.

The other basic objection which Sir Robert voices to X12 was that the low-level conception was wrong because ground defences within the timescale envisaged will be able to destroy it. I tactfully suggested that this was perhaps not the field in which MOA should spend a lot of time, as this involved operational as well as economic factors which should eventually be a subject for the DRPC as a whole and perhaps the Chiefs of Staff. He argues that the results from Bloodhound and Thunderbird trials indicate that the Russians could in the timescale produce a defensive system around all likely targets, with their detection radars mounted on towers ... I reminded him of the magnitude of this problem, together with the complications involved in tying it in with defences against other forms of attack posed by manned aircraft, ICBMs etc, he still contended that it was feasible.

I was left in no doubt that the whole of the MOA approach to the X12 proposals was coloured by their conviction that the operational concept was wrong and it was, therefore, their duty to cast doubts upon it wherever possible. I was also convinced that Sir Robert still feels very sore indeed about the cancellation of Blue Streak. The RAF are held largely responsible for giving up this weapon which he and a lot of his people in the MOA feel most keenly should have been continued and the attitude that we must now put up with the difficulties which this cancellation revolved was made quite apparent.[6]

One further addition to the proposal was for the missile to be able to 'jink'—that is, to have the ability to alter course during flight so as to confuse the defences. The missile was required to be in service by 1966, but the Air Staff were prepared to accept some reduction in range and complexity in order to get the missile in service as early as possible, but with the proviso that it could be subsequently upgraded.

The Royal Radar Establishment (RRE) was asked to write a report as to the feasibility of a Russian defence against such a missile. In the summary to the report, it was noted:

> It is concluded that, from a limited study, that an effective low-level defence could be mounted at an initial capital cost, for the basic technical equipment, of about £M15 to £M25 per city ...
>
> Work services, spares and training and exercising would add considerably to the above costs. An addition of 100% is not unlikely.[7]

The CGWL, Sir Steuart Mitchell, was of much the same opinion:

> The advent of C.W. [Continuous Wave] radar techniques, and of semi-active C.W. homing systems, has opened up a major breakthrough in defence against low-level attack.
>
> Given nuclear warheads, a very effective defence for cities by heavy S.A.G.W. [Surface-to-Air Guided Weapon] could be provided against medium or high attack by both manned winged aircraft and unmanned winged guided weapons. The chance of a kill per S.A.G.W. fired would be of the order of 80% against such targets.
>
> The same heavy S.A.G.W. system deployed ... but using H.E. warheads, could also provide a good defence against both manned and unmanned low-level attack, if the acquisition and TIR radars are sited either on buildings or towers 100 ft. above the ground.
>
> A light S.A.G.W. system using semi-active C.W. homing and H.E. warheads and mounted on 50-100 ft. towers or buildings could provide a good defence against both manned and unmanned low-level attack. The chance of a kill per S.A.G.W. fired would be of the order of 50% against manned aircraft and 30% against unmanned guided missiles.
>
> The cost of missiles, launches, and their radars to give this level of defence to a city of 1M inhabitants, but not including supporting costs such as crew accommodation, roads, power, etc, and not including the national early warning system, would be of the order of £7–12M per city at UK prices.

With the supporting services this might be increased to £10–15M. To provide this for a total of, say, 50 Russian cities so located as to be within range of this type of attack would cost £500–£750M …

Raising the speed of the manned aircraft to supersonic figures—say Mach 2—would give it very little extra protection against S.A.G.W. defence, except in the case of attack against Coastal towns where early warning is difficult.[8]

Although the UK did have plans for a nuclear-tipped Bloodhound missile, they were soon dropped. However, the US did deploy two such systems: the BOMARC and the Nike Hercules.

Nike Hercules was the first to be deployed and had a very respectable performance; one was fired at a simulated aerial target, which was at an altitude of 100,000 feet and 55 miles distant, detonating within 50 feet of the aiming point. The BOMARC was ramjet-powered, similar to Bloodhound; initial deployment began late in 1959 and was taken out of service in the early 1970s. Each missile carried a W-40 nuclear warhead, with a yield of around 6.5 kT. Approximately 400 missiles were produced. There was also an air-to-air missile deployed by the United States, which carried a 1.5-kT warhead, known as Genie. The lethal radius of the warhead was estimated to be about 300 metres or 1,000 feet. However, a missile the size and shape of X12 would be a great deal less vulnerable than a standard aircraft design. The Russian equivalent to Nike Hercules or Bloodhound was the SA-2 Guideline, a nuclear-tipped version of which came into service in May 1964.

Yet there are other factors to take into account when considering the effects of a nuclear explosion. As well as the blast effect, there is, of course, thermal radiation, and also X-ray and neutron bombardment. X-rays and neutrons can disable semiconductors, such as transistors, thus destroying the guidance if not the missile itself. Nuclear warheads are also very vulnerable to X-rays and neutrons. Certainly, the UK was aware of this in the late 1950s, describing it as the 'R1 effect', and devoting considerable effort to develop what were described as 'immune' warheads. Fairly obviously, the core of the nuclear weapon, made as it is of uranium or plutonium, would be extremely vulnerable to neutrons in particular, which could cause the weapon to 'fizzle'.

AVRO did some analysis on the vulnerability of the W130 missile mentioned above. The W130 was described as a boost-glide vehicle, and the glide started at an altitude of 108,000 feet after boost termination, and ended at an altitude of 90,000 feet, followed by a dive on to the target. Avro considered its vulnerability against four possible Western systems. These were the Bloodhound Series 2 surface-to-air missile, Bloodhound Series 3 (never deployed) and the American Nike Hercules and Nike Zeus. The Nike Zeus

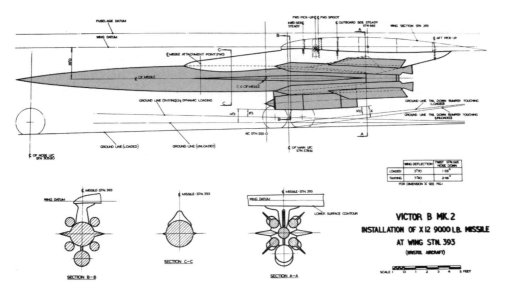

The Bristol X 12 missile mounted under the wing of a Victor bomber.

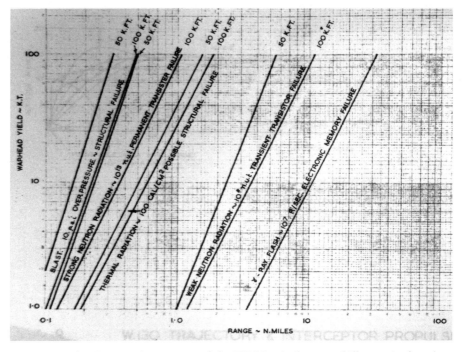

An estimate by Avro in the context of the W130 missile as to 'kill range' of nuclear warheads. Blast is the least effective; much more damage is done by neutrons and X-rays. Later re-entry vehicles had to be 'hardened' against such effects.

was the most capable of these, having a maximum interception range of 150 miles at altitudes of up to 60,000 feet. Command guidance was used for the greater part of the trajectory, with active radar homing for final interception. The final stage used a thrust vectoring rocket and was, therefore, highly manoeuvrable at all altitudes. AVRO considered that the W130 was safe against Bloodhound and Nike Hercules, but not against Nike Zeus.

There was also an attempt made by the RAE to assess the vulnerability of what was described as 'a supersonic flying bomb' (in other words, Blue Steel) to attack by guided weapon warheads. These were taken to be conventional high explosive warheads, not atomic warheads. After a fairly lengthy analysis, the conclusion reached was as follows: 'it has been tentatively concluded from the survey that, on the evidence of available information alone, the supersonic flying bomb is a target of low vulnerability'.[9]

In the reverse context (that is, fitting nuclear warheads to British surface-to-air missiles), a Ministry of Defence briefing for the minister had various points to make:

> The question of the future use of nuclear warheads in surface-to-air guided weapons may be raised during the debate. If it is, the Minister is advised to avoid getting involved in a full discussion because:—
> (i) The matter raises exceptionally thorny political problems.
> Examples are:
> (a) The amount of 'fall-out' to which the inhabitants of the UK be exposed if the weapons were used;
> (b) The methods used to ensure that the weapons do not fall in flight and crash—as atom bombs—on British or Allied cities.[10]

The following is in a slightly different context:

> But the prospect of firing atomic missiles into the air over our own or our allies' heads, with the object of intercepting enemy bombers or missiles, reminds me of the Iron Duke's comment on a contingent of raw troops:—
> 'I don't know what effect they will have on the enemy, but, by God, they terrify me'.[11]

While such weapons might not have been acceptable to the British public, the same was not true in America or Russia, although the chances that the Russian leadership would be greatly concerned by public opinion would be remote.

In September 1960, the British Nuclear Deterrent Study Group had been discussing the TSR 2 and concluded the following:

> Strategic missions could be carried out with a low-level flight plan over the whole flight path ... With this mode of operation, the TSR 2 would be practically invulnerable to known forms of air defences.[12]

If the TSR 2 'would be practically invulnerable', why should a supersonic missile be more vulnerable? In this context, it is worth noting that in 1953, Northrop in the United States began the development of a supersonic target drone (known as the Q-4 or AQM-35), which could achieve speeds of Mach 1.55. The drone bore a considerable resemblance to the later Hound Dog missile. However, it never became fully operational with the USAF, and only twenty-five missiles were built. One of the reasons given for the cancellation was that the performance of the drone was too high for the surface-to-air missiles of the early 1960s. Given that the drone was very similar to the proposed missiles, it seems that the threat was considerably exaggerated.

Only twenty years later, in 1980, NATO began deploying ground-launched cruise missiles at RAF Greenham Common. These were subsonic, flying at low altitude over enemy territory, and had a range of approximately 1,500 miles. Presumably, NATO would not have been convinced by CGWL's arguments. There were also many in the Air Ministry who were not impressed by the reports produced by the RRE and CGWL. A memo to DCAS was typical:

> I believe it quite incredible that the Russians would spend £4200M to provide a defence against cruise type weapons, particularly since the conclusions of the R.R.E. memorandum themselves indicate that it would be pointless to do so unless simultaneously a further vast sum was spent on providing an anti-ballistic missile defence ...
>
>   To sum up my general advice is that you should ... endeavour to ensure that somewhat more balanced and less selective advice on the technical aspects of this study is put forward to Ministers in the name of the D.R.P.C., without raising any issues or major principle about the manner in which the feasibility study is being conducted.[13]

Supporters of the missile took the line that defending forty cities at a cost of £50 million per city would mean that the Russians would have to spend at least £2 billion, and if further cities and other sites were to be defended, this cost would rise very considerably. Opponents of the missile took the line that such a defence was feasible and hence the missile would be vulnerable (similar to the arguments that led up to the cancellation of Blue Streak).

One of the conclusions of a joint report written jointly by the Ministry of Aviation and the Air Ministry into the requirement was as follows:

The appropriate Russian defence would be an S.A.G.W. point defence of vital
targets, both specialist low altitude defences and high altitude defences being
required. Technical considerations suggest that the defence could be highly
effective; the cost would be high, but not definitely outside the limits which the
Russians might afford. If the deterrent value of a weapon is to be discounted,
the defences must have a very high probability of success. The factors which we
have, within our terms of reference considered, lead us to conclude that a weapon
of the type considered would be a valid contribution to the Western deterrent.[14]

This led to a clash of opinions, as can be seen in a paragraph near the
beginning of the report:

Some differences of opinion between the Air Ministry and Ministry of Aviation
members of the Working Party as to the conclusions drawn in this Report
remain unresolved. The Air Ministry members consider that the defence
capability credited to the enemy has been exaggerated, and, while accepting
that it is for the Ministry of Aviation to assess weapon feasibility, they
regard the assessment in this Report as unduly pessimistic. The Air Ministry
members accordingly believe that a detailed feasibility study of Operational
Requirement No. 1182 should be commissioned from Industry.[15]

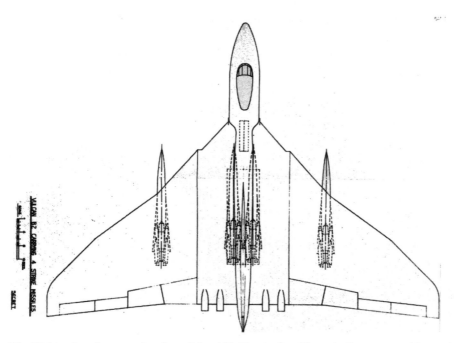

The Vulcan bomber carrying four Bristol X 12 missiles. The missile was very 'draggy'
and the range of the combination would have been very limited.

In an earlier draft of the report, the same paragraph originally read: 'Despite the limitations, the broad conclusions of the report are believed to be reliable'. As part of a progress report, Bristol noted:

> A study of the vulnerability of the missile to S.A.G.W. defences based on improved Nike Hercules and Blue Anchor Illuminator [the radar used for Bloodhound] have now been completed. With a deployment based on the general idea of the NATO missile belt calculations have shown that in order to ensure destruction of 100 diverse targets the delivery aircraft requirement will be of the order of 40 or 50 for this missile.[16]

Presumably, this is assuming four missiles per aircraft, and thus a total of between 160 and 200 missiles were launched.

Whereas the Air Staff and Bristol thought an interim weapon could be in service by 1968, the Ministry of Aviation was far more pessimistic. They thought that the interim weapon could not possibly be ready before 1967–68 and that the interim weapon would delay the final weapon even later than 1968–69. In other words, they were suggesting that development would take at least eight years.

Meanwhile, the Admiralty had been following events with dismay. Thorneycroft had said the project might cost £100 million, and that money would have to come out of the existing defence budget. Once again, the Admiralty saw their funding been threatened by yet another missile for the RAF:

> I attach a copy of a Minute to the Prime Minister from the Minister of Aviation....
>
> The outstanding points are:—
>
> (a) extremely costly (of the order of £100M R & D).
>
> (b) major new project.
>
> (c) such a weapon could not be ready before 1968/69 at the earliest AND that defence against it would be fully feasible at that time (i.e. cruise-type missile—pre-emptive attack against aircraft arguments are all valid).
>
> (d) The Air Ministry wish to ensure a weapon in service by 1966 and are prepared to accept an interim weapon WITH NO FINAL LOW-LEVEL APPROACH—later achieving full performance.
>
> Mr Thorneycroft's points are detailed in his paragraph 5—of which the most worrying with regard to the Navy is paragraph 5 (d) which states:—
>
> 'If the proposed weapon is introduced, there will be no question of cutting, or probably even of holding R and D expenditure unless some other major project is deleted from our programme'.[17]

AVRO Enters the Scene

The only other aircraft firm with experience of producing a long-range air-to-ground missile was AVRO, who were heavily involved ironing out the bugs in Blue Steel. They had produced a proposal for a long-range missile known as the W.130, which did not impress the Ministry of Aviation, as a note from the Director General of Guided Weapons shows:

W.130, on the other hand, is as yet a very nebulous proposal which amounts really to a Meccano set of weapons which they claim could provide a longer range air-to-surface missile at 750 miles when adequately boosted ... Very little detail work has been done on it and I suspect it is in the stable simply because Sir Roy Dobson insisted on having something of that kind of future weapon to talk to Mr Watkinson about when he was at Woodford. The studies have not been carried out at any length and Francis was quite sketchy about it.

It inevitably suffers all the drawbacks of Meccano set arrangements and I do not believe in the end that we will ever go for such a scheme.

The Bristol offer on the other hand is, to my mind more worked out and more attractive although its study has not been carried very far ... it uses Bristol's own ramjets, one of which is fully developed and is the same motor which goes in the Bloodhound II, the alternative being a motor which was under development for OR1159, but on which work is now proceeding at the moment.[18]

The W.130 was a proposal was described by Francis of Avro as follows:

A graphic of the rather nebulous W130 AVRO missile.

... a complex of offensive weapons systems, both deterrent and tactical, all built around a single basic missile design. This basic missile weighs (including a 700 lb warhead) approximately 4500 lb and is 20 foot long with a span of 7½ feet. It could be launched as a single stage missile from such aircraft as the TSR 2, NA 39 [Buccaneer] and Mirage IV, giving from the Mirage, for instance, a range of about 280 n miles. Alternatively, with suitable boosters, it would be capable of ground launching or launching to long range as a two-stage missile from such aircraft as the Vulcan. Highly variable trajectories could be programmed to defeat defensive systems, both in plan and altitude.

Ground-launched, using boosters weighing 7500 lb, the range would be 400 n miles with a peak altitude of 100,000 feet. The range would, of course, increase rapidly with increased poster size. The launches would be highly mobile—mounted on railway tracks, lorry trailers, etc.[19]

The letter was not at all well received by the Air Staff or the Ministry of Aviation. CGWL commented:

I do not know what requirement the 'small general-purpose tactical weapon' version of Blue Steel is intended to meet. I would state firmly however that if there be such a requirement it should be analysed in the customary way by this Ministry, and the various possible ways of meeting it should be examined. To buy a pig in a poke out of an AVRO sales brochure would, in my view, be inexcusable. Let us see this requirement if it exists, and having competently analysed by our own resources.[20]

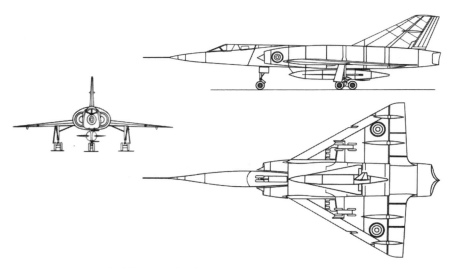

An attempt to sell the W130 to the French, showing the installation on the Mirage.

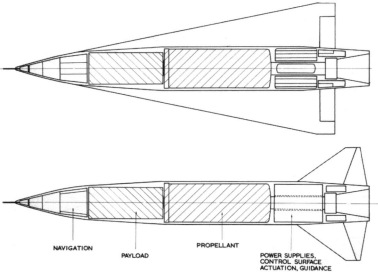

FIGURE 2   AVRO MISSILE TYPE W130   INTERNAL ARRANGEMENT

This view of the internals of the W130 shows how sketchy a design it was.

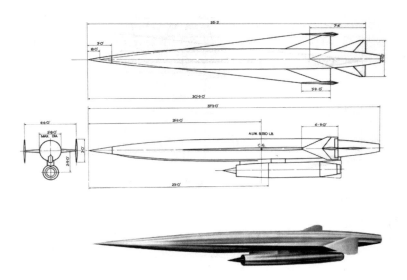

Avro's submission for OR 1182 together with an artist's impression. It appears to be a 'clean sheet' design—in other words, owing nothing to Blue Steel. Simple and straightforward, it could be carried easily by either the Victor or Vulcan. In performance, it would be roughly equivalent to the American Hound Dog missile.

The Director General of Guided Weapons gave a very similar response:

> Mr Francis's letter of the 21st of October … gives a very brief description of one variant of the Blue Steel weapon and also in Paragraph 2 of the letter, under the heading W.130, mention of 'a complex of offensive weapons systems all built around a single basic missile design'. The W.130 suggestion is certainly not at all intelligible from this letter and one doubts from the way in which it is written whether there is any sense in the notion at all. In view of this it is quite impossible for us to give close consideration to this particular proposal before the meeting …[21]

Undeterred, AVRO also produced a proposal to mount the W130 on the French Mirage. The brochure describes how it would be carried and makes discussion of range, navigation, and trajectory, but the illustration of the internal layout is very schematic, without any substantial detail. Certainly, if the design details passed to the Ministry of Aviation had been equally skimpy, then it is not surprising that it got a very cool reception.

AVRO then went on to produce brochures specifically for OR1182—one in March 1961, designated an 'Interim Report on Feasibility Study to O.R. 1182', and a follow-up report in May entitled 'Design Study to O.R. 1182'.

The report is rather dismissive of ramjets, which might well have been aimed at the Bristol project:

> Ramjet missiles can readily give the required high altitude performance but offer, within the required time scale, only very limited low altitude range. There are also some special development problems associated with air-launched ramjet missiles, which necessarily lengthens their development time scale: their tolerance of weight and drag increase is comparatively poor; there are special control problems in the boosted phase; penalties associated with provision of ancillary power during the transition from carriage to free flight are substantial; additional trials are necessary to prove boost separation and engine light-up …
>
> Any turbojet missile cannot be given a high altitude speed significantly greater than $M \approx 3$ and in this, of course, inferior to the ramjet. However, it has a high altitude range equal to that of the ramjet and, in addition, it can be given a good low-level range. No boosts will be required. The engine can be lit before launch and could provide all ancillary power so that, during development, all missile systems could be run for long periods in captive flight; a feature of great value in a project of short timescale. With any available turbojet the low altitude speed is restricted to less than the $M \approx 2$ called for in the OR, but we consider that the control problems involved in contour flying at speeds greater than $M \approx 1.5$ are so severe that it would be unrealistic to attempt to exceed $M \approx 1.5$ during the next two years …

The missile design … does not fully meet the range requirement stated in the OR, but it can fly a 750 n.m. trajectory, including 100 n.m. contour flying at M=1.5 or alternatively a high altitude-only trajectory of 1300 n.m. To meet the range requirement fully its launch weight would have to be increased from 8200 lb to 9400 lb and its linear dimensions increased by about 4½%.[22]

The RAE was given the task of evaluating the proposals produced by the two companies from a technical point of view. They were not particularly impressed with the arguments against the ramjet. However, they did admit that using a ramjet meant also using a rocket boost, which would mean the development of a satisfactory separation technique. They also conceded that being able to light the engine before launch might be useful in the development stage, but that when it came to operational use, the engine should be capable of reliable ignition after release. Indeed, the RAE argued that in some respect, the ramjet was simpler and easier:

> More serious is the fact that the turbojet engine requires from the outset a variable geometry inlet which also entails a closed loop control system. This need arises in the main from the difficulty of reducing thrust in the turbojet engine in the decelerating dive to low altitude. Turning off reheat alone is not enough, and throttling the engine back to idling speed will send the intake into 'buzz' (unstable sub-critical operation) if there is no provision for varying its capture and throat areas. Both the intake types suggested by Rolls-Royce are in a fairly early experimental stage and a good deal of work will be required on the intake alone, the control system and on the intake-engine combination, in simulated flight before missile flight tests can begin in earnest.
>
> By comparison, in the ramjet engine, the dive is made with the secondary fuel turned off and only a pilot flame burning. A variable geometry intake is therefore not required for this phase of the flight …
>
> In our view the cost must be considerably greater and the development time longer than the corresponding figures for the Bristol ramjet.[23]

There were some very considerable criticisms of Bristol's initial proposal, which seems to have been thrown together in a rather hasty manner. According to the RAE, the centre of gravity of the missile was in the wrong place. This could be compensated for by adjusting or trimming the aerodynamic controls, but doing so would add very considerably to the drag on the missile. A large amount of redesign work would be needed to overcome the problem. More work was needed on the overall structural design in order to achieve the optimum structure weight, and in the overall weight estimates, there appeared to be a serious omission: the weight of the pylon structure required for installation on a V-bomber. This weight could be significant at 2,000 lb or more for four missiles. Bristol produced a revision of the design, which is the version considered in the final RAE report.

The height at which the missile could fly at low level was dependent on the terrain clearance radar. This would be provided by Ferranti, and over the Air Ministry's typical Russian terrain, simulation work showed that the missile should maintain a mean height of about 300 feet. To obtain maximum reliability and small size, a simple system was proposed and, as a result, it would be unlikely that electric transmission lines towers in the missile's path would be detected. Three different systems were examined:

Fixed Dish—This was the simplest system and over the difficult Russian terrain digital simulation showed that a mean height of about 320 feet would be obtained. The disadvantage of this system is that it tends to oscillate in pitch and this might have repercussions on the missile structure.

Angled Tracking System—In this system, the aerial moved in pitch to keep the range to the ground along the boresight constant and the missile follows the aerial. With this arrangement, the pitch instability was reduced and the mean height above the typical Russian terrain fell to 300 feet. This improvement in performance was obtained at the expense of extra mechanical complexity and the moving aerial made the radome problem more difficult.

Nodding System—This was the system being developed for the TSR 2 and was probably the system which enabled the best terrain following to be obtained. Over the Russian terrain, it would give a mean height of under 300

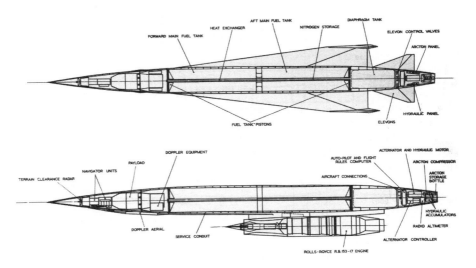

A drawing showing the internal layout of the AVRO W140 missile to Operational Requirement 1182.

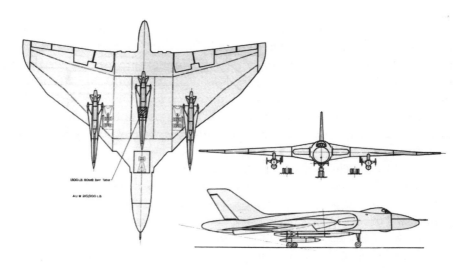

FIG.23   INSTALLATION OF THREE MISSILES ON VULCAN MK.2

The Vulcan carrying three Avro W140 missiles.

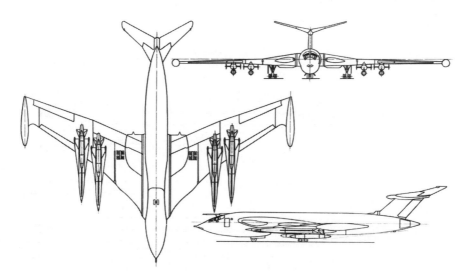

FIG.25   INSTALLATION OF FOUR MISSILES ON VICTOR MK.2

The Victor carrying four W140 missiles.

feet, but this performance was only obtained with a considerable increase in complexity and it would involve serious radome problems.[24]

The later AVRO brochure had drawings of a Vulcan carrying two, three, or even four missiles in a manner so reminiscent of the Bristol proposals that it does seem as if they might have had some inside information. There are also drawings of the Victor carrying the missiles, which this is somewhat surprising since AVRO and Handley Page were rivals in this respect.

Despite the fact that the Victor was supposed to have a higher performance than the Vulcan, virtually every project considered by the Air Staff features the Vulcan almost exclusively. Sir Frederick Handley Page had refused to join in the 'rationalisation' of the aircraft industry, and so the firm had fallen into disfavour with the powers that be.

The AVRO missile was also a good deal cleaner than the Bristol proposal, which had four wraparound solid-fuel boosters, which must have given an immense amount of drag. This was emphasised in a report giving what was described as the 'Aircraft Carry Radii'—in other words, how far the missiles could be carried, allowing one hour's fuel reserve and the missile being dropped at the turning point.[12]

Number of missiles	Two	Four
Vulcan 2 with Avro W140	1,514 nm	1,026 nm
Vulcan 2 with Bristol X12	1,180 nm	350 nm
Victor 2 with Avro W140	2,050 nm	1,390 nm
Victor 2 with Bristol X12	1,540 nm	500 nm

The superiority of the Victor-W140 combination is very considerable.

The W140 is also one of the relatively few AVRO proposals which seems to owe nothing to Blue Steel. Unfortunately, by this time, the reputation of the AVRO missile department was such that any proposal from the firm was regarded as suspect and a distraction from the job of actually getting Blue Steel to work.

Bristol's Bloodhound missile was also ramjet-powered and used Gosling rocket motors to boost the missile to a speed where the ramjet could be lit up. Naturally, Bristol proposed using the Gosling motors on the X12. The RAE was very dubious about this:

Firing failures of the Gosling boosts might result from prolonged carriage on the V bombers at medium to high altitude. The lowest temperature to which the rocket motor can be cooled and then fired was -20°C, with 100 per cent failures if cooled to -60°C. As the boost skin temperature was likely to be about -29°C for about six hours, it was not certain whether failure would occur; this would require further investigation. Other boost motors of less thrust should also be studied. Drag penalties of carrying the Gosling motors on the missile on the V-bombers appear to be quite severe.[25]

The high speed of the missile gave rise to other problems. Kinetic heating of the metal skin gave rise to explosions risks towards the end of the flight due to the ignition of fuel leaks by spontaneous combustion, since the skin temperatures would be greater than 240°C, which was the spontaneous combustion temperature for a fuel-air mixture in closed compartments. It also gave problems with the radome. The missile used a terrain clearance radar mounted in the nose, and, as a consequence, the nose would have to be made of a radar-transparent material. GRP is often used for this, but the temperatures would be too high. Instead, the radome would have to be made from ceramic on a suitable glass, and the manufacture of this type of radome would present considerable difficulties. Additionally, to cater for the loss of signal, which can occur over water, a radio altimeter would have to be fitted. There were various other problems, which Bristol had not considered:

Little information was given on the subject of what guidance equipment would be used and no accuracy figures were quoted. The Blue Water system, as proposed, was not suitable. A new system would be required, and it would be necessary to start R&D trials with this missile in 1963. Also, if an in-service date of 1965–6 was to be met the design of such a new system would therefore have to start immediately and use existing components.

Bristol's seem to underestimate the problem of setting the correct azimuth into the missile launch; an accuracy of about 1 milliradian is required. The rapid take-off requirement being applied to air-launched deterrent weapons will preclude pre-flight alignment without continuous running of the navigation system which has a limited life. The only airborne means of meeting the accuracy requirement of 2½ miles is likely to be by astro means. This is not favoured by Bristol's and would not be feasible as a British development in the timescale.

A possible alternative to pure inertial navigation would be a system using Doppler in the missile itself and for this the fix monitored azimuth technique would be applicable. The system would give a reasonable CEP of about three miles at 1,000 miles range, but the penalties would be about 140–150 lb and loss in space required for fuel. Also, the Doppler system would have to be developed over the speed range of the missile and would have to work satisfactorily at all heights from 70,000 feet down to 200 feet.

Bristol do not appear to have considered the possibility of difficult problems related to weapon release. The weapon must not diverge too far from the desired flight path by the time the boosts have separated and the boost must not strike the aircraft after separation. The dispersion during boost may be too great unless the missile is deliberately rolled or is controlled by its autopilot. Autopilot control would probably be very difficult because the control surfaces are shrouded by the boosts.

The omission of any wind tunnel programme is particularly noted. Many of the difficulties to be expected of such a new design can only be investigated by wind tunnel methods. Model construction alone can take some 6–8 months before supersonic testing begins.[26]

None of this sounds very impressive. Bristol revised their proposal very considerably, and after AVRO's proposal had been submitted, the Working Party produced a new report on the two proposals. This was much more optimistic about both designs, and it would seem that most of the bugs had been worked out.

Both AVRO and Handley Page submitted brochures for carrying the OR 1182 missiles on the Vulcan and the Victor respectively. Not entirely surprisingly, AVRO confined their brochure to the carriage of the W140 missile only, whereas Handley Page considered three missiles. These were Bristol's X12, AVRO's W140, and a ballistic missile proposed by de Havilland named the RG12B. This latter missile does not appear in any Air Staff or Ministry of Aviation files or memoranda, so its presence here is somewhat unusual.

From the drawings provided by Handley Page, this does seem to be something of a Skybolt rip-off. The weight given for the missile is 14,000 lb. It appears to be slightly shorter than Skybolt, but its diameter is 40 inches rather than 36 inches. The configuration of the fins and tail cone seem to be identical. There is no mention of a star tracker.

Thorneycroft, who was then the Minister of Aviation, obviously did not favour the project. He wrote a memo to the Prime Minister, copied to other Cabinet members of the defence committee, in which he described the proposal as 'extremely costly', said that the experts in his Department thought that 'such a weapon could not be ready before 1968–69 at the earliest, and that a defence against it would be fully feasible at that date'. He also suggested that 'It might be worthwhile to examine the possibility of achieving our objects more cheaply with the TSR 2'. As to whether an insurance policy against Skybolt was needed, he wrote:

> Our present view in the Ministry of Aviation is that if the Americans give up SKYBOLT the cheapest and most effective course for us to take would be to carry on with it where they leave off. This we can do under our agreement with them.[27]

This does seem distinctly unrealistic and would not be the line he would take eighteen months later, when the Americans did indeed give up Skybolt.

There was also some obvious scepticism about the cost estimates produced by the two firms:

> BAC estimate a total cost for the X 12 project of £28.5m over five years. AV Roe put the cost of their project at £10-20m again over five years. The RAE Working Party does not accept these figures and estimates that total costs could be £50m or more in either case. The main reasons, aside from the consequences of a seven rather than a five year project, are that they doubt the allowance made for trials missiles and for the very expensive range instrumentation and radar coverage that would be needed for terrain clearance tests. In forwarding the report Sir Steuart Mitchell increases the estimated cost still further to £75–100m. It would be contrary to precedent if a Ministry of Aviation estimate turned out to be too low.[28]

The last sentence seems to have been written without any sense of irony. There was obviously considerable frustration in the Air Ministry about what they saw as deliberate obstruction. Talking about the report from the Ministry of Aviation, a senior RAF officer noted:

> This CGWL report opens up a wide and delicate principle. If the M.O.A. are to continue as the Government's official advisers, how can we ensure that reports are truly impartial and not couched in terms which tend to reinforce

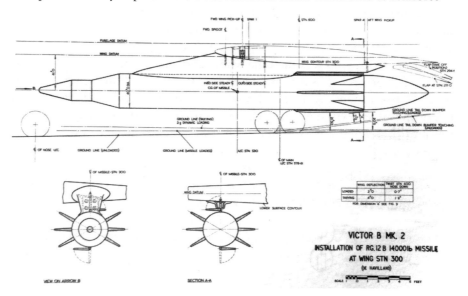

The Victor carrying a de Havilland ballistic missile design.

the ideas of future strategy, assessment of the threat, etc? If we insist that Air Ministry members are included on any future assessment groups, we are, in effect, interfering with their rightful province.[29]

Slanting a report by emphasising technical difficulties was nothing new (as in the Blue Streak and Skybolt cancellations). The problem lay in the bureaucratic procedures then in place for weapons procurement for the RAF. The RAF had to rely on assessments made by outside bodies such as the RAE, and also on industrial policies of the Ministry of Aviation, whereby contracts were given to firms partly on the basis of keeping them in business, rather than to firms most competent to deal with the project.

By August 1961, the Air Staff were reluctantly coming to the conclusion that there was no point trying to press ahead with this requirement, and it was allowed to lapse. Whether Pandora/X12 or the Avro proposal would have lived up to its role, and whether it would have produced a worthwhile substitute for Skybolt, is an interesting question. Despite the report of the RRE, defending Russian cities against OR1182 would have been a considerable task if the missile were flying at supersonic speed at low level. More interesting is the question as to whether either of these missiles would have lived up to their promise: a fair amount was standard technology, but the terrain following radar and autopilot would have been a considerable challenge, and whether it could have been in service by 1966 is doubtful.

Was a British designed ballistic missile possible? There is an interesting memorandum from CGWL about the possibility.

The Chief of Air Staff invited me to have a personal talk with him on 27th January on the present position regarding Air-to-Surface Weapons.

At this discussion, CAS expressed much anxiety at the situation which would arise if Skybolt was dropped by USAF, and said that he was somewhat dismayed by the Ministry of Aviation's attitude towards further work being done on the Pandora/X 12 weapons. He asked if we could not accelerate the further studies of these weapons and, if possible, get development work started.

I replied that from our knowledge of potential advances in defence against low-level attack we had serious doubts as to the ability of these cruise type weapons to penetrate the defences they were likely to meet by the late 1960s. I said I could not understand, if the Air Staff wanted an Air-to-Surface insurance against the cancellation of Skybolt, why they insisted on it being a cruise type missile rather than a ballistic type. This insistence on the cruise-type seemed to me to be technically quite wrong because of its vulnerability. Why did they not ask for a ballistic type? I could see no reason to think that a ballistic type will be more difficult, more expensive, or take longer to develop than a cruise type. Further, if Skybolt were cancelled by USAF the quickest and cheapest solution for the UK might be to make use of the Skybolt development, rather than to start ab initio on one of our own.

To this CAS replied that nobody had ever suggested to him that a ballistic type should be called for, but that the idea attracted him greatly.[30]

This does show the nervousness among the Air Staff as to whether Skybolt would actually materialise. CGWL was quite right to say that a ballistic missile would have been better than a cruise missile. The question is whether the UK could actually have produced one. The biggest issue with Skybolt was that of guidance, yet it seems from all the technical reports that the star seeker lived up to expectations, and was, by the time of cancellation, a fully worked out system. As Sir Steuart remarked, it would be relatively simple for the UK to simply ask for the work that had already been done. This is not always as easy as it sounds, since taking over the project started by people not only in a different firm but in a different country is not a trivial task. The bigger problem would have come with the computer: whether there was any British firm that could cope with a task of that size is another matter.

The Chief of Air Staff seems to have passed the idea up to his minister, the Secretary of State for Air, Julian Amery, who wrote to both the Minister of Aviation and the Minister of Defence suggesting a feasibility study. However, this seems to have got no further, and shortly after, OR 1182 was effectively abandoned.

Yet there was one other political point, made by Amery in a letter to Thorneycroft: 'If we decide now to abandon any attempt to build up a British deterrent system, we shall be accepting complete dependence upon the goodwill of future American administrations ...'[31]

He was quite right; the UK has been completely dependent on the goodwill of American administrations from that day until this day. In the end, it did not matter since Polaris was obtained in place of Skybolt, and the V bombers with Blue Steel soldiered on until 1969, but OR1182 is interesting in that it was probably the last ever proposal for an entirely independent British delivery system for the deterrent.

Skybolt: The Test Firings

The first dummy missile test drop took place at the Eglin range in Florida on 27 February 1961, when it was dropped from a B-52G at 40,000 feet and Mach 0.8. The missile hit the ground 300 feet from the predicted point, showing excellent stability during the drop. Results of these dummy drop tests showed that the free-fall trajectory of the missile was predictable for high-altitude drops. Later drop tests used missiles that were instrumented with rate gyros and accelerometers to establish the separation dynamics of the missile from the launcher under various conditions and investigate the bomb drop mode trajectory. These drops were completely successful and proved that the missile control system could control the missile after having being dropped. The third and instrumented final drop test was made over the Eglin range in Florida on 6 October 1961.

In the UK, the first Skybolt captive mechanical flight test was on 7 July 1962, with the missile mated to a Vulcan bomber. Additional environment and compatibility testing continued in July and August. A second series of captive flight tests started on 16 October using a structurally modified Vulcan, allowing aircraft manoeuvres at higher accelerations. The instrumented drop dummy programme ended with a successful drop over the West Freugh range, with the last of six drop tests made on 8 February 1962.

Skybolt made its first powered flight over the Atlantic Missile Range on 19 April 1962. This was the first of four programmed missiles flights. During these tests, the guidance system would be inoperative, but instead, the missile would go through a pre-set programme to test the flight and control systems. The missile would also have a dummy re-entry vehicle, and so all systems were to be tested during these programmed flights except for the re-entry vehicle and guidance system.

After a smooth drop, the missile was properly oriented and controlled by the interim guidance and flight control systems. The missile dropped away from the aircraft, the first-stage rocket motor ignited and flew successfully, but although it separated at the proper time, the engine of the second stage failed to ignite. The guidance and control systems attempted to control the missile as it tumbled, but without the rocket motor, there was no way to steer the vehicle since the second stage was steered by swivelling the exhaust nozzle. The re-entry vehicle separated at the correct interval, impacting in the water about 151 nautical miles from the launch point.

On 29 June 1962, the second programmed launch was attempted, and the missile operated normally until the first-stage motor failed to ignite. The elevons which steered the missile in the atmosphere unlocked and properly oriented the missile, the tail fairing unlatched and the missile continued to fall toward the sea while responding to command elevon deflections. The missile then pitched up beyond its stability limit, the nose dropped below the horizontal position, and the missile developed a coning motion which increased until the first stage separation. The second stage igniter fired properly, but ignition of the propellant did not occur until 13.8 seconds later, by which time the missile was tumbling end-over-end. Two seconds after the second stage ignited, the missile was destroyed by command when it fell below 10,000 feet. No structural failure seemed to occur.

Since both launches had failed due to ignition failures, a special group was set up to investigate the problem. Telemetry showed that there had

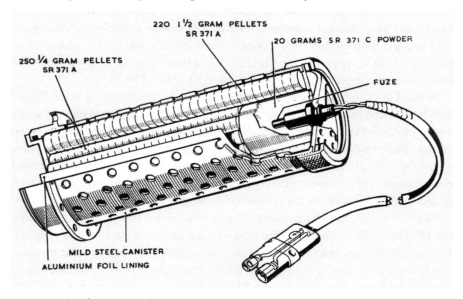

An example of an igniter for a solid-fuel rocket motor, in this case from the British Rook motor.

been a small pressure rise in the motor chamber when the igniter operated, but since the propellant did not ignite, pressure fell back to normal.

Following the first ignition failure, two specially instrumented second-stage motors were test fired at about 140,000 feet in an altitude chamber at the Arnold Engineering Development Center to find out what had gone wrong. In the first of these tests, the igniter operated correctly but the motor did not fire. This was attributed to a failure of the altitude chamber and to the fact that the motor had not been stored properly, becoming thoroughly damp in the process. The second test was completely successful and preparations for launching the next programmed round were continued.

Following the second failure, Douglas and Aerojet concluded that the igniters for both first and second stage motors were inadequate even though they were typical of those employed with success in Genie, Minuteman and Polaris and the results of the ground firing tests had all been good. Although the fault had not been found, a new type of igniter was designed, which contained much more ignition material, and the shape of the igniter was also changed. It later appeared that the problem arose from the break-up of the foam retaining pellets, which then jammed the orifice in the centre of the head, thus raising the pressure to the point where the igniter body ruptured and failed to set the rocket fuel burning.

On 13 September, the launch of the third programmed missile also met with little success. Due to a failure in the programmer timer circuitry, the missile failed almost immediately after launch. As soon as the missile had been released, the second-stage gas generator ignited at the same time as normal ignition in the first-stage gas generator. Within a few seconds, the first stage with tail fairings still attached separated and underwent automatic destruction. Second stage motor ignition occurred about forty seconds later. Command destruct was ordered when the erratically flying second stage approached the range safety limits. The only consolation was that the failure had occurred in the programmer, which was not intended to be part of the final missile. The piece of good news was that the igniters had after all worked successfully.

The fourth programmed missile was launched on 25 September 1962. Although first-stage performance appeared normal, all telemetry data was lost at the time of second-stage ignition. Thrust reversal action occurred early during second-stage performance, resulting in less than the programmed range and trajectory. This was the last of the programmed flights, and all future flights would use the guidance system intended for operational use.

The primary objective of the early guided rounds was to check out the operation of the guidance system in both the pre-launch and post-launch modes, and also to check the compatibility of the guidance system with the flight control system. The fifth and sixth launches in the flight test programme were fully guided launches and employed the tactical guidance system. On 28 November 1962, the prelaunch alignment and navigation function was satisfactorily demonstrated for four and a half hours, then on 22 December, the equipment operated flawlessly for three more hours. These tests included 292 successful star acquisitions with stars down to 2.75 magnitude in full daylight; a total of twenty-five hours flight test time was accumulated on the tactical system carry flights.

While the prelaunch operation of the guidance system was successful, the initial guided launch on 28 November ended prematurely. The primary in-flight failure occurred during first-stage burning and involved the hydraulic power unit. The ballistic computer malfunctioned after thirty-seven seconds of flight, including twenty-three seconds at vibration levels, which exceeded those for which the equipment was designed. A mission review panel convened at Eglin Air Force Base on 29 November concluded that the missile loss of stability after fourteen seconds of free flight was the direct result of a malfunctioning gas generator and hydraulic subsystem. All other systems operated within limits up to the time of failure.

The second guided launch occurred on 22 December 1962, one day after the meeting between President Kennedy and Mr Macmillan.

The missile fell from under the wing of its B-52 carrier, and the first stage ignited correctly. The missile soared into the Atlantic Range, giving every indication of a successful flight. Although no ablative re-entry vehicle was used, Air Force computations made from the missile's position and velocity at the precise time that the guidance system commanded thrust termination and re-entry vehicle separation showed that the vehicle would have impacted approximately 847 nautical miles downrange. Duration of the flight would have been approximately 700 seconds and all planned test objectives appeared to have been achieved.

The Department of Defense later argued that further calculations indicated the missile's impact point would have been about 100 statute miles beyond its predicted target area. Since the missile had not been carrying a re-entry head, it would not have impacted in the sea but instead would have burned up on re-entry.

The success of this test was, in many ways, a considerable embarrassment. Skybolt had been cancelled for 'technical reasons', yet on this test, it had done all that it had been asked to do. Kennedy was highly displeased; he had been watching the television news, together with the British ambassador, David Ormsby Gore. Ormsby Gore, when writing to Macmillan, described Kennedy's reaction thus:

> The President had had reports of the generally hostile reaction in London to the Bahamas agreement and then he was confronted with the news of the first

successful firing of Skybolt. He felt that the timing was appalling and that whoever was responsible in the Pentagon must be out of their minds. He told me that this was the first bad mistake that McNamara had ever made. He had understood that McNamara had made arrangements to postpone the firing for some time. Fortunately for his sake, McNamara was not immediately available as he was on his way to a skiing holiday in Colorado. It was therefore the luckless Gilpatrick who received the full blast of the Kennedy fury. It was an awe-inspiring exhibition and was notable for the fact that the President again and again emphasised with the most vivid choice of words the trouble it would cause you in London. He asked Gilpatrick [Deputy Secretary of Defense] to prepare a statement for publication putting this single test in perspective and he stressed that this statement should be in a form best calculated to help us. When Gilpatrick telephoned back with a draft statement, he made him speak to me and told me to suggest any amendments and additions which I thought would be helpful. This I did, and I also told Gilpatrick that it would be valuable if he would send an immediate message to Peter Thorneycroft explaining just what had happened and why. This he readily agreed to do. The President then discussed with me the line that should be taken with the American press and left me to brief Salinger over the telephone while he went for a swim. I then suggested that I might explain direct to you in Nassau what had happened. He thought this an excellent idea and I am only sorry that the White House line to your house was not still open, with the result that my explanation must have been extremely hard to hear.

The only excuse for this ill-timed firing that the president thought a valid one was after several previous postponements on political grounds, a further postponement at McNamara's request would have looked as though the Administration were determined to prevent a successful test. This would add to their troubles with Congress, which are likely to be formidable in any case. Nevertheless, he still thought that the problem could have been circumvented by giving the Air Force definite permission to fire the missile a week or two later ...

What vexed him particularly were the accusations that the United States were using the troubles over Skybolt to drive Britain out of the nuclear business. He kept repeating that this was an absurd suggestion in view of the fact he had offered to pay half the cost of the further development of Skybolt although it was a weapons system for which the Americans no longer had any requirement. He had then offered Hound Dog, which his experts estimated would prolong the active life of our V-bombers, and finally he had offered us Polaris, which extended our period as a nuclear power far beyond anything even we had previously planned for. As it is these accusations seem most likely to adversely Anglo-American relations, he hopes very much that they can be vigorously countered.

As a postscript to the Skybolt episode, Salinger telephoned to me when I was back in Washington to say that the President's anger over the test firing had become known in certain press circles. He explained that it would not do if it was thought that the President was displeased by the successful outcome of the test. It was therefore important that the story should be killed, otherwise it would add to the Administration's troubles with Congress over the decision to abandon Skybolt.[1]

A few hours after the test, Gilpatric issued a statement saying that the test firing had been scheduled prior to the Kennedy-Macmillan meeting.

> Today's single test did not conclusively demonstrate the capacity of the missile to achieve the target accuracy for which the Skybolt system was designed ... It is always expected that some tests of this sort should succeed and that others will fail ... Doubts as to the prospect of success of the Skybolt system in its entirety and its reliability when operational were among the factors responsible for the recommendation of the Secretary of Defense against further funding the program. The results of today's test have not caused any change in that position.
> Programmed flights:
> 1—ignition failure in second stage
> 2—ignition failure in first stage
> 3—programmer failure (not part of the final design)
> 4—failure at second stage ignition.
> Guided flights:
> 1—hydraulic power failure
> 2—completely successful[2]

At the time of cancellation, Thorneycroft was very keen to demonstrate that Skybolt was not a technical failure, but was being cancelled for political reasons. Therefore, he asked for information on other missile tests:

> You asked for information about the early successes or failures which had occurred with test missiles which ultimately have been developed successfully.
> Blue Steel. Of the first eight unguided rounds, the first two were successful; the third and fourth were failures; the fifth was successful and the six, seventh and eighth were failures. The first three guided rounds failed; the fourth was successful; the fifth failed; the sixth was successful and the seven failed.
> Thor. The first four Thor firings were failures; the fifth succeeded; the sixth and seventh were failures and the eighth was successful.

Minuteman. The first Minutemen firing was a success but the second, third, fourth and fifth failed; the six, seventh and eighth were successful.

Polaris. We have no information on the advanced (A-3) Polaris firings, but press reports state that the first six firings were failures. Of the first eight original Polaris firings in 1959, the first was successful; the second third and fourth failed; the fifth and sixth were successful but the seventh and eighth were failures.[3]

There may have many reasons for the Skybolt cancellation, but technical failure was not one of them.

Skybolt and the V Bombers

The V bombers were originally designed to carry free-fall atomic weapons at a time when the warheads were extremely large and heavy. The Fat Man bomb, dropped on Nagasaki in 1945, weighed 10,300 lb and was over 10 feet in length and 5 feet in diameter. The first British free-fall bomb, Blue Danube, was 24 feet long, 5 feet in diameter, and weighed 10,000 lb. By the time the Victor and the Vulcan were coming into service, Blue Danube was basically obsolete and was being replaced by the much lighter and smaller Red Beard bomb. These were fission devices, with a yield of between 10 and 20 kT, and again, for strategic purposes, they were becoming obsolete. The kiloton fission weapons were giving way to weapons in the megaton range, which were usually some form of fusion device.

The RAF briefly deployed the horrendously dangerous Violet Club megaton device, whose warhead was then transferred to a new design of free-fall bomb, Yellow Sun. This warhead, known as Green Grass, was derived from the Blue Streak warhead, Orange Herald. The warhead was not a fusion device, but instead, a very large fission weapon, and it contained several critical masses of weapons-grade uranium in the form of a hollow sphere. If this became deformed as a result of an accident, a small scale nuclear explosion was possible. To prevent this happening, the inside of the sphere was filled with several hundred ball bearings which had to be removed before the weapon could be used. This warhead was replaced with the Anglicised version of the American W-28 under the codename of Red Snow, a fusion weapon with a yield of just over a megaton, the new weapon, being named Yellow Sun Mark 2.

Another problem with using free-fall megaton weapons is that the aircraft dropping the bomb has to turn away very rapidly to avoid being caught up in the blast of the much bigger weapon. Yellow Sun was designed deliberately with a blunt face, which would mean that the bomb would fall very much slower, giving the aircraft time to escape. One of the major hazards was thermal radiation, which is why all the V force were painted white as an anti-flash measure.

However, Yellow Sun did not have a very long operational life, since free-fall bombs of this type had to be dropped from at least 10,000 feet. In reality, any bomber flying towards Moscow at 10,000 feet or higher would have been shot down long before it got there. A stand-off weapon was needed, which was the point of Blue Steel, and then Skybolt. However, carrying a stand-off weapon meant considerable modification to the aircraft.

The V bombers were already equipped with a very sophisticated navigational system. The advances in technology between 1940 and 1950 revolutionised navigation. In 1940, the only navigational aids available to the aircraft of Bomber Command were compass, stopwatch, and airspeed indicator. One of the major sources of error was that airspeed and ground speed are not the same. The air is moving relative to the ground; in other words, a wind is blowing. This can be allowed for to some extent with a good weather forecast, which tells the navigator what winds to expect. Alternatively, a navigator might be able to get a fix as the aircraft flies over some particular distinctive landmark. However, in the hazy atmosphere of the industrial Ruhr, very little was visible. It became increasingly apparent that the bombing campaign was almost completely ineffective as a result of aircraft losing their way.

Two techniques in particular improved accuracy. One was the use of radio beams, the other was an improvement in radar technology. The use of radar at centimetre wavelength meant that the navigator now had a picture of the ground—in effect, a map of what was underneath the aircraft. The use of radar gave rise to a further idea—Doppler radar.

A radar works by sending out electromagnetic waves that are reflected by the target. If the aircraft sending out the radar signals is moving towards its target, then it will pick up the reflection sooner than if it had been stationary. Effectively, the waves will seem to have been compressed; to put it another way, the frequency of the reflected waves will be higher. If the reflected signal is mixed together with the original signal, the result will be a new signal whose frequency is the difference of the two. By measuring the frequency of this new signal, the velocity of the aircraft can be determined very accurately, perhaps to within a tenth of a knot. It is also possible to measure the drift of the aircraft—that is, by how much it is being blown sideways by the wind. The great advantage of this technique is that it measures ground speed and not airspeed. The one problem came when flying over calm water, where there was nothing to reflect the radar waves.

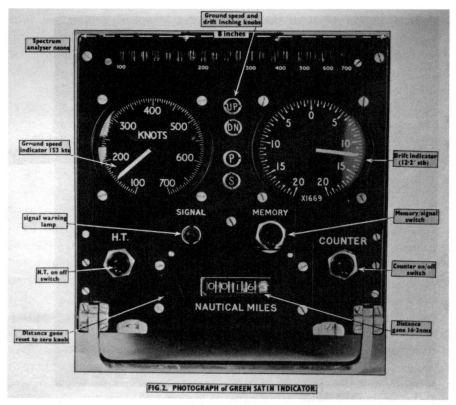

FIG. 2. PHOTOGRAPH of GREEN SATIN INDICATOR

The Green Satin navigation system, based on Doppler radar. This is the unit as mounted in a Canberra test aircraft.

The UK Doppler system was known as Green Satin, which worked on a wavelength of 3 cm. During trials carried out in a Canberra aircraft in the second part of 1953, it was found to be accurate to +/- 0.1 per cent in distance and +/- 0.1° in drift.[1]

There is another method for position fixing, a method that has been in use for centuries.

But I am constant as the northern star,
Of whose true-fixed and resting quality
There is no fellow in the firmament.
The skies are painted with unnumbered sparks.
They are all fire and every one doth shine,
But there's but one in all doth hold his place.

Julius Caesar, Act 3 Scene 1

Using a sextant, it became relatively straightforward to measure your latitude on the Earth. This could be done by measuring the angle of the sun at its highest point during the day, or by measuring the angle of various chosen stars. This would only give you your latitude on the earth, not your longitude. Even so, given the cloudy skies of the Atlantic, sun and stars might not be visible for days. In the days of sail, ships coming from the Americas would line themselves up with the latitude of a line running into the English Channel—somewhere between Land's End in Cornwall and Ushant in France. Sadly, the squadron of four ships of the line commanded by Admiral Sir Cloudesley Shovell had not seen the sun for some days on their approach and were further north that they thought they were. The four ships in succession were wrecked on rocks in the Scilly Isles with the deaths of the admiral and 1,550 seamen.

Like the sun and moon, the stars rotate across the sky from east to west with one exception. The Earth spins around its axis, which points to a star known variously as the Pole Star, the Northern Star, the lodestar, the guiding star, Stella Maris, or Polaris. A watcher of the night sky would see all the other stars rotate about this one 'whose true-fixed and resting quality/There is no fellow in the firmament'. Polaris has not always been the pole star, nor will it remain so. There is a slight wobble to the axis of the Earth's rotation (nutation), the wobble taking 26,000 years to complete. Yet for modern navigational purposes, it can be taken as fixed.

Many British bombers of the 1930s and '40s were fitted with an astrodome so that the navigator could use a sextant to find the latitude of the aircraft, but doing so in a noisy, draughty vibrating aircraft was not at all easy. The RAE and the RRE set about producing an automatic system, whereby a telescope was used to observe the Polaris, and then using a combination of gyroscopes and servo motors, the telescope could lock on to the star.[2]

This system was known as Blue Sapphire. The first attempt to try it out was not a success, but during a second attempt on 28 February 1950, Polaris was satisfactorily locked for the whole flight of one hour and fifteen minutes.

The RRE report noted that five variables were involved in the relative positions of camera and stars—latitude and longitude of point of observation, and course, pitch, and roll angles of the aircraft. Thus, if the course, pitch, and roll of the aircraft are known, latitude and longitude could be calculated.

The system also had another use; if the telescope was pointing at Polaris, then it was pointing at true north. This effectively made it a compass, and a much better compass than the standard magnetic compass. The magnetic compass does not point at true north, but at magnetic north, and the two are not in the same place. Thus, a correction has to be applied, known as compass variation. Furthermore, a magnetic compass may be affected by metal in the aircraft system and also by of magnetic fields associated with wires carrying an electric current. This can be allowed for some extent, but not entirely.

Thus, by the time the V bombers had entered service, they were equipped with a sophisticated navigation system. For the purposes of flying from the UK to Moscow in order to drop a megaton weapon, this was more than sufficient. However, when it came to using a stand-off missile such as Skybolt, there were problems.

Ground-based ballistic missiles know exactly where they are at the moment of launch, they know exactly where their target is, and they start from rest. Air-launched ballistic missiles need to be told not only where they are, but also the speed of the carrier aircraft, the direction at which it is flying, and its height above the ground. Very small errors in, for example, the direction will be magnified correspondingly over a direction of 1,000 miles. An error of 1 degree in the heading will mean an error of around 17 miles over 1,000 miles distance. The accuracy of any air-launched missile will depend on the accuracy of the data it is given at the moment of release, and the accuracy of the missile's inbuilt guidance system after release. In the 1950s, this was primarily governed by the quality of the gyroscopes available; over time, the axis of the spin would wander. Thus, time of flight was an important factor, and for Skybolt, the period for which the guidance had to operate would have been under two minutes, since once the second stage had burned out, the missile was on a ballistic trajectory.

The Victor

As early as February 1960, the Air Staff had decided that the Victor would not be used as a Skybolt carrier. This is rather surprising in many ways; as a Skybolt carrier, cruising at high attitude, the Victor was probably more efficient and longer ranged than the Vulcan. Nevertheless, Handley Page persisted with attempts to persuade the Air Staff to change their mind.

One major problem with the carriage of Skybolt on the Victor was that of ground clearance. Although Douglas and the USAF had agreed that a new design of the missile would be compatible with the V bombers, the Victor was always going to be problematic. It did not help that the missile design went through so many variants before the final Delta configuration was finalised, and by that stage, the RAF and the Victor could not have been further from the minds of Douglas and the USAF.

The issue arose because of the size of the fins. Handley Page issued some drawings to show the ground clearance. Different drawings seem to

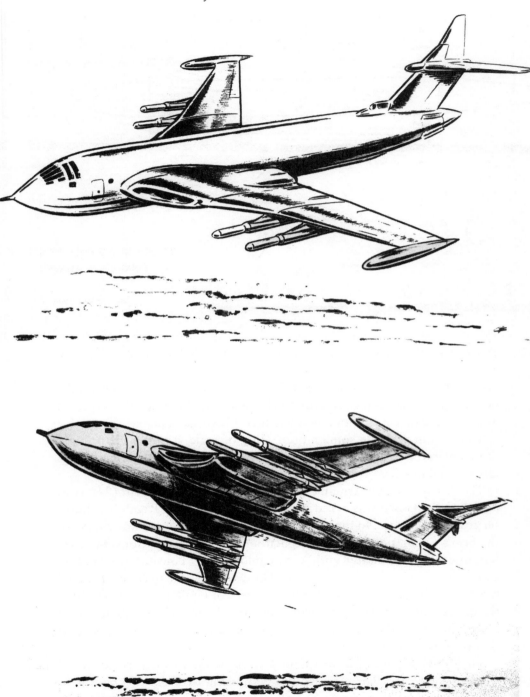

An illustration of the Victor carrying four Skybolt missiles from an early brochure, before the issue of ground clearance assumed such importance.

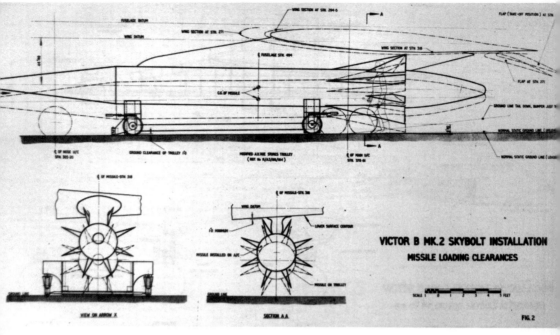

This illustrates the relatively small ground clearance of the missile mounted on the Victor.

give slightly different values for the ground clearance, but it seems to be between 8.5 and 9.5 inches (ground clearance for the Vulcan was quoted as 22.5 inches). The question was whether this was adequate.

To give the drawing some more feeling of scale, a rather charmingly drawn picture of a mechanic clutching a spanner was drawn alongside the aircraft and missile.

The Aeroplane and Armament Experimental Establishment (A&AEE) at Boscombe Down was asked to comment on Handley Page's brochures on ground clearance. In their reply, they said they had not made checks of the firm's calculations and the implicit underlying assumptions, but they had discussed the matter with Victor pilots. They consider the landing case to be more critical than take-off. This would be due to crosswind, and the pilots consulted suggested that 2 degrees of bank would be probably the greatest needed. This represented one set of wheels being about a foot lower than the other, and this they considered was the worst case that needed to be considered.

They were a good deal less happy about what was described as the slow taxying case. The aircraft will be passing over various bumps or ruts, which would lead to the aircraft suspension being compressed as the aircraft bounced up and down, reducing the clearance to only 6 inches. The A&AEE thought that this would mean operation only on the best of

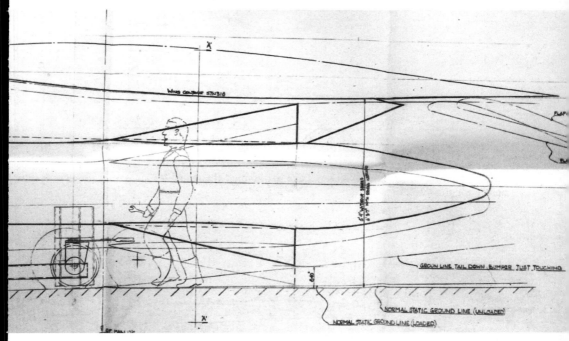

Ground clearance issues on the Victor aircraft. The mechanic gives some feeling of scale.

surfaces, very gentle turning when taxying, no overhang of the weapon beyond the edge of the perimeter track, keeping clear of landing lights, and there must also be no possibility of setting up a forced vertical oscillation during the taxying. They were also worried about the consequences of a burst tyre or tyres in the ground roll.

There was another option, which was to mount the missile at a slightly different angle (in effect, rotating it by 22.5 degrees) and making some of the fins fold or retract. Handley Page suggested that the retracted fins could be held in the closed position by a solenoid-operated release mechanism that would be actuated on release of the weapon, and then a spring could be used to thrust the fins out, whereupon they would lock in this position. This was a non-starter. The USAF would not be interested in modifying the missile in that way, and the Air Staff were determined to maintain complete compatibility between the USAF and RAF.

In one respect, there was no problem; the missile would fit on the Vulcan without any problems, and it was abundantly clear that the Air Staff much preferred the Vulcan to the Victor. The other official reasons given by the Air Staff to limit carriage of Skybolt to the Vulcan that the number of missiles to be purchased (around 120) could be carried by the planned front-line force of Vulcans, which would eventually number seventy-two—that is, eight squadrons of nine aircraft. As a result, the cost

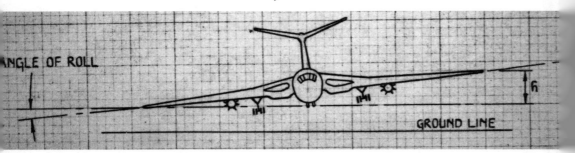

This shows the maximum angle of roll at take-off or landing before the fins of the missile touched the ground. Handley Page maintained that the ailerons would touch before the missile.

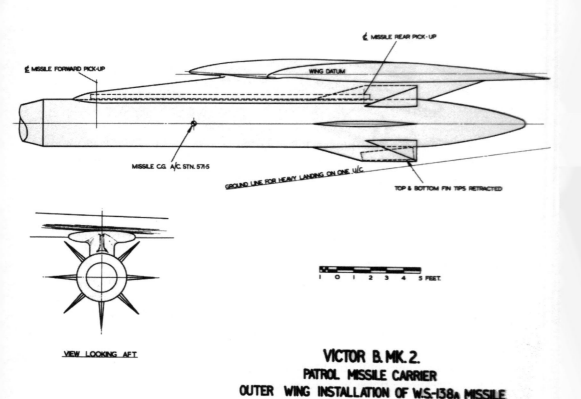

VIEW LOOKING AFT

VICTOR B. MK. 2.
PATROL MISSILE CARRIER
OUTER WING INSTALLATION OF W.S-138a MISSILE

One way of curing the ground clearance problem would be to make some of the fins retractable. This would have been unacceptable to the Air Staff.

of developing and fitting the installation of the missile on the Victor would be saved. Thus, the Vulcan was chosen as the only Skybolt carrier.

Handley Page did not give up and retreated to give the matter some more thought. The result was a brochure entitled 'Report on Ground Clearance'.

Handley Page's defensiveness can be seen from its comments in the introduction to the report:

> When the Skybolt configuration having an 8 fin layout with an overall diameter of 73 inches was introduced, the somewhat arbitrary method of determining ground clearance is by considering the aircraft tail down position with oleos and tyres collapsed, showed an adequate ground clearance on the Victor B Mark 2.
>
> The situation was reassessed and a report dated 11th July, 1960 issued showing the effect of making a more realistic appreciation of the actual dynamic conditions during take-off and landing. This showed positive clearances under all conditions and proved that the Victor B Mark 2 Skybolt installation was quite acceptable from ground clearance considerations. The report was discussed with representatives of MOA and Air Staff at a meeting on 11 July, 1960, when it was agreed that the clearances then offered were quite adequate.
>
> This current report brings up to date that issue previously by incorporating the latest missile dimensional data. In general, this has had little effect on clearances, if anything they are increased.[3]

The missile was moved forward on its pylon by 22.5 inches, and under normal circumstances, the ground clearance would be 9.5 inches. If the oleo of the undercarriage collapsed, this would be reduced to 5.5 inches. Of course, these were static conditions. The situation was eased in some respects during take-off and landing since aerodynamic lift on the wings tended to bend them upwards. The report concluded:

> Adequate ground clearance is available under static conditions and during taxiing with two Skybolts and are now greater by some 1 inch than in the previous report.
>
> During a take-off as laid down in the Pilot's notes, at the moment of 'unstick' a fully deflected aileron will touch first at 7½ degrees.
>
> Landing straight and level, adequate Skybolt fin clearance is available at all permissible rates of vertical descent. Even with bank at normal vertical velocities, the fully deflected aileron will touch first.[4]

That '1 inch' does not sound too impressive. Unfortunately for Handley Page, the report was issued on 30 November 1962, which was only eleven days before McNamara's visit to London to inform Thorneycroft that the

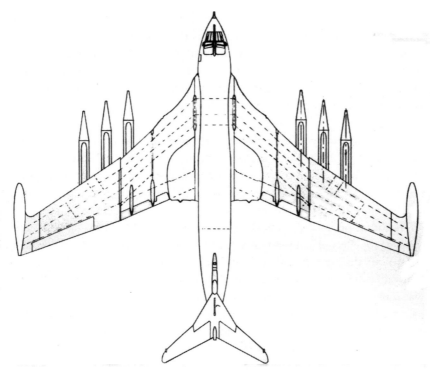

A Victor modified to carry six Skybolt missiles and to act as an airborne alert. These would have been reconditioned Victors, which would have become available after Blue Steel was withdrawn and would have cost a fraction of the cost of a VC 10 fleet.

missile had been cancelled. Even if the project had gone ahead, the chances of the Air Staff agreeing to the Victor as a Skybolt carrier were remote.

Handley Page also produced a proposal designed to appeal to the Air Staff. The existing Victors were designed to carry a freefall nuclear weapon (Yellow Sun) and also Blue Steel. The free-fall weapon was becoming strategically obsolete, and Blue Steel itself would be going out of service at the end of the 1960s. The proposal was for a retrospective modification programme designed to give existing aircraft a life extension from 1970 to 1980, when it would then operate with six Skybolt missiles in the air alert role.

After two aircraft were modified for test purposes, the idea was that three aircraft a month would be withdrawn from service, starting in 1969, each aircraft being at the factory for nine months. A total of thirty aircraft would be modified. The resulting aircraft would have a maximum all up weight of 310,000 lb, an endurance of 8.25 hours, and a fatigue life of 30,000 hours.

Most of the modifications would be to the wings. There would be a new outer wing with heavier sandwich panels, mountings for two Skybolts each side, and new 650-gallon tip tanks. The intermediate wing would be modified by having one bottom panel replaced and mountings added for one Skybolt each side. The centre wing would be modified for a new main undercarriage to accommodate the higher all up weight and to improve Skybolt ground clearance. New electrical installations will also be needed. Costings were provided. The complete programme would cost £2,630,000, which amounted to £344,000 per aircraft, assuming a total of thirty aircraft.

The new aircraft would in effect be a competitor to the VC 10 in the air alert role, and if Handley Page's costings were correct, this would be far cheaper than buying modified VC 10s at £3–4 million each. Indeed, if their costings had been realistic (which does seem a little unlikely), then the entire modified fleet of thirty aircraft will be cheaper than one single VC 10. However, whether Handley Page would have got the contract was another matter. The Victor aircraft that were withdrawn from service were due to be converted to tanker aircraft. The aircraft were flown to the Handley Page works, and the firm waited to be given the contract for the conversion. The Ministry of Aviation withheld the contract until it became obvious to Handley Page that they were not going to get it. At that point, the firm folded, and the contract went to AVRO.

The Vulcan

Modifications to the Vulcan fell into two main areas: structural modifications and modifications to the navigational system.

Apart from the pylon to carry the missile, other structural amendments were needed. These included outer wing strengthening and fixed fittings for the wing pylons. Some of these could be incorporated in production, but for those Vulcan already constructed, the modifications would have to be retrospective. The total cost for the retrospective modifications amounted to more than £1 million, but the total cost for the programme would be much higher. Fitting the pylon and the missiles on to the aircraft had an unexpected effect on the aircraft handling.

When an aircraft is flying low to the ground, the aerodynamics of the aircraft are affected by the surface underneath. On a simplistic level, the ground acts as a cushion increasing the lift on the aircraft, and the ground also affects the vortices produced at the wingtips, reducing the drag on the aircraft. This is known as 'ground effect'.

The Vulcan, with its very large wing area, was particularly prone to this effect, and pilots had to be aware of this when landing the aircraft, otherwise the aircraft would 'float' above the runway for some considerable distance. The pylons and the missile had a marked effect on the handling of the Vulcan, increasing the ground effect. This seemed somewhat surprising, but the islands were effectively acting as 'fences'. The pilots on the test flights of the converted Vulcans were not prepared for this, and had to adjust their landing technique accordingly.

There were also contracts with Douglas and the USAF for all the work to be done in America associated with fitting Skybolt to the Vulcan. These costs were defined as follows:

> All costs, including costs relating to the use of United States or contractor facilities, which, with the prior agreement of the United Kingdom, the United States incurs as a result of the participation of the United Kingdom in the development programme and which would not have been incurred but for such participation.[5]

This also included the cost of the Skybolt trials at Eglin Air Force Base. The estimate for these amounted to more than £23 million.

Early Deployment

The Air Staff were anxious to deploy Skybolt as soon as possible, and one possibility was to borrow American missiles so as to achieve an earlier operational date. When the Deputy Chief of Air Staff (DCAS) made enquiries as to the possibility, he was told:

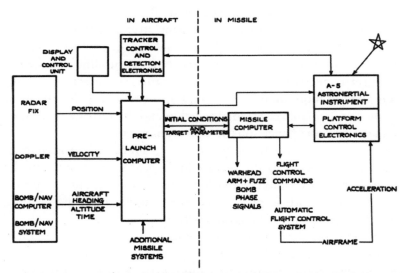

FIG. 8. SCHEMATIC LAYOUT OF GUIDANCE SYSTEM IN AIRCRAFT AND MISSILE.

FOR SKYBOLT MISSILE CHECKOUT

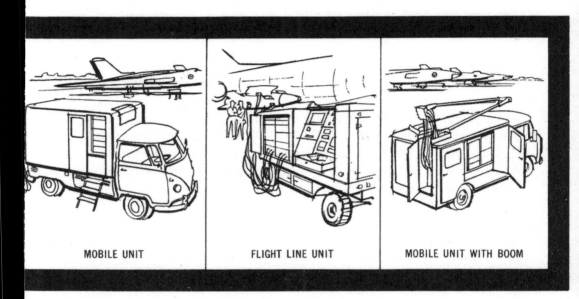

MOBILE UNIT   FLIGHT LINE UNIT   MOBILE UNIT WITH BOOM

Now in quantity production at Bendix is the PC-300 Checkout Sequence Programming Set (equivalent of the U.S.A.F. Type AN/GJQ-9). This universal programmer-comparator is designed for automatic GO, NO-GO checkout of Skybolt, air-launched hypersonic ballistic missile built by Douglas Aircraft Company. Capable of making as many as 100,000 test evaluations, the PC-300 can also reduce checkout time to minutes on a wide range of other weapons systems—both manned and unmanned. Some PC-300 functions are:
• Selection of stimuli control channels for application

to system under test. • Regulation of program continuation in accord with measurement and evaluation results, or holding program conditions, as directed by tape intelligence and selected operating mode. • Operation of printed and visual read-out devices to indicate test data in accord with selected mode of operation.

We have *proven* experience in engineering analysis of controls, aircraft, and missile systems; computer functions; and field service. Whether your support equipment needs are commercial or military—airborne or ground—you can count on Bendix for efficient answers.

For full details on the PC-300, write:

Bendix International DIVISION   

205 E. 42ND ST., NEW YORK 17, N. Y., U. S. A.   CABLE ADDRESS: "BENDIXINT," N. Y.

The RAF would have had to provide support equipment for Skybolt, and this is an advertisement for the missile checkout equipment provided by the Bendix Corporation. A drawing of the Vulcan can be seen in the background of the left-hand frame. (*aviationancestry.co.uk*)

There was very little hope of deliveries of warheads before the end
of 1964;

There was only just sufficient time to complete the first RAF station by
September 1964, and more rapid procedures would be costly;

The first delivery of ground equipment was scheduled to arrive in the UK
in September 1964 by which time the Americans will have only four sets
themselves. It seems unlikely that we could advance delivery of this even if
we could get the missiles;

Weapon system would trials would not be complete until October 1964.
Even under pressure, the Ministry of Aviation would not give a promise of
clearance before March 1965;

Although the first modified aircraft should be available by July 1963, the
RAF would not get the first 'B' until May 1964 (the 'B' kit is that part of the
modification kit which is of American manufacture). Neither the aircraft
installation nor the 'B' kits can be properly checked out until the first station
facility is in operation.[3]

The author of the memorandum finished by noting dryly, 'I think,
therefore, that we should only embarrass ourselves if the Americans were
able to lend us missiles before our first delivery in September 1964'.

A view of the V bombers in formation: Victor, Vulcan, and Valiant. (*Image courtesy of T. Panopolis*)

The Fritx X weapon, seen here at the RAF Museum in Cosford, was one of the earliest stand-off weapons. It was guided by radio signals from the attacking aircraft. The Navy quickly produced countermeasures to jam the radio signal, hence the guidance. (*Author's collection*)

Above: A Vulcan
and B-52 in
formation over
America.

Left: The three
V bombers in
formation. *Front
to back*: Vulcan,
Victor, and
Valiant.

A Vulcan carrying the Blue Steel stand-off missile. (*Image courtesy of T. Panopolis*)

The Blue Steel missile used 85 per cent hydrogen peroxide (HTP) and kerosene as fuels. Extreme care had to be taken when handling HTP, which is why the men working on the missile are in protective clothing. Any spillage of HTP had to be washed away with copious amounts of water.

A Victor carrying a Blue Steel missile. The original intention was for the aircraft to fly at high altitude until it was within 100 miles of the target, at which point it would release the missile and turn away. (*Image courtesy of T. Panopolis*)

A Blue Streak missile on the test site at Spadeadam in what is now Cumbria. The tanks were made of extremely thin stainless steel and had to be pressurised at all times, otherwise the missile would crumple under its own weight.

The Bold Orion missile mounted on a B-47 aircraft. (*Image courtesy of T. Panopolis*)

The Hound Dog missile, which was carried by the B-52. The B-52 was a high-wing aircraft, and ground clearance was not a problem. This would not be the case with the V bombers.

The first powered test firing of Skybolt on 19 April 1962. This test would not use the guidance system, but instead, it was intended that the missile should follow a pre-determined programme. The trail behind the missile in the first two frames must be a vapour trail since the rocket motor had not yet ignited. The tail fairing can be clearly seen. First stage ignition and flight went as programmed, but the second stage failed to ignite. (*Image courtesy of T. Panopolis*)

A B-47 takes off, carrying a Bold Orion missile. (*Image courtesy of T. Panopolis*)

A Vulcan carrying two dummy Skybolt missiles. These have the earlier re-entry vehicle designs fitted. (*Image courtesy of T. Panopolis*)

A dummy Skybolt missile in the RAF Museum at Cosford. This version carries the later re-entry vehicle design. (*Author's collection*)

A Skybolt missile being loaded onto a B-52 prior to a test flight. (*Image courtesy of T. Panopolis*)

A Vulcan preparing for take-off. Notice that one missile has the earlier re-entry vehicle, and the other the later version. (*Image courtesy of T. Panopolis*)

A doctored photograph (almost certainly that of a Vulcan with two Skybolts) showing X12 or Pandora on a Vulcan; today, this would be described as 'photoshopped'. However, the image is distinctly misleading as the missiles are shown without any wraparound solid-fuel boosters.

The aircraft clears the runway for a test flight. (*Image courtesy of T. Panopolis*)

Blue Water had originally been intended as a short-range tactical ground-to-ground missile for the British Army in Germany. It would have been armed with a 10-kt nuclear warhead. It was easily transported by road using an adapted Bedford lorry as shown in the picture.

A Vulcan with two dummy Skybolt missiles. (*Image courtesy of T. Panopolis*)

The Russian surface-to-air missile known as the SA-2 or Guideline.

FIG.3.   SIGHTING HEAD, *VIEW FROM WEST SIDE OF LATITUDE PRISM*

Blue Sapphire—an early attempt at an astrocompass. Once the telescope had locked on to Polaris, it would stay locked on, acting as a celestial compass.

Above: A two-stage Black Knight set up for launch at Woomera. This is BK 22. All the firings took place at night so the re-entry phenomena could be observed by camera. It was powered by kerosene and hydrogen peroxide, which could have been stored in the rocket for at least some weeks, if not longer.

Below: This is how the Vulcan would have looked if Skybolt had ever entered RAF service. The two missiles carry the later re-entry vehicle design. (*Image courtesy of T. Panopolis*)

The Black Arrow satellite launcher was developed at a total cost of £10 million and would have made an excellent MRBM.

A prototype of the TSR 2 under development.

Left to right: Gen. Maxwell Taylor, chairman of the Joint Chiefs of Staff; Robert McNamara, Secretary of Defense; and President Kennedy.

The Russian SA-2 guideline missile.

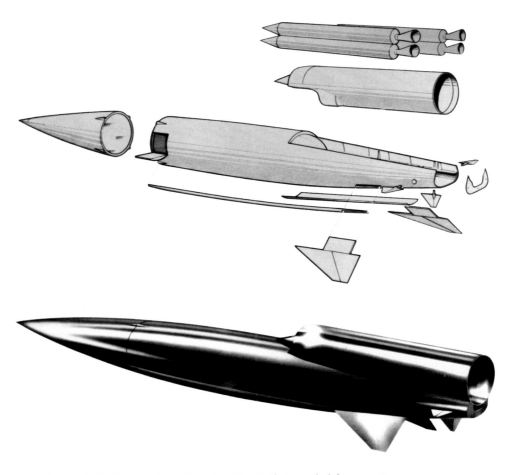

An 'exploded' view of the Avro W170 missile intended for TSR 2.

A High Virbo rocket being prepared for a test flight. (*Image courtesy of T. Panopolis*)

Prime Minister Macmillan and President Kennedy.

The Doubts Grow

Although the British Nuclear Deterrent Study Group had effectively ruled Blue Streak out of court, it would take some months before the cancellation would become official. After the report of the study group, the Chiefs of Staff wrote to the new Minister of Defence, Harold Watkinson, to say that they thought that Blue Streak no longer had any military value. That was effectively the death knell for Blue Streak. However, the decision had to be pushed upwards towards the Defence Committee of the Cabinet and then the Cabinet itself. Even then, it took several meetings before the decision was final.

Cancelling a project such as Blue Streak, on which very large sums of money, equivalent to some billions in today's currency, had been spent is never an easy political decision. In an adversarial chamber like the House of Commons, the opposition can have a field day, asking questions like 'Why was the project started in the first place?' and 'If it was a failure, why was it allowed to go on so far?' Indeed, George Brown's (then the Labour defence spokesman) immediate response to the announcement of the cancellation was: 'This brings to a head a most incredible chapter of obstinacy and of determination to go on with something long after all kinds of people everywhere were clear in their minds that it was wrong'. In addition, no announcement about the cancellation could be made until a viable alternative was ready and waiting; although, in Skybolt, as one Labour member of Parliament put it, the Government were buying 'a pig in a poke'. That turned out to be truer than he might have thought.

During the Prime Minister's visit to Camp David in March, Eisenhower and Macmillan came to an agreement whereby the UK could buy 100 Skybolt missiles (minus warheads). Macmillan later said in Parliament:

Looking back over my meeting at Camp David with President Eisenhower, in 1960, it was clear why it was agreed that we should have Skybolt. At that time, as I recall it, the emphasis was on mobility. We were just deciding to abandon the fixed rocket. There were two possible systems in the mobile ballistic rocket field. One was Skybolt and the other was Polaris. Neither system had been fully perfected, and both were complicated and costly. At that time I must say frankly that I was greatly influenced by the fact that we in Britain already had a bomber force, with all that that implies in morale, men and material. The V-bombers were being constructed and large orders had been placed for them. I reached the view—and I think that it was not unreasonable—that if the Americans would sell us the Skybolt missile, although it would not be a permanent solution—nothing is ever permanent in the defence field—at any rate it would get us through a long period of years with the least disturbance.[1]

At the same time, Macmillan agreed that the US could base Polaris submarines at Holy Loch in Scotland. Such a decision was politically sensitive for the British Government, and although there was never any formal linkage between the two, it was taken very much for granted by the British that this was a *quid pro quo* situation. This was one of the reasons why the government felt badly let down when eventually Skybolt was cancelled. In the same speech, Macmillan went on to say about the American bases:

> In return, the only offer that I was able to make, and was glad to make, was that when the Polaris system was developed we would, by making facilities available in this country, add enormously to its strength and efficacy.[2]

This was at the time when CND and the Aldermaston marches were at their peak, and the anti-nuclear and anti-American sentiments in the country were running high. Providing yet another American base for nuclear missiles in the UK would be a hard sell politically. Watkinson appreciated this, and, during his talks with Gates, the American Secretary of Defense, proposed that this should be a joint project.

> They believe that we are morally committed to allow them to use the Gare Loch as the base for their POLARIS-carrying submarines, in return for getting SKYBOLT. If we refuse facilities at Gare Loch they are ready to use Bremerhaven instead, reluctantly. They need a decision by the end of June. They take the point that our public will only swallow this if the project is made a joint one.

I think this is a case for a package deal, under which we should get POLARIS for use at sea, treat this as our contribution to the MRBM scheme and allow the Gare Loch to be used for their submarines and ours. Without any commitment, I discussed the deal of this kind with Mr Gates.

The proposition is that we should provide ourselves with two submarines each carrying 16 missiles. The Americans are anxious that a total of 80 missiles should be produced at this stage because SACEUR mentioned that figure as a first instalment. It looks as if our first POLARIS submarine may have to be bought from the Americans because we could not build one ourselves quickly enough; but we need not decide this at once. We should need to make it clear that these submarine-launched missiles were our only MRBMs contribution and that we should not pay now or later for any MRBM on the Continent.

This proposal has obvious drawbacks but I think it would be on balance be distinctly to our advantage. We could easily find ourselves faced with other possibilities that would cost us a great deal more and be highly dangerous politically.[3]

There was a complication all of this, a complication that would also rear its head in the later Nassau negotiations. There was a long-running proposal by the American Government to provide medium-range ballistic missiles (MRBMs) for use by NATO. They would come under the authority of the Supreme Allied Commander Europe (SACEUR), or, if they were carried on Polaris submarines, the Supreme Allied Commander Atlantic (SACLANT). The British Government was not at all happy about such a scheme since it meant that long-range nuclear missiles came directly under the authority of a military commander rather than a head of government such as the President or Prime Minister. This would effectively be Polaris with strings; the missiles would not be under the control of the UK Government but under a NATO commander.

The idea produced considerable consternation in the Treasury. The chancellor and his senior officials had not been happy with the idea of buying Skybolt. Indeed, the Treasury would be quite happy if the deterrent were abandoned. At the same time, the Treasury also got the mistaken impression that Watkinson was going to go ahead with Blue Streak Mark II. The costings provided for the chancellor looked alarming (and were almost certainly wildly overestimated):

Skybolt—£235 million or £335 million if VC 10s are needed.
Two Polaris submarines—£150 million
Blue Steel II—£110 million
Development of warhead for Skybolt and Blue Steel Mark II—£15 million.

This came to a total of £610 million. By purposes of comparison, a figure of £470 million was given for the development and deployment of Blue Streak.

Yet, as far as Macmillan was concerned, there was a moral commitment if not a formal commitment. The government had taken an extremely unpopular political move in providing the bases for American Polaris submarines, effectively as a *quid pro quo* for buying Skybolt. Unfortunately, the cancellation would occur under a subsequent Administration, where recollections of the deal had faded into the mists of time.

However, the Americans did make it very plain that Skybolt was not a certainty; it was merely a project under development, and that development could be discontinued at any time. In the words of Mr Gates, Secretary of Defense, in the agreement signed by him and Watkinson: 'Mr. Gates affirms the intention of the United States Government to make every reasonable effort to ensure the successful and timely completion of SKYBOLT'.

'Every reasonable effort' is no guarantee the project will be carried through to completion.

> In a memorandum handed to the Prime Minister, the Americans:
> (i) said they wished to assist in improving and extending the effective life of the V-force;
> (ii) stated that there would be no conditions as to their use other than those usually attached to the supply of US weapons. In a reply to a Parliamentary Question on 26th April 1960, the Prime Minister announced this as meaning that the missiles would be completely under British control, except that we could not sell them without American consent or use them for aggressive purposes.[4]

The Government pressed ahead, and in June, Watkinson signed an agreement with Gates. This was then presented to a meeting of the Cabinet in the House of Commons, where the two items on the agenda were Skybolt and the American base in Scotland. The minutes stated:

> The Minister of Defence said that, following the agreement in principle which the Prime Minister had reached with President Eisenhower in March, he had during his recent visit to Washington concluded a memorandum of understanding with the United States Secretary of Defence about SKYBOLT to give effect to our intention to order this weapon if it were successfully developed in a form suitable for the Mark 2 V-Bombers of Bomber Command. He now sought approval for the negotiation of a more detailed technical and financial agreement with the United States authorities.
>
> There could as yet be no absolute certainty that SKYBOLT, which was not due to be tested as a complete weapon for about a year, would be successful and it must be recognised that the Americans would not develop it for our

use alone. However, the United States authorities were confident that it would be effective and they attached importance to it both for their own Air Force and as a means of prolonging the effectiveness of our V-Bombers, which they recognised were an important part of the strategic nuclear deterrent. By acquiring 144 missiles, with spares and associated equipment, we should be able in the later 1960s to maintain with the Vulcan Mark 2 bombers a deterrent force equivalent to that previously planned for BLUE STREAK .... It would be in our interests to respond without delay to the American desire to expedite the joint development of SKYBOLT, in order to ensure that it would be fully compatible with our requirements.

On present estimates, the cost of our requirement would be between £76 million and £115 million (depending on the unit cost of the missile), with a dollar content of up to £108 million. We would have to ensure that the price would be based on the cost of production, without any contribution from us to the underlying development costs. We should only be committed to purchase if the price were on this basis and if the weapon was successful.

The Chancellor of the Exchequer said that, while he felt there was a danger that the bomber force itself might have become unduly vulnerable by the time SKYBOLT was available, he recognised that, if the weapon were successful, the proposals of the Minister of Defence might be the cheapest means of maintaining an effective contribution to the Western deterrent. It was not possible to foresee at this stage the burden that the dollar costs would ultimately involve, but if this proved excessive our policy might have to be reconsidered at a later stage.

Discussion showed that the Cabinet were in agreement with the course recommended by the Minister of Defence. They were informed that there was a promising prospect that the Vulcan Mark 2 aircraft would give longer service than originally planned; and that no need was foreseen at the present time to order additional replacement aircraft of this or another type, such as the VC-10, that would add to the cost of the programme.[5]

In fact, the dollar expenditure was quite considerable. Watkinson noted:

If SKYBOLT is obtained at £0.25 millions each the total capital cost is therefore estimated at £76.5 millions of which perhaps £68 millions would be in dollars. With SKYBOLT at £0.5 millions total costs might be £115.5 millions with a dollar content of £108 millions. The assessment is that the full cost of the weapons, two-thirds of the aircraft modifications and equipment and the bulk of the research and development would be in dollars. In addition, there would be a dollar element in running costs for spares, etc., which might amount of £5 millions a year [*sic*.] when the force was fully built-up.[6]

Dollar expenditure was a considerable financial obstacle in the days before the easy conversion of currencies. Watkinson also commented that this would not include the cost of the nuclear warheads.

Cost estimates for the project were already rising in America; by June, the cost had risen to $350 million, and by August this had been revised up to $372 million. Rubel remarks about the cost estimates:

> The original cost projections had conveniently left out provisions for spare parts, training, manuals and many other essentials, without which no project is complete. Including them now, well after the start of development, meant greatly exceeding cost estimates that had served as a basis for project approval only have a few months before. This, too, was a familiar tactic often used in playing budget games under the pre-McNamara rules.[7]

Secretary of Defense Gates was having considerable doubts about the project, and although the development was allowed to continue, it was under a considerably restricted budget.

Watkinson was given a warning by James Douglas, Deputy Secretary of Defence, when they met in October to the following effect:

> He wanted to let the Minister of Defence know straight away that he believed that we might be in real trouble with SKYBOLT. The development costs of SKYBOLT were turning out to be much higher than expected, and there was an opinion in the US Air Force that would prefer the B.70 to SKYBOLT. He did not mean to imply that the SKYBOLT programme would necessarily be cancelled; but there was no doubt that it was an area where more money was badly needed. How much we wanted it would have some effect on the decision.
>
> THE MINISTER OF DEFENCE said that, if SKYBOLT went wrong, it would be an extreme embarrassment to Her Majesty's Government. He had already cancelled BLUE STEEL Mark II and other BLUE STEEL developments on the expectation of getting SKYBOLT. He hoped that Mr Douglas or Mr Gates would keep him in close touch and would inform him immediately there was any sign of trouble.[8]

Watkinson wrote a fairly lengthy letter directly to Macmillan:

> I am sure that we should take this calmly and be seen to be doing so. From the start we have foreseen it as a possibility and for that reason you and I have been at pains never to say that we were certain of Skybolt. I have purposely talked in public about other possibilities.
>
> One possibility would be to pin everything on getting POLARIS. I do not advise this. That would be proclaiming that we were at the mercy of

the Americans. No one in America, until after the Election, can promise us anything. Even after the Election I doubt if they will promise us the chance of buying POLARIS missiles for our national use until the plan for a NATO POLARIS scheme has succeeded or failed, and perhaps not even so.[9]

Macmillan asked Watkinson to prepare a memorandum outlining the possible alternatives if in fact the Americans did decide to abandon Skybolt. One possibility was, of course, to try for Polaris, but Watkinson warned of the difficulties, difficulties that would still apply two years later:

> As matters stand at present, this is not in fact a possibility, because the Americans are not willing to allow us to buy or copy POLARIS missiles, except for a scheme for providing SACEUR with strategic missiles. Such a scheme would not give us the control over the weapon system that we need. We should need to be able to purchase outright and without strings. It might be possible to negotiate on this basis with the US administration, if Skybolt were denied us.[10]

The only other indigenous alternatives were the TSR 2 and the cruise weapons proposed by Bristol and Avro under OR 1182. Watkinson did suggest putting a design study in for the cruise missile but warned that it would have to be very low profile so that news of difficulties with Skybolt did not leak out.

As a result of all this uncertainty, Macmillan sent a cable to Eisenhower:

> Dear Friend,
>
> I have been disturbed to hear that there is some talk of the possibility that you may reconsider your SKYBOLT programme in view of the high costs of development and the reinstatement of the B70 in the U.S.A.F. programme.
>
> You will remember that we cancelled our BLUE STREAK rocket and our further steps of BLUE STEEL development on the understanding that (so long as it proved technically feasible) SKYBOLT would be available for our V-bomber force. We are therefore relying very heavily on you in this.
>
> I hope you will be able to reassure me.
>
> With warm regard,
>
> as ever,
>
> HAROLD[11]

Eisenhower replied:

> Dear Harold:
>
> Replying to your letter of October 25 with regard to Skybolt, I believe we fully appreciate your concern with the prospects for the continued

development of the weapons system. I can at least assure you that we are still proceeding with the project as outlined in my Camp David memorandum to you of March 29, the Gates-Watkinson memorandum of June 6, and the subsequent technical and financial agreement on September 27.

I am still hopeful of seeing you later this year, at which meeting we could discuss the matter further. In any event, our people will continue to keep yours informed on any problems relating to Skybolt and we will similarly appreciate your people keeping ours advised from time to time of the place this project occupies in your plans.

With warm regard, Sincerely, Ike.[12]

In the meantime, Macmillan asked Watkinson to prepare a report for the Defence Committee on the likelihood of cancellation and on the possible alternatives. The Cabinet Secretary wrote to Macmillan to say:

If it does turn out that the Americans wish to discard SKYBOLT, and if the knowledge of this leaks, we should have to take a more positive line about our alternative plans. The difficulty is that we have at present no alternative in sight which will fill the gap for the whole period 1965-70, unless it should prove possible to obtain POLARIS at the beginning of this period. The British Nuclear Deterrent Study Group have, since the Minister of Defence wrote his minute, concluded that there is no justification for proceeding with the improved version of BLUE STEEL.

I understand that the capability of two other weapons systems are being studied, but that these, like the T.S.R.2., could not be effectively in service before about 1969.[13]

Meanwhile, Watkinson had asked for a senior officer to be based in America to report directly to him on the progress of Skybolt. The civil service rather disapproved (not the way things were done; a memo describing his role and function noted that 'He must not travel around unaccompanied'!) but complied with his wishes. The man chosen was Group Captain Fryer. A memo describing the group captain makes for interesting reading:

Group Captain Fryer, aged 44, is at present Requirements Interchange Officer on the Staff of the British Joint Services Mission in Washington. Under the terms of the redundancy scheme Group Captain Fryer applied for premature retirement ... The Group Captain intends to take up permanent residence in the United States ...

Group Captain Fryer is a rugged, forthright type of officer with a wealth of experience in practical flying and staff work in Research and Development

... As a result of his work with the Americans, he has not only obtained their confidence, but has shown himself to be extremely successful in working with them in all respects.

It is Group Captain Fryer's knowledge of all the difficulties and doubts about the SKYBOLT project, which the Americans have experienced since they decided there was a requirement for such a weapon, which makes him, in my opinion, the best man to monitor the project on your behalf ... In short his contacts are such that it would be extremely difficult for American contractors or Service personnel to pull the wool over his eyes.

It is a paradox that a Group Captain who is so well-qualified for this task has been granted early retirement. Group Captain Fryer, as will be apparent in an interview, is not necessarily an officer well suited to higher command, nor is he particularly smart in dress.[14]

One can only speculate on the meaning of that last paragraph. However, taking up the post would mean that he would have to retire from the RAF, and so, as a result, he would be technically a civilian. The question then arose as to whether he would be able to wear the uniform 'as and when appropriate'. Enquiries were made in the Department of Defense and the USAF, and apparently, 'the Americans were emphatic that a man not in uniform would be at a serious disadvantage as USAF officers controlled the project at all levels'.

His first progress report was made in January 1961; he concluded:

There is no reason to suppose that the Skybolt weapon system will not continue in development. It has suffered a setback in the last month but it still enjoys solid support from the Research and Engineering Directorate and the principal figures of the USAF.[15]

Yet it was not the USAF that was the problem, but, as we have seen, the Department of Defense in Washington. Gates had almost brought development to a standstill by restricting funds; he had been annoyed by the Air Force and so was not convinced by the project. January 1961 saw a big change. Gates had been at the tail end of the Eisenhower administration. Now Kennedy had been inaugurated, the new Secretary of Defense was Robert McNamara, who had been president of the Ford Motor Company. McNamara had a reputation as a technocrat, and Kennedy relied on his advice in many other areas as well as defence. McNamara had been briefed about Skybolt as one of the problem projects and decided to restore funding. It seemed that the missile's future was now secure.

However, Skybolt's main opponent, Rubel, stayed on in his previous post and became part of a group known as McNamara's 'whiz kids'. These were a group of experts from the RAND Corporation, who McNamara enlisted to help change the corporate culture of the Department of Defense. Rubel also became friends with someone many would regard as one of the villains in the debacle that would follow—Solly Zuckerman.

Zuckerman had recently been appointed to the new position of Chief Scientific Adviser (CSA) to the Ministry of Defence. He formed a close personal and professional alliance with Mountbatten, and for that, and for other reasons, was regarded with considerable suspicion by the Air Staff. The historian Richard Neustadt says of him, 'In the Ministries of Air and Aviation he was tagged as something of a "traitor". His warnings roused more anger than attention'.[16]

He was undoubtedly a brilliant man but had the capacity to be all things to all men. He aroused controversy by some comments made during a visit to the United States, which he claimed were misreported:

> The CSA to the Minister of Defence returned from a visit to the US and reported to the Minister on Skybolt ... In one of his minutes Sir Solly said 'If it were not for the US concern with the British problem, I have little doubt that the chances are that Skybolt would be cancelled... In fact I do not believe that it will be ...' And he then went on to substantiate his case for this statement. It is important to note that these minutes were not sent to the Air Ministry as direct guidance on the Skybolt position. They were sent to help clear up a misunderstanding that had arisen in the conversation between Sir Solly and Mr Wiesner when sceptical remarks Sir Solly had made about the NATO MRBM were misreported back to CAS by General Wilson to the effect that Sir Solly had said the British Government were losing interest in Skybolt.[17]

A cable from the British joint services mission to the Chief of Air Staff was unequivocal in its opinion of Zuckerman:

> The challenge which Sir Solly has done to our interests has certainly been sufficient to lead the anti-Skybolt lobby to believe that we should not oppose too strongly a decision to cancel. In the last few months we have done our best to retrieve the situation by representations at all levels culminating in the recent Thorneycroft visit and if we can have an unequivocal letter from Sir Solly it may finally convince Rubel and Brown that we mean business.[18]

When cancellation seemed imminent, he also made some rather injudicious remarks to the effect that there were no British experts capable of assessing the technical aspects of Skybolt competently. The waves caused by these remarks were considerable: they prompted Julian Amery, the new Minister of Aviation, to write to the Minister of Defence, Thorneycroft, saying, 'Your Chief Scientific Adviser questions the competence of my staff to have an independent view on the state of Skybolt development. I have gone into this matter'. Amery then listed those of his staff who were working in America, together with their qualifications. He ended by saying, 'I conclude that your Chief Scientific Adviser's doubts of our ability to judge Skybolt development are ill-based'.

This obviously got back to Rubel, who commented:

> However, Solly was not and never pretended to be up on the engineering problems afflicting the Skybolt concept. Indeed, he wrote, surprisingly, that the UK did not have 'have "experts" to match John Rubel or Jerry Wiesner in assessing the technical feasibility of the Skybolt concept as a whole', implicitly recusing himself out of an excess of modesty. The British had experts, all right, but few or none were sufficiently detached from bomber die-hards, or from ties to the USAF and the Skybolt project itself, to assert a needed objectivity.[19]

This seems to be an astute summing up. The reports from Group Captain Fryer and the others who were attached to the project concentrated as much as anything on the technical progress of the missile. It was natural that RAF personnel should be on good terms with their opposite number in the American Air Force. Few of them were paying any attention to the political scene in Washington.

Yet, on the other hand, Neustadt, in his account, remarked that: 'Zuckerman, like his American friends, had never been a SKYBOLT partisan—far from it. He never made a secret of his disdain for its guidance system'. It is difficult to see how someone who claimed no technical expertise could express such a strong opinion on a technical matter. Indeed, some of his reports back to the UK were very complimentary about the guidance system, as shown in this letter of May 1962:

> My two hours at Nortronics were even more illuminating, and I was much impressed by the obvious technical capacity of Mr L.L. Balsam, who is the Manager of the guidance part of the system. Here, too, considerable evidence of progress was seen in the shape of the pre-launch computer, the star tracker, with its navigational and guidance platform etc. etc. They have carried out extensive environmental testing of the gyros and accelerometers of the system …
>
> About a fortnight ago, Nortronics started testing out guidance equipment in an old aircraft which is being fitted up as a flying laboratory. All appears to be going well here, and they have succeeded in searching for, and tracking, stars …[20]

Scribbled on the letter is a comment from Harold Watkinson: 'Thank you this seems re-assuring'. It does seem that Zuckerman was adept at telling people what they wanted to hear, irrespective of the merits of the story.

During 1961 and 1962, progress on development work appeared to be going well, even though there was some inevitable slippage in the programme. The British Government had been reassured by American officials that the project was going ahead. In October 1961, Eugene Zuckert, the United States Secretary of the Air Force, visited Julian Amery, the British Secretary of State for Air and said that the Skybolt programme was going well. Even as late as August 1962, Thorneycroft sent a telegram to McNamara:

> I understand that you are being invited to approve allocation of production funds to SKYBOLT. I am glad to know that this project is so well balanced that this step can be taken as we are relying completely on the successful development of SKYBOLT in planning our V bomber force. In considering the production programme for the weapon, I should be grateful if you would take account of a UK requirement for 100 missiles.[21]

This was no doubt intended to demonstrate to McNamara that the British Government not only still had a keen interest in the missile but emphasised its importance to the UK's defence policy. McNamara replied to say that he was very glad to have such definite reassurance and thanked the Minister. Thus, no doubt could have been left in McNamara's mind as to the importance that Thorneycroft was placing on the missile.

Yet clouds were gathering, and McNamara was less and less convinced for the need of such a missile. Minuteman and Polaris were being successfully deployed in large numbers. Skybolt came to be seen increasingly as an expensive luxury to keep the Air Force happy. Then at the beginning of November 1962, McNamara asked the British ambassador in Washington, David Ormsby Gore, to come and see him. As an ambassador, Ormsby Gore had no executive authority but could only listen to what McNamara had to say, give some sort a response, and report back to London. It is a fairly lengthy telegram but is worth reading in full:

> Mr. McNamara asked me to come and see him today to discuss the future of Skybolt. He said that he was in the middle of considering the defence budget for the fiscal year 1964 and this meant that all the major weapons systems had to be subjected to the closest scrutiny. The Skybolt programme had recently been giving him particular concern. He then rehearsed the history of the project and reminded me that the original estimate for the cost of research and development had been $200 million. As soon as he had taken over in the Defense Department he had come to the conclusion that

Douglas were not performing in an efficient and satisfactory way. Costs had been examined and the estimate had gone up to $373 million. Late in 1961 he had still been dissatisfied and had asked for a firm figure which the Air Force would be asked to certify would be sufficient to complete the development programme. This figure had come out at $492 million and he had accepted it. Unlike the Eisenhower Administration, since taking over he had ensured that Douglas had sufficient funds to proceed at optimum speed but it now seemed that the estimated cost of development would once more exceed the most recent figure. As for the cost of producing the number of missiles ordered by the United States, this would rise from around $1.75 billion to something over $2 billion. In addition the date when the missiles would come into service would probably slip several months. In view of this background, McNamara had asked the Chiefs of Staff to examine the whole project and make recommendations to him about its future. They would need to review all aspects of the problem including the ability of the United States bomber force to remain effective after 1965 if they did not have Skybolt and the possible alternative missile systems they might buy instead. Here he mentioned that the cost of a Minuteman installed in its hardened site was approximately $5 million. They could, therefore, buy an additional 200 for half the cost of the Skybolts. The number of Skybolts available for firing at any given time would only constitute a comparatively small proportion of the United States total strike capability. For instance, after 1967, counting only bombers on 15 minutes alert, 50% of Polaris submarines which would be on station and missiles ready to fire, the Americans would be able to make nearly 4,000 first strikes all, of course, nuclear.

2. He thought that the Chiefs would take about two weeks or more to come up with their recommendations. McNamara would then examine their conclusions and having addressed his own mind to the problem would prepare a paper to send to the President. At this stage he envisaged further discussions and it would, therefore, be safe to assume that the United States administration itself could come to no decision for four or five weeks at least.

3. McNamara then went on to say that, he fully recognized the American obligations to the United Kingdom. There were those set out in the joint technical and financial agreement but he accepted that there were moral obligations as well. He wished to emphasize that no decisions had yet been reached nor would they be reached without consultation with us as provided for in the agreement, but he was nevertheless anxious that we should have an early and frank exposition of his own thinking. He had of necessity to make up his mind at this time since he was now wrestling with the estimates for defence expenditure with a view to submitting them to the President.

4. I replied that I was most grateful for this full account of the present position. I said I was sure he would realize that a decision to abandon the Skybolt programme would be political dynamite so far as the United Kingdom was concerned. The whole of our defence policy in the strategic nuclear field in the second half of this decade was founded upon the availability of Skybolt. We had received repeated assurances from successive Administrations and from the Douglas Corporation that the system could be made to work and would be available to us. As a result, we had abandoned Blue Streak as a weapon, we had planned the modifications needed for our bombers and we were developing special nuclear warheads for Skybolt. We had no alternative delivery vehicle such as the Americans had got. I must tell him that the repercussions of such a decision by the United States would be extremely grave. A major part of the United Kingdom's defence policy would be in ruins which would have serious internal political implications. Our military posture, not only in Europe but in other parts of the world, would be radically changed and Anglo-American relations would be put under the severest strain. I feared that there would be people who questioned the United States' motives in arriving at this decision. They would say that this was a means of bringing pressure upon the British Government to abandon their independent nuclear deterrent. For all these reasons I was sure that the British Government would wish to see the programme continued in spite of the increased costs which might indeed be a small price to pay in view of the political considerations. I asked him to confirm that he was not suggesting that the system could not be made to work. He said that he thought that in the end it could be made to work but there must be some limit to the cost and while he did not wish to give the impression of making a premature judgment he did suspect that a system so incredibly complicated might well prove to be unreliable and difficult to maintain in a serviceable condition in any case. He fully realized the political implications I had put to him and both he and the President would wish to have frank discussions with us at every stage. He also recognized that the Americans would be under a continuing obligation to us if they decided to cancel the project. He said quite categorically that, of course, there was no question whatever of the United States wishing to put pressure on us to abandon our nuclear effort. We were the only judge of our interests and he entirely recognized the disastrous reaction which would result from any such pressure not only in the United Kingdom but in the rest of Western Europe.

5. If they felt they had to cancel, there seemed to him to be three alternative ways in which they could help us:-

(a) As provided for in the agreement, we might decide to continue with the project on our own, the Americans handing over to us all their research up to date. He thought that this would make the missiles prohibitively expensive.

(b) They might provide us with an alternative such as Hound Dog or another missile. In answer to a critical comment from me about Hound Dog he said that his experts were quite confident that it would have a capability of penetrating any likely Soviet defences up to 1970.

(c) They might provide us with an alternative missile system such as Minuteman or Polaris.

I said that I doubted whether any of these alternatives would be satisfactory from our point of view but I could, of course, give no final judgment.

6. McNamara replied that all these questions would need a great deal more careful thought. However, he had felt that we should know as soon as possible that the Skybolt programme was in trouble and under review. He recognized the paramount necessity of giving us the maximum amount of time to consider the position. If the United States did finally arrive at an unfavourable decision he thought it possible, barring leaks, to keep it entirely quiet until January or February which would give us time to work out alternative solutions that might be satisfactory to the United Kingdom. The cost of continuing the programme for two or three more months was not a major consideration. Indeed, if the Chiefs of Staff came up with recommendations showing only a small margin in favour of abandonment he recognized that it might be right to continue the programme on political grounds and in order that the Americans should fulfil their obligations to us. He finally re-emphasized that no decision had as yet been taken and he did not exclude the possibility that the Chiefs of Staff might recommend a continuance of the programme.[22]

Thus the stage was set. McNamara was due to come to London in December to meet Thorneycroft, and the BNDSG had what was probably its last meeting at the beginning of December. It was chaired by the Permanent Secretary at the Ministry of Defence, Sir Robert Scott, with the usual representatives from the Treasury, Foreign Office, Ministry of Aviation, the Vice Chiefs of Staff, and Sir William Cook from Aldermaston. After Nassau and the choice of Polaris, the BNDSG would become redundant. There was only one item on the agenda—alternatives to Skybolt.

It was fully accepted that any suggestion on Mr McNamara's part that Skybolt might be dropped should be strongly resisted. It was necessary however to consider what line the Minister of Defence should be advised to take if Mr McNamara made it plain that the Americans threatened to cancel the Skybolt programme, whatever protests we might make.[23]

Unfortunately, the options were distinctly limited.

... the Study Group agreed that fixed or mobile site land-based missiles must be ruled out as a means of providing a full strategic deterrent. All the arguments used against Blue Streak applied in some degree to Minuteman, the mobility of which on land was in any case limited. Similarly cruise type missiles would have to be ruled out; it was possible that airborne alert might be practicable with Hound Dog, which had a considerable range, but the Air Staff could not regard it as capable of penetrating Soviet defences in depth in the later 1960s. To adapt the V-bombers to carry Hound Dog would involve a major modification, while it was hardly worth investigating the possibility of acquiring B-52 bombers to carry it, in view of the limitations of the missile itself and the undesirability of giving up the V-bombers in favour of American aircraft. One possibility was for the UK to go on with Skybolt herself or to make a sufficiently large contribution towards its cost to induce the Americans to continue development; but this looked like being a dubious and expensive proposition.[24]

At this stage, the Admiralty was thinking in terms of what were described as hybrid submarines. The UK was building what were described as 'hunter-killer' submarines, whose main purpose was to track and destroy Russian submarines. A hybrid Polaris submarine would attempt to carry out this role and also be available for launching the missiles if required. It was soon realised that this was not a good idea. A Polaris submarine should hide deep in the depths of the ocean undetected, whereas a hunter-killer submarine should act aggressively against the opposition. The two roles are diametrically opposed.

The hybrids would carry eight missiles instead of sixteen, and a force of seven submarines would be needed. The Admiralty estimated the cost of each of the submarines at £32 million each, but there would be some saving if they were built as part of the existing hunter-killer programme. Missiles and other equipment would add another £6 million per submarine. Even with a crash programme, they would take seven–eight years to complete.

Thorneycroft sent a letter to the Prime Minister setting out what line he intended to take during his meeting with McNamara.

I have been considering how best to handle the SKYBOLT question with McNamara next week. Much depends on whether, when I see him, I am told that the Americans have decided that they will not proceed with the development of this weapon for their own purposes. If things have not gone that far, I propose to press very strongly that the Americans should see the project through to the end.

2. If, however, I am told that a decision against SKYBOLT has been taken on their side, I may be offered with alternatives of taking over the project

and continuing with it, either here or in America. I propose to reject both of these alternatives: I am sure that we could not afford to complete the project in this country and that, even if we could afford it, we would not do it without a long period of delay before the weapon came into service. For us to continue with it in America would be most unlikely to be acceptable to the American firm since our production order would be too small for them and I doubt whether we could afford to pay what this alternative would cost.

3. I should therefore have to bid for an alternative weapon completely free of political strings as SKYBOLT would be. The Americans have no worthwhile air-launched missile to offer and we would not, I'm sure, accept a ground-launched rocket such as MINUTEMAN. This only leaves some kind of arrangement to provide us with POLARIS and, for the reasons set out in the attached note, I would propose to bid for this missile to be supplied to us for fitting in hybrid submarines which we would build ourselves.

4. If you agree with this line, and on the assumption that I cannot persuade McNamara to proceed with SKYBOLT, I will take it with him: the brief for your meeting with the President will have to be prepared after my talks have been completed.[25]

Just before McNamara's visit, he met Zuckerman, almost by chance, who gave a report of the meeting by telegram to Thorneycroft:

At end of meetings with Rubel, I went to McNamara's office to pay my respects. Nitze and Rubel were present. McNamara immediately asked what I thought of the Skybolt problem. I replied that I certainly knew there was a problem but I was hardly prepared to discuss it. He urged me to say what I would do and I answered that the issue was of paramount political importance to the United Kingdom regardless of the technical difficulties into which the project had run. Whatever else, our position as an independent nuclear Power in the public eye should not be shaken. In the course of the subsequent discussion the following possibilities were raised:

(1) that we take the programme over;

(2) that the United States assign to us a number of Minutemen in the United States which would be targeted in such a way as to blaze a path for a V-force not armed with Skybolt;

(3) that we should try to fit Hound Dog (which has a 500-mile range); and

(4) Polaris.

I raised Polaris and said that I felt that it was the only system alternative to Skybolt which did not appear to suffer from technical or political objections or both. It was indicated that a submarine Polaris system might be more difficult for them to provide than one adapted for surface ships. McNamara also observed that the Polaris solution was likely to cause as embarrassment in our negotiations over the Common Market. To this I observed that Skybolt implied the same difficulties. McNamara is clearly preoccupied with Skybolt to the exclusion of almost any other issue and I gained the strong impression that he is determined to be helpful. From snippets of conversation that I picked up earlier in the day, it had also become clear that he was being heavily advised to offer us Hound Dog, technical details of which were being assembled in various briefs. Until the matter of Skybolt was raised by McNamara I had studiously avoided talking about it with Rubel and his colleagues.[26]

The idea of targeting Minutemen missiles to clear a path for the V bombers does seem distinctly bizarre, and it would suffer from the obvious political drawback that the UK deterrent would no longer be independent, but instead would have to rely on the willingness of the United States to launch nuclear missiles on the behalf of the UK. However, McNamara was certainly correct when it came to Polaris and the Common Market; de Gaulle used the British acquisition of Polaris as a pretext for his famous '*Non!*' declaration.

Thorneycroft and the Air Staff also received a warning from Group Captain Fryer in Washington to the following effect:

McNamara will be bringing Rubel (Deputy Director of Defense Research and Engineering) with him as his Technical Expert for discussions with Foreign Secretary and Minister of Defence. Rebel knows the SKYBOLT programme fairly well but he has never been enamoured of the system and I have reason to believe that he would like to see an early end to it and that he has slanted his advice to McNamara correspondingly.

In my view therefore you will only be able to save SKYBOLT on the most compulsive political arguments (and even then you may have to be content with an emasculated programme) despite the fact that Montgomery of Rubel's staff admitted at Zuckert's meeting last Thursday ... that there was nothing technically wrong with the system as it now exists.[27]

McNamara and his team flew into London on 11 December to meet Thorneycroft. Henry Brandon, the veteran foreign correspondent, described Thorneycroft as 'a pugnacious right-wing Tory with little patience for Americans'. As for McNamara and Thorneycroft, Brandon considered that 'the two disliked each other intensely'.

McNamara gave a statement to the press which was very downbeat about the prospects of Skybolt: 'It is a very expensive program and technically extremely complex. It is no secret that all five flight tests attempted so far have failed and program costs have climbed sharply'.[20] The writing was on the wall; Skybolt was to be axed. All that remained to be the official announcement.

Rubel took verbatim notes of the subsequent meeting (in his memoir, written very much later, he refers to Gatwick airport as 'Gatskill', which is a warning that people's recollections many years after the event may well have unintentional errors).

At their meeting, McNamara suggested that he read out the paper he had brought with him. Since it was twenty pages long, this apparently took an hour, which does seem a bit pointless. Thorneycroft responded to McNamara by telling him that the British had depended upon Skybolt, and now had been let down. Rubel relates:

> He said it in a way that invoked images of the direst betrayal. I remember reflecting on his skill in evoking a sense of guilt, of obligation on the part of the Americans who had, in fact, done nothing more than cancel a development that should never have been started, to which the British had contributed nothing, for which the Americans have no real military need, and which the British had identified as their independent nuclear deterrent …
>
> He made it appear, moreover, that he was almost surprised by all this, that his remarks were entirely unrehearsed, a spontaneous, heartfelt response to an unexpected confrontation, although he had known about the likelihood of the decision to cancel for more than a month.[28]

Rubel was wrong about one thing; although the British had made no financial contribution, it had made a very substantial contribution in political terms when it allowed a base for American submarines to be built at Holy Loch. When Rubel was first appointed as Assistant Director of Defense Research and Engineering, he naturally had briefings on all the missiles under development. He remarked in the case of Skybolt:

> I was astonished to learn only after that briefing that British RAF officers had collaborated in writing the basic military 'requirements' for Skybolt in 1958, and had sat in on the selection of Douglas Aircraft as the prime contractor early in 1959, a collaboration that American officials above the Air Force level, not to mention the President, apparently knew little or nothing about at the time. It would appear, however, that British collaboration in the Skybolt initiative was well known up to the top of the British government, perhaps from its early stages.[29]

Presumably, Rubel was ignorant of the policy of 'interdependence', which had then currently been in vogue. The idea that the US might depend on the UK for any aspect of its defence programme was distinctly optimistic, but the UK took advantage of the policy to become involved in various

American projects. The USAF was more than happy for the RAF to become involved since it improved the chances of getting approval for Skybolt. Most of the British officials involved in Skybolt were working in co-operation with the USAF and tended to close their ears to any contrary messages coming from the DoD.

Indeed, the co-operation went deeper than he thought as this proposal from the American Government in 1959 demonstrates:

> The United States Government believes that in order to advance co-operation among United States, United Kingdom, Canada in research and development and military fields where the three countries have mutual defence interests, it would be useful to establish some supervisory institutional arrangement. It is suggested that for this purpose the Combined Policy Committee be reconstituted with appropriate new guide-lines.
>
> The Combined Policy Committee was established by the Agreement of August 19, 1943, in order to facilitate co-operation and atomic matters among the three allies. After the end of World War II such co-operation became much more limited, and the Combined Policy Committee for some years now has functioned only to a small extent and through correspondence...
>
> In the fields of non-atomic weapons research and development various arrangements for co-operation among the three countries have now been established, principally among the military services. Some of the co-operation carried out under these arrangements is quite extensive and it is desired that this should continue the fullest possible way.[30]

He also seems to be unaware of the reason why the UK felt so let down; British had, as they saw it, upheld their part of the bargain and allowed an American submarine base in Scotland. As a *quid pro quo* situation, the Americans had promised Skybolt. Now, it seemed that the Americans were reneging on that agreement. It was not only political matters on which Rubel seemed uninformed; the British delegation at the later Nassau talks was not impressed by Rubel's grasp of technical matters when they discussed Skybolt with him. James Lighthill, Director of the RAE, noted in his report:

> In the meantime, on the technical soundness of Skybolt I had a long discussion with Rubel ... On the influence of terrain on Doppler velocity readings and the alleged consequential need for a more extensive flying programme than had been planned he had no satisfactory reply at all. On numbers of launches he was very unclear and did not seem to appreciate the large volume of data derived from telemetry and other instrumentation from

even an unsuccessful launch. He admitted however, that the partial failure of each of the first five firings was not of major significance. On the reliability of flight trials of the pre-launch computer he had no knowledge at all and generally lacked solid arguments to substantiate DoD doubts on reliability. He gave it as his opinion that the project could have been brought to fruition. Summing up, the evidence is that the DoD [Department of Defense] damning of Skybolt on technical grounds was a trumped-up affair.[31]

Rubel was shown a copy of Lighthill's comments after the papers had been released. He says in his defence:

> If my talks with him were not my finest hour, it remains that I was a senior member of the Hughes team that designed, built and demonstrated (1950) the first airborne celestial-navigation navigation system in the world.[32]

Air Vice Marshall Hartley, ACAS (OR), was not impressed with Rubel either when they met at Nassau:

> Nothing of significance occurred until the evening, when I had a conversation with Lighthill, Wilson and Rubel of DoD (who we have known for some time was an under-cover opponent of Skybolt). Wilson asked him point-blank why he was against Skybolt and his immediate answer was—'Because it won't work'. He went on to elaborate this in terms of cost-effectiveness, on the basis of a preconceived war. I suggested that there might be some factor that he had not thought of and was offered in return a shower of Minute Men and 42 Polaris submarines. Lighthill was manifestly so disgusted by Rubel that he took no part in the conversation, which was in any case abruptly terminated by the passage of McNamara. In retrospect, I was horrified at the thought that the workings of the largest Democracy in the West could anyway be influenced by someone so shallow as Rubel.
>
> To complete the Rubel story, since I did not meet him again, he lunched with Zuckerman and Lighthill next day. Lighthill told me afterwards that Rubel appeared to know little about missile development in particular and to have wide gaps in his general knowledge. For example:—
>
> (a) he was unaware that telemetry was fitted to Skybolt during R and D, and appeared to think that a missile trial was rather like a gunnery trial.
>
> (b) it was news to him that Doppler did not work over the sea.[34]

To be fair to Rubel, he was quite right to say that the existing missile systems being deployed by the US (Minuteman and Polaris) meant that Skybolt was no longer needed, certainly not in the light of the anticipated cost. He was not the only one in the Kennedy Administration who held that view. Jerry Weisner was chairman of President Kennedy's Science Advisory Committee and, writing to the Deputy Chief of Air Staff (DCAS) shortly before the Nassau conference, AVM Hartley related, albeit at second hand, Weisner's views on Skybolt:

> Dr Wilson told me today that the Head of Chancery had approached Weisner about ten days ago to find out whether the Administration was under any misapprehension about the strength of UK interest in Skybolt. The gist of Weisner's reply was:—
>
> (a) 'You realise that I am Skybolt's principal enemy, I have never liked the system and have always opposed it.'
>
> (b) 'I think you have grossly over-estimated your need for this weapon. This is because you over-estimate the Russian anti-aircraft defence capabilities. Your V-bombers will be able to penetrate the U.S.S.R. for some time to come.'
>
> (c) 'If Skybolt is cancelled and you must have a weapon, you could have Minuteman.'
>
> (d) 'You realise of course that if we go on with Skybolt it will be at least two years late.'
>
> (e) 'You do not need Skybolt in order to retain your independent deterrent capability. This capability will exist as long as you are able to destroy either Leningrad or Moscow.'
>
> (f) 'We in the administration have always been perfectly clear on the extent of UK interest in Skybolt. If we had not taken full account of the interest we would certainly have cancel Skybolt a year ago.'[35]

The issue of whether Skybolt was to be cancelled for political or for technical reasons was very important to the British. If the reasons were technical, the UK Government would have to accept the decision, whether it liked it or not. If the decision was political, then that was a different matter. Thorneycroft had asked McNamara directly: 'If you are going to cancel the project, are you going to say that it won't work, or are you going to say it will cost too much?' The reply he got was, 'We won't say that it is impossible, but we will say that technical problems dominate the decision'.

One feature that was muddying the issue was that the American administration had made it very clear that small, so-called independent nuclear forces such as those of Britain or France were an unnecessary complication. McNamara himself had said as part of a speech in July 1962:

> In particular, relatively weak national nuclear forces with enemy cities as their targets are not likely to be sufficient to perform even the function of deterrence. If they are small, and perhaps vulnerable on the ground or in

the air, or inaccurate, a major antagonist can take a variety of measures to counter them. Indeed, if a major antagonist came to believe there was a substantial likelihood of it being used independently, this force would be inviting a pre-emptive first strike against it. In the event of war, the use of such a force against the cities of a major nuclear power would be tantamount to suicide, whereas its employment against significant military targets would have a negligible effect on the outcome of the conflict. Meanwhile, the creation of a single additional national nuclear force encourages the proliferation of nuclear power with all its attendant dangers.

In short, then, limited nuclear capabilities, operating independently, are dangerous, expensive, prone to obsolescence, and lacking in credibility as a deterrent.[36]

That last sentence was quite an accurate summing up of Britain's deterrent. His remarks were picked up in the British press and quite widely publicised, but McNamara was not only giving his opinion as Defense Secretary but reflecting a view quite widely held in Washington, particularly in the State Department. Thus, there was a good deal of suspicion, if not paranoia, in British Government circles that Skybolt was being cancelled as part of a policy to force Britain to abandon its deterrent, which is why Thorneycroft had pressed McNamara so hard to admit that he was not abandoning Skybolt for technical reasons but political reasons. In reality, it was both.

McNamara then proposed:

The UK government might wish to continue the SKYBOLT programme in order to obtain the number of missiles planned for the Vulcan II force, either (a) through cut-back production programme in the US, or (b) through production in the UK employing US technology.

The HOUND DOG missile system might be adapted to some British aircraft. This alternative would involve a number of technical problems and uncertainties.

The UK government might wish to participate in a sea-based MRBM force under multilateral managing and ownership, such as NATO is now discussing.[37]

It was very obvious from this that the UK was not going to get Polaris without strings. The terms being proposed would be totally unacceptable to the British Government, since it removed any pretence of 'independence' from the deterrent, and one of the major selling points of the deterrent, which had cost so much, was that it was independent.

From the political point of view, the Government was in a very awkward position. The 'independent deterrent' had been a major plank in Conservative policy. It was becoming clear that while Skybolt was being cancelled, the alternatives on offer seemed derisory by comparison. Thorneycroft had to face a distinctly critical House of Commons on 13 December, which re-opened old questions as to whether the UK truly had an independent deterrent. The most critical comment came from a Labour member, Emrys Hughes: 'Is he aware that it is very humiliating indeed to see the Minister of Defence and the Prime Minister going cap-in-hand, crawling to the Americans, for something that is no use, and which will prove exorbitantly expensive to the people of this country?' Even allowing for the partisan nature of the debate, it was a widely held opinion.

Any hope that help might come from the US Air Force was soon dismissed, as this telegram sent by Group Captain Emson from Washington to the Chief of Air Staff illustrates:

> Following my discussion with S of S [Secretary of State for Air] I arranged to see General LeMay this afternoon on his return from Europe.
>
> The Vice Chief General Mckee asked me to see him this morning in order that he might brief General LeMay before my appointment. I brought him up to date with the situation in the UK, including the results of the McNamara/Thorneycroft meeting and I left him a copy of the US aide memoir to show to General LeMay. We went over the well-known ground and discussed the USAF position ...
>
> Subsequently, he rang me to say that he had been thinking over the situation and that for a number of reasons which he did not specify in any detail, he must advise me not to press for the interview. Although I had previously assured him that any report I might give to you and S of S would be in the strictest confidence, but not used in the forthcoming negotiations he obviously feels that the slightest hint that there has been collusion between the USAF and RAF could well result in destroying altogether LeMay's usefulness and the already difficult relationship existing between him and McNamara.[38]

The question then was what the government should do next. Skybolt was obviously on its way out, and the only other acceptable American missile was Polaris. Any attempt at a British missile had been dropped more than a year ago. Yet it would seem that the offer of Polaris would be hedged about with various strings. Thus, it seemed that the options are running out for the British Government.

The Nassau Agreement:
Kennedy and Macmillan Meet

Macmillan and Kennedy had already agreed to a meeting in the Bahamas, which would take place after Macmillan's visit to Paris to talk to de Gaulle. The original purpose of the meeting was to be merely a friendly exchange of views about the state of the world. This changed very drastically in view of the imminent Skybolt cancellation; Skybolt and its replacement took up almost the entire meeting.

The Skybolt crisis had not gone unnoticed in America, and neither had the effect that the crisis was having on Anglo-American relations. This was summed up in an editorial in *The Washington Post* just three days before the meeting:

> Skybolt was an experiment and some experiments can be expected to fail. The State Department is not an experiment and it cannot be allowed to fail. Most especially, it cannot and must not fail in sensing the things that are of capital importance putting aside everything else for them. Foreign officials who do not instinctively perceive the signs of decay in this country's relations with its closest and best ally must be operating a Foreign Office that is in alarming disarray. The British are feeling ill used. It does not matter if we intended to ill use them or if they have a right to feel so. In any case that is the way they feel. They have ventured at our urging into a politically dangerous, but eminently right economic policy. In the view of the way we have dealt with them in the past few weeks they feel wronged and outraged. If we don't respond as a friend or to respond to that feeling, their emotions will be justified and fears about the adequacy of the State Department confirmed.

The editorial summed up a general opinion in America that the State Department has not been up to the mark in dealing with the crisis.

The meeting began on Tuesday 18 December and finished on Friday the 21st. Although much has been written about the face-to-face meetings of Kennedy and Macmillan, what went on behind the scenes is equally interesting.

Fortunately, several of the backstage participants have written their own accounts of the meeting, some as official reports written straight after the meetings, others as part of autobiographies. These should be treated with a little caution since each report reflects the particular position and prejudices held by the author.

On the political side, Macmillan was accompanied by the Foreign Secretary Lord Home, Thorneycroft, and Duncan Sandys. The presence of Sandys is slightly surprising; at that time, he was the Secretary of State for the Colonies and Commonwealth Relations, although in the past he had been Minister of Supply, Minister of Defence, and Minister of Aviation. David Ormsby-Gore, the British ambassador in Washington, was also present.

Thorneycroft took with him a number of advisors from the Ministry of Defence. The Chief of the Defence Staff, Lord Mountbatten, was not invited since the Americans would then be forced to include the chairman of the Joint Chiefs of Staff, which the President preferred not to do. Thorneycroft's advisors included Sir Robert Scott, Permanent Secretary at the Ministry of Defence; Harry Lawrence-Wilson, Under-Secretary (the next rank down); Sir Solly Zuckerman, Chief Scientific Adviser at the Ministry of Defence; Vice Admiral Le Fanu, Third Sea Lord and Controller of the Navy; James Lighthill, Director of the RAE; Dr Harry Wilson, Director-General, Defence Research Staff; and Air Vice Marshal Christopher Hartley, Assistant Chief of Air Staff (Operational Requirements).

AVM Hartley began his report with the wonderful opening: 'In the course of a partridge shoot near Coltishall on Monday, 17th December, I was given a message at 14.00 hrs that I was to accompany the Ministry of Defence and his party to Nassau ...' His report exudes a general air of disgruntlement, which may have begun when his partridge shoot was interrupted, but was then exacerbated by events on the aircraft:

The journey was relatively uneventful except that I was told firmly by the Private Secretary that I was not required at the Minister's table, the fourth seat been reserved for him (the Private Secretary). I told the Private Secretary that I was at his disposal for any professional advice about the flight, after which I occupied the jump seat on the flight deck (except when sleeping) in preference to one of the rear seats. The PS did not see fit to consult me with the result that the initial rather nebulous directive to the Captains to get the minister there 'as soon as possible' was implemented, to the embarrassment of the Governor of the Bahamas.[1]

According to Zuckerman, the main British and American parties were both comfortably housed in the Lyford Cay Club, although the President and the Prime Minister had their own separate villas. However, working space was very much more restricted, as the Air Vice Marshal reports:

We ... assembled for our first Advisors' meeting at 10.45, in the cottage next to the PM's house, where the main meetings were to be held. Apart from the Signals and Cipher Office, which was housed in another building, this cottage appeared to be the only roof under which the UK delegation could operate. It consisted of three relatively small rooms and one hall-way, which were used as follows:-

(a) Smallest room: Typing Pool

(b) The large room: Minister's conference room, overflow from typing pool, and bar (because it had a sink).

(c) Smaller room: apparently reserved for FO and PM's Staff: penetrated by others at their peril in order to reach the only lavatory.

(d) Hall-way: used by Lord Hood [Deputy Under Secretary at the Foreign Office] and occasionally Sir Robert Scott for private drafting sessions. Tactful advisors used the back door on these occasions.

This cottage was used on and off by up to forty people: fortunately there was a good veranda and Nassau weather is delightful. However, it rapidly became one-upmanship (and at times very important) not to be left out in the sun. The organisers apologised for the lack of space by explaining they had picked the site for a cosy chat between the President and the PM, having at that time no idea that Skybolt would be on the menu.

In these conditions any system for distributing and handling papers was conspicuous by its absence. It became a matter of initiative to get a sight of papers and of skill verging on subterfuge to retain possession of those which appeared important. The only papers readily accessible were copies of FO telegrams, which did not appear to me to be in this category.

The same problems applied to hearsay information on the progress of the talks, on which I was heavily dependant [*sic*.] since I was never once called in to them. This information could be obtained, but usually only by direct questioning of the source; it was seldom volunteered, and if it was volunteered at a meeting of Advisors, there was no guarantee that one would be invited to be present.[2]

At their first meeting, Kennedy told Macmillan that he had decided to cancel plans for the introduction of Skybolt into the USAF. Among the reasons which he gave was that Skybolt was an advanced and complex weapon that probably could not be completed within the timescale projected when the programme was begun, that costs were rising, and because there were doubts about the eventual value of Skybolt as a weapon system. However, he was prepared to go ahead on the basis that the further development costs be shared between the two countries on a 50-50 basis, after which the UK would be able to place a production order to meet its requirements.

Macmillan described this as a 'generous offer', but turned it down, using a rather vivid turn of phrase:

> Mr Macmillan said that while the proposed marriage with SKYBOLT was not exactly a shot-gun wedding, the virginity of the lady must now be regarded as doubtful. There had been too many remarks made about the unreliability of SKYBOLT for anyone to believe in its effectiveness in the future.[3]

There were a variety of reasons for this rejection. AVM Hartley put it in a rather cynical fashion:

> Harry Wilson and I were at pains to brief Thorneycroft and Scott that control of the programme in the US from the UK would be impossible. The difficulties about priority, both in the use of government facilities and within the firms involved, would be augmented due to certain DoD reputations having been staked on its failure.[4]

Lighthill made exactly the same points in his report. Thorneycroft reinforced the point when he told Kennedy the following:

> It was incontrovertible that SKYBOLT would be late, expensive and unreliable. This had been publicly stated by Mr McNamara. It would be difficult for him to recommend to Parliament that Britain should now, as it were, buy shares in the company. He did not think it a defensible position for the United Kingdom to continue the SKYBOLT development.[5]

McNamara was distinctly sceptical about the chances of completing Skybolt successfully.

> He had gone to Nassau determined not to tell untruths about Skybolt and indeed it was confirmed from the American side that he sat in the corner of the room uttering a plural monosyllable whenever the possibility of completing Skybolt was mentioned.[6]

What that plural monosyllable was, we shall probably never find out, but the words 'Balls' comes to mind.

Macmillan also pointed out what the UK was already doing for the American Government. This was not entirely a gentle hint at blackmail, but more to underline what he felt was an American obligation to the UK.

> Mr Macmillan added that he did not wish to suggest in any way that the United Kingdom would retract from the agreements they have already reached with the United States. The POLARIS depot ship could stay in the Holy Loch, the advanced radar station could operate from Fylingdales. He did not wish in any way to retreat from these obligations. At the same time the United Kingdom had run risks by having these facilities stationed in their country. So it could be said that they were to run all the dangers and exercise none of the power ...[7]

A briefing paper prepared before the meeting by the Ministry of Defence makes exactly this point but in rather more detail:

> But if, in addition, the President refuses to let us have Polaris missiles on the same terms as Skybolt, then a most serious situation will arise. The full implications will take time to work out, but the President should be warned at once that this makes it impossible for us to associate ourselves with him in jointly sharing the responsibility for the cancellation of Skybolt. This will have to be presented as a unilateral American decision, with most damaging consequences for Anglo-American relations.
>
> Moreover, he should be warned that without an independent strategic system of our own we refuse to consider taking part in any multilateral medium-range or tactical force, partly because of the political impact in this country and partly because of the military risks. A country that lacks a strategic deterrent system of its own as much less chance of deterring a massive attack on its homeland. It must be exceedingly prudent. It should not take part in a lesser force, not only under its own control, when this might invite the destruction of its homeland. Such a refusal would also have profound consequences for the Atlantic Alliance and from NATO.[8]

This paragraph was discussing the possibility that the UK would be offered Polaris 'with strings'—in other words, not under independent British control but under control of a NATO commander. The briefing went on to say:

> There are, of course, bound to be pressures in Britain to review the Holy Loch arrangement [the stationing of American Polaris submarines in Scotland] and possibly the stationing of American aircraft in this country.[9]

If matters were to get to the state where American Air Force bases in the UK were threatened, then the rupture between the two major NATO allies would be vastly damaging to the whole alliance.

Macmillan went on to say that if necessary, Britain could develop its own missile-launching submarines, but warned of the consequences:

> He did not wish President Kennedy to be under any illusion about the effect of such a decision in the United Kingdom. If they had to go ahead and develop a submarine-fired missile themselves. This would inevitably lead to a deep rift in United States-United Kingdom relations. That is not to say that the Government would in any way lessen their efforts to cooperate with the United States Government. But public opinion could not be controlled.[10]

The second US offer was that of the Hound Dog missile. There were two fairly serious objections to this. The first is that it would be almost impossible to fit to the V bombers, and the second is that its performance was much lower than Skybolt. It would certainly have been an improvement on Blue Steel, which is not saying very much.

Hound Dog was 43 feet long, 8 feet longer than Blue Steel and so there was no possibility of fitting it into the bomb bay of a Vulcan, which was only 30 feet long, or that of a Victor, which measured 33 feet. As Hound Dog had its jet engines mounted under the body of the missile, it had a vertical dimension of 9 feet. The ground to wing clearance of both V bombers was only about 5 feet, so this virtually eliminated any consideration of carrying it. Furthermore, even more allowance would have to have been made for a pylon of about 15 inches depth if the missile was going to be slung under the wing, which would demand clearance of some 10.25 feet for the missile in this position. The alternative would have been to cut a hole in the wing for the fin of the missile, as shown below.

The Ministry of Aviation made a rough estimate of the costs of fitting Hound Dog to the V bombers, which came to a grand total of £100 million:

R & D and Production cost of modifying the Vulcan, say—£20M
Proving trials (including trials missiles but assuming free use of US range)—£10M
Purchase of, say, 100 HOUND DOGS—£50M
Purchase of support equipment, say—£20M [11]

These do seem to be more in the nature of guesses rather than estimates.

In many ways, particularly in performance, Hound Dog was very similar to the designs produced by Avro and Bristol for OR1182, although the layout was obviously very different.

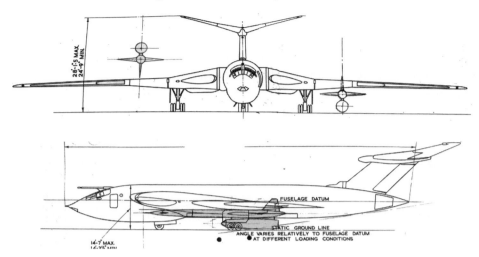

An Air Ministry drawing of the Hound Dog missile mounted on a Victor. As can be seen, any attempt to mount it underneath the wing meant cutting rather a large hole. It would be difficult to mount the missile further back, since the centre of gravity of the missile needed to be fairly close to the centre of gravity of the aircraft. Mounting it on top of the wing was equally problematic.

The third offer was, as the British delegation put it, Polaris 'with strings'. There were several factors at play here. It was certainly true that there were many in America, including McNamara himself, who thought that small independent deterrents were an unnecessary complication and potentially dangerous. Yet Kennedy had other concerns, in particular, the relations between America, France, and Europe generally. This came out in such comments as follows:

> He was, of course, aware in a general way of the history of Anglo-American co-operation in the nuclear field. He knew that the two countries had co-operated very intimately. The United States, however, had not supported the French in the nuclear field and the result of this policy had been to sour American relations with France.[12]

> President Kennedy said that if the United States gave POLARIS to Britain, it would be difficult in logic not to say that if any country developed a nuclear bomb the United States should give them a missile system.[13]

One of the questions revolved around the word 'assigned', the meaning of which was debated with all the earnestness of mediaeval theologians. Kennedy remarked: 'For their different reasons, the United Kingdom wanted the word "assign" interpreted as loosely as possible and the United States wanted it defined as tightly as possible'.

In the end, it was emotion rather than logic that broke the deadlock, in the form of an appeal from Macmillan to Kennedy:

> Accordingly the President and the Prime Minister agreed that the United States will make available on a continuing basis POLARIS missiles (less warheads) for British submarines. The United States will also study the feasibility of making available certain support facilities for such submarines. The United Kingdom will construct the submarines in which these weapons will be placed and they will also supply the nuclear warheads for the POLARIS missiles. British forces developed under this plan will be assigned and targeted in the same way as the forces described in paragraph 6 (i.e., such forces would be assigned as part of a NATO nuclear force and targeted in accordance with NATO plans). These forces, and at least equal United States forces, would be made available for inclusion in a NATO multilateral nuclear force. The Prime Minister made it clear that these British forces will be used for the purposes of international defence of the Western Alliance in all circumstances, except where Her Majesty's Government may decide that supreme national interests are at stake.[14]

This was spelt out more clearly:

> Only in the event of a dire National emergency—an emergency in which it might be necessary to act alone—an emergency which we cannot envisage and we must all trust will never occur—would Her Majesty's Government be faced with a decision of utilising such forces on its own—of course after adequate notice to all its partners will.[15]

This would later be described as 'the bargain of the century'. This was not the feeling at the time of most of the British delegation, and many in Whitehall and the Cabinet. Robert Scott, one of those at Nassau, drafted a letter to Thorneycroft, which he persuaded Zuckerman to sign:

> We have thought hard about the outcome of yesterday's discussions, and feel we must draw your attention to the very serious risks of the proposed arrangement.
>
> A formula has been sought and found whereby POLARIS is substituted for SKYBOLT in the maintenance of the British deterrent. The claim that it is 'independent' can be made, but only with difficulty—the more so as we know that to the President it is a cardinal feature of this policy to deny his allies independent nuclear forces. In fact, we shall be spending vast sums of

money in order to make a contribution to a multilateral force the object of which is political rather than military.

We shall lose some of our freedom of action to support NATO militarily, in both the nuclear and non-nuclear fields, and we shall be under constraints in freely negotiating and discussing the military policy of the Alliance and the shape and size of its forces. To the extent that we are put in a straitjacket in the NATO area we shall correspondingly lose some liberty of choice and action elsewhere.

Timescale is very relevant. Such an arrangement might conceivably be tolerable if we could have a POLARIS force quickly. But for six years or more we shall be spending vast sums of money without being certain that we shall in the end get the missiles.

These seem to us to be grave risks. There are risks also for the Americans: Anglo-American relations will be under severe strains arising directly and indirectly after the conclusion of this agreement.[16]

Opinion in London was not favourable either. Sir Maurice Dean, Permanent Secretary at the Air Ministry, also wrote a long report on the events. He says:

There were a number of telegrams ... the third turned out be the substance of the final communiqué under which we had Polaris but on the condition we committed it to NATO, although we reserved the right to use it for our own purposes where supreme British needs were involved. As the price of this, however, we were committed to a multilateral policy under which we put over some unspecified part of the 'V' force to NATO as of now.

None of us liked this, and the Secretary of State, who had already left for the Cabinet, was sent a minute. My own view, of which I informed the Secretary of State on several occasions ... is that this proposal is thoroughly unacceptable.

At the Cabinet discussion Mr Butler opened with a strong plea that the Prime Minister should be supported and, despite the great deal of uneasiness expressed, this was a view which was finally held. The Prime Minister was, however, invited to secure her a strengthening of the passage which reserves the right to serve our national interests in emergency.[17]

Even after the conference had ended, he noted:

The Minister of Defence held a 'working dinner' on the night of Sunday, 30th December. This was ostensibly to discuss the central organisation of defence. In fact, so Mr Fraser told me, it was occupied exclusively with discussion about Skybolt. All the Service Ministers and the Minister of Aviation attacked the Nassau Agreement in strong terms and the Minister can have been left under no misunderstanding as to the extreme unpopularity of the bargain which has been struck with the US President.[18]

Rubel was present at Nassau, although he was not involved in the negotiations, since, as he puts it, they were primarily political rather than technical. However, his final comments on the outcome are distinctly bizarre and wrong in almost every detail:

> The Bermuda meetings ended with the announcement that the US would sell the UK two Polaris submarines which would then comprise the British independent nuclear deterrent.
> A Labour Party government took over a few years after the end of the SKYBOLT affair. Britain's independent nuclear deterrent was abandoned. The POLARIS forces that we had made available to the British were made part of the UK contribution to NATO.[19]

It was the missiles that were sold to the UK, not the submarines. As far as his point as to whether the UK still had an independent deterrent or not, he seems to have misunderstood the negotiations completely. Perhaps this is a salutary warning that people's recollection of events many years later can be very much in error, and we should be wary as to how much trust we put in them.

There is an interesting footnote to this. Early in January, a British MP, Sir Arthur Vere Harvey, was visiting America on private business. He had been involved in aviation for most of his life, having been in the RAF in the 1920s and '30s and rejoining at the start of the war. He had a distinguished war record and left the RAF with the rank of air commodore. At the time, he was chairman of the Conservative defence backbench committee. He could, therefore, be regarded as someone who knew what he was talking about.

During his tour of America, he visited the Douglas Aircraft Corporation to discuss Skybolt with them; he then went on to Washington, where he visited the Pentagon. He was naturally accompanied by British officials, who made a record of events. These were written up by Mr Blair-Oliphant, the director of Aircraft Defence Research Staff, and a copy ended up on the desk of the minister, Julian Amery.

He was met by Colonel Dallam, chief of foreign liaison division, USAF. Blair-Oliphant goes on to say:

> They were accompanied to the office of Hon. John Rubel, Assistant Secretary for R&D. Sir Arthur Harvey, who is Chairman of the Conservative

Parliamentary Defence Committee, explained to Mr Rubel the difficult position brought about by the cancellation of Skybolt and the resultant gap in deterrent capability of Bomber Command. Apart from the political capital made by the opposition, he was embarrassed also by the Conservative back-benchers, who insisted not only on the continuation of an independent British deterrent, but also on the ability of the Royal Air Force to exercise it. They realise that ad hoc developments such as extending the range of Blue Steel were not only ineffective but a waste of money.

Sir Arthur told Mr Rubel that he had visited D.A.C. and Nortronics and heard for himself about the state of development of Skybolt and its trials. He was satisfied that development was going well and that the guidance system, in particular, promised a high degree of reliability. He was surprised that technical reasons had been quoted in connection with cancellation of the project. Mr Rubel admitted that the technical reasons given in public statements have not been well founded. Sir Arthur then went on to discuss the possibility of continuing the development of Skybolt in UK, using the guidance system developed at Nortronics. He had discussed this with the firms concerned … who considered that successful development could be completed in the UK with a delay of no more than 18 months resulting from the changeover. Mr Rubel, speaking as an engineer, doubted whether such a change in management could be successfully achieved with the transfer of know-how, skills and techniques involved. He was not disposed to consider such a possibility very seriously or to discuss it further with Sir Arthur.

Mr Rubel outlined very briefly the history of Skybolt as a whole and said, frankly, that he had never held much belief in the reliability of this weapon system. He had said as much on a number of occasions … and when, about 18 months ago, his opinion had been requested by Sir Solly Zuckerman, he had told him the British should go for Polaris. He went on to explain that it was not the present as much as potential cost of development that had given rise to the Administration's decision to cancel Skybolt. Even discounting the first five failures, only one out of two guided launches had been successful; bearing in mind that there will be a further 51 R&D launches, it could be seen that very expensive costs could result. The Administration had felt that there were other more reliable systems on which to spend their money …

Sir Arthur then made a courtesy call on Mr Zuckert, Secretary of the Air Force, who received him very warmly. He was acutely aware of and sympathetic towards the situation in following the cancellation of Skybolt and offered to co-operate to the fullest extent in any proposals might subsequently be made. Sir Arthur discussed with him a possibility of continuing the development of Skybolt in UK using Nortronics' guidance system. Mr Zuckert doubted the feasibility of this proposal in view of the very small production order that would be involved. In reply to a direct question he said that it was unlikely that the USAF would have Skybolt now or in the future.[20]

One line in the report was underlined in Amery's characteristic violet ballpoint pen: 'Mr Rubel admitted that the technical reasons given in public statements have not been well founded'. It was obviously still a sore point in London.

Vere Harvey touched on this in the subsequent debate in the House of Commons on the Nassau Agreement:

> Officials in Washington admitted that it was a mistake ever to say that Skybolt was 'ditched' for technical reasons. I think that the Americans are now being frank enough to say that it would have been better not to adduce technical reasons for stopping the work, and I think that it ought to be seen in that perspective.[21]

Concerning the agreement itself, he went on to say:

> We have been told that the Prime Minister did well, and I think he did extremely well, to get what he did. However, the Americans having ditched the Skybolt agreement as they did, there ought not to have been any question of the Prime Minister's battling hard to get Polaris. I should have thought that if one broke an agreement with a friend and ally one should say, 'We are sorry this has happened. Will you have this instead?' But the Prime Minister had to battle for it. What has disturbed me is that in dealing with a close ally we have had to go to extremes to make our case.[22]

Feathers were still obviously ruffled, but politics moves on, and Skybolt would, in the minds of politicians and the public, fade into the past.

The Stopgaps

Most unfortunately Skybolt is gone. Attacking Polaris will not bring it back. I think we must accept that and turn all our energies to building up the Royal Air Force to fill a 'limited war' role. We cannot afford to antagonise Ministers upon whose support we must rely for success.

The Deputy Chief of Air Staff (DCAS), 28 December 1962.

Written underneath: *I agree with DCAS's comments. M.J.D.*

Sir Maurice Dean, Permanent Secretary, Air Ministry.[1]

The degree of consternation and confusion caused in the Air Ministry by the cancellation of Skybolt can be seen in the number of wild schemes thrown up as possible substitutes. Even when the government had obtained Polaris on acceptable terms, there was still what was called the 'gap'. The deterrent programme had been based on the assumption that Skybolt would be coming into service with the RAF in 1964 or 1965. Even on the most optimistic assumptions, Polaris would not be available until around 1970. If Polaris had not been available, the situation would have been even worse; the government would be faced with having to develop an entirely new delivery system from scratch, and the chance of getting that into service before 1970 was even more remote. Now there would be a lengthy period when the V bombers, even armed with Blue Steel, would no longer be able to penetrate the Soviet defences, and as a consequence, many 'stopgap' proposals were thrown up.

By now, Blue Steel was just entering service, but given its limited range, it still required the Vulcan and Victor bombers to fly over the Russian defences at high altitude, where they would undoubtedly suffer a large number of casualties. Blue Steel's range was only 100 miles, which meant that in order to reach Moscow and the other major Soviet cities, the bombers would be vulnerable to the Russian air defences, although perhaps some of the estimates of the vulnerability of the V bombers seem to be somewhat exaggerated. A paper from the RAE of January 1963 estimated that 'in the western USSR and the satellite countries there are currently, in round numbers, some 10,000 interceptor aircraft, 30,000 SAGW and 20,000 AA guns'.[2]

What threat was it that the V bombers would be facing? The RAE analysis of the deployment of Russian systems was as follows:

We are assuming that:—

(a) the SA 3 is a low altitude air-to-air system and is starting deployment now and will be intensively deployed by 1964/5—this is assumed to be a city perimeter defence...

(b) the SA 2 medium and high altitude defensive system is more or less fully deployed now—it is largely a city perimeter defence ...

(c) an ABM system may be deployed during the period (note there are already some indications that a system which may be ABM is being initially deployed now).

(d) a fighter air-to-air weapon system ... with capabilities of efficient interception of low flying aircraft up to M = 1 will be deployed by 1968/70. This is assumed to be an area defence.

(e) light A-A radar-controlled guns will continue to be widely deployed during the period, but that they are likely to be taken from the city defences to form an area or 'iron curtain' defence ring.[3]

If the V bombers were to attend to penetrate the Iron Curtain at high altitude, they would have around 1,000 miles to cover while being observed on Russian radar. The flight time for that distance would be around two hours, which would give the air defences plenty of time to scramble interceptor aircraft. As they approached Moscow itself, they would encounter Soviet missile defences. Moscow itself was extremely well protected by surface-to-air missiles. The two principal missiles which were then in service were the SA-2 and SA-3, which were respectively high-level and low-level missiles. The RAE produced a diagram showing the interception capability of each of the missiles.

The SA-2, known to NATO as Guideline, was an extremely successful design, exported widely to Soviet satellite countries and other states. It was

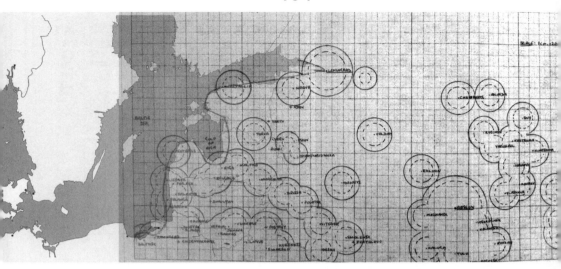

This is a sketch map of the Soviet surface-to-air missile bases superimposed on a map of the Baltic. It is not complete: for example, the island at the top of Riga Bay, Saaremaa, also had several surface-to-air missile sites.

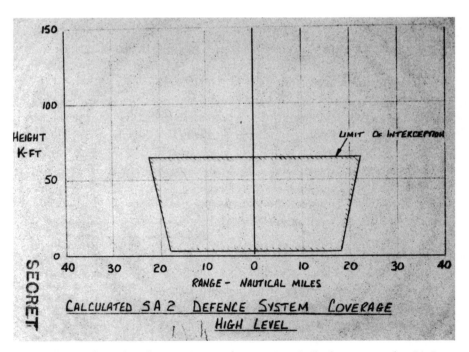

The 'kill' envelope for the Russian surface-to-air missile known as the SA-2 or Guideline.

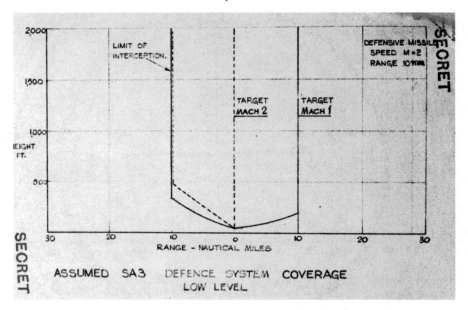

The 'kill' envelope for the Russian surface-to-air missile known as the SA-3 or Goa.

extremely effective in the Vietnam War—during the Linebacker bomber offensive between 18-29 December 1972, fourteen B-52 aircraft were shot down and five were seriously damaged by the missile. The SA-3 was equally effective but in a different height and range envelope. Although both the systems could be confused by effective electronic countermeasures (ECM), the US Air Force found that considerable experience was needed to do so. Whether the V force, on their first and only penetration of Russian airspace, would have been able to jam the guidance radars is questionable.

The Treasury, of course, was alert to the possibility that money would be requested for these stopgaps.

> The Minister seemed most doubtful whether the USA would in fact agree to hire us POLARIS submarines while their own build-up was in progress. This is a blow, since it leaves the field open to the Minister of Aviation and the Air Staff to press a variety of expensive dodges for keeping the V-bombers more or less viable up to 1970 (more BLUE STEELS, more bombers, more tankers, better BLUE STEELS, airborne alert and so forth).[4]

The author of that note might have given a wry smile if he had seen a memorandum written by Julian Amery, Minister of Aviation, to Hugh Fraser, the Secretary of State for Air:

The decision to take Polaris instead of Skybolt implies that on present plans for the credibility of Bomber Command's deterrent will decline between 1965 and 1970/72.

If we are to correct this it will be important to take decisions as soon as possible. I should accordingly be grateful if you would consider the following questions:—

1. Blue Steel. Will you want more? If so, in the present version or one of the stretched versions?

2. T.S.R.2. Could it be used in a strategic deterrent role? If so, will you want more? Will you want a laydown bomb?

3. Should we consider developing a weapon such as Pandora (OR1182) as an insurance against delay or defection on the Polaris programme? This would have the advantage of retaining the V-bomber force as an effective deterrent (including airborne alert) well into the 1970's. But it would take about eight years and might cost about £100M.

4. Would you want more advanced E.C.M. [Electronic Counter Measures] to extend the penetrative power of Bomber Command?

5. Would you want more tankers?[5]

Yet the Treasury had its own dodges to avoid spending more money than it thought necessary. The Treasury note continued:

Even if we can shoot down most of this, it is clearly going to make the task of getting compensating savings in this field virtually impossible. We may therefore have to look at an alternative which will be equally unpopular, though in the Navy's quarter this time. We are in fact given a lead by a point the Admiralty made on the POLARIS build up. It is this.

The Admiralty say that one of the limiting factors on the build-up will be design staff; they will need, they say, freedom to recruit these in large numbers and at fancy rates. The obvious suggestion for the Chancellor to make, at a suitable early moment, would be that the first step on the design side is to switch the staff employed at Bath on the aircraft carrier successors from this work to work on the POLARIS submarines. This ought to have the effect of putting back the carrier successors by several years and thus giving us useful relief in the late 'sixties. The Admiralty, of course, will fight this tooth and nail.[6]

It has often been remarked that as far as the Treasury is concerned, money came before security.

The major problem was that of timescale: a relatively sophisticated solution would have taken a long time to develop, as would any solution that involved starting from scratch, and the whole point of a stopgap was that it should be available as soon as possible. To paraphrase a well-known saying, you can have cheap, quick, or effective, but not all of them at the same time. This limited the possible options considerably. V bombers flying at high altitude were no longer a viable option. The robust Vulcan could fly at low level, but even so, it would be vulnerable to the defences close to the cities that were targets. Some form of stand-off weapon was still needed, as the free-fall megaton bombs then in service were intended to be dropped from a height of at least 10,000 feet, and to fly a V bomber over Moscow at a height of 10,000 feet was suicidal; in reality, the bomber would never even reach the centre of Moscow.

Therefore, the Air Staff considered a whole variety of proposals, some of which were more realistic than others. They put them into one of three categories: short range (less than 100 NM); medium-range (100–500 NM); and long range (over 500 NM). The information below gives an indication of some of the weapons considered, together with cost, time scale and Air Staff evaluation:

Type: Long-Range Ballistic Air-Launched
Proposal: Martin Co./BAC—Modified Pershing
Range: 1,000 NM
Timescale: 4–5 years
Cost: As for Skybolt
Notes: Technical problems indicate that this proposal cannot be made quicker or cheaper than Skybolt, and is considered unsuitable on grounds of timescale and cost.

Type: Medium-Range Air-Launched Subsonic Low-Level Cruise
Proposal: A. V. Roe—Blue Steel with Viper jet engines
Range: 400–500 NM
Timescale: 4–5 years
Cost: £35–45 million
Notes: Low speed implies the missile would be vulnerable (M 0.9); can only be carried on V-bombers; time scale and cost preclude this proposal.

Type: Medium-Range Air-Launched Ballistic
Proposal: B.A.L. Grand Slam 1 Toss Bomb
Range: 100 NM
Timescale: 3–5 years
Cost: £20 million
Notes: Firms cost considered gross under estimate, system too complex for the range required, not considered suitable.

Type: Medium-Range Air-Launched Ballistic
Proposal: Skylark motors plus Inertial Navigation from Blue Steel
Range: 200 NM
Timescale: 4 years
Cost: Not given
Notes: This proposal was too sketchy to allow adequate comment, the missile is likely to be very heavy, and is not considered suitable.

Type: Medium-Range Air-Launched Ballistic
Proposal: D.H. Report R.C.17/1
Range: 120 NM
Timescale: 5–6 years
Cost: £75 million
Notes: Although this proposal is feasible, timescale and cost preclude it from consideration. The range quoted gives no significant increase in invulnerability over a range of 60 NM so we would, therefore, be paying for range which was not required

Type: Medium-Range Air-Launched Ballistic
Proposal: BAC—Blue Water modified for air launch.
Range: 150–200 NM
Timescale: 5–6 years
Cost: £40–45 million
Notes: Range unsuitable. Refer above. Proposal cannot be considered suitable on grounds of time and cost.

Type: Short-Range stand-off cruise type
Proposal: B.A.L.—Extension of AST 1168 [the Martel missile]
Range: 150–200 NM
Timescale: 4–5 years
Cost: £20 million
Notes: Range insufficient for timescale.

Type: Short-Range stand-off missile cruise type
Proposal: RAE
Range: 30–50 NM
Timescale: 4 years
Cost: £15–20 million
Notes: This is a possible Gap Filler. Mach 2.0 low-level Cruise gives approx. 30 NM. Toss Launch Techniques could give up to 50 NM.

Type: Short-Range stand-off Ballistic
Proposal: DH—Hatchet
Range: 55 NM
Timescale: 2 years
Cost: £0.865 million
Notes: This is a possible proposal but firms' estimates of timescale and cost considered a gross under estimate, accuracy forecast could be in error by at least a factor of 2.

Type: Short-Range stand-off Ballistic
Proposal: RAE
Range: 100 NM
Timescale: 4 years
Cost: £14 million
Notes: Prospects of reduced echoing area and limited decoys: considered a suitable 'Gap-Filler'.

The RAE produced a report evaluating all these proposals. Only one was considered to have any merit:

> A ramjet missile of about 2500 lb, using one of the ramjets very slightly modified from the Bloodhound missile, could be developed to give around 50/55 miles range. This missile could fit in all the aircraft considered—V bombers, Buccaneer and TSR 2. The missile could use an existing motor as a boost and this boost might sensibly be retained in the missile for simplicity. The speed of the missile can be maintained at M = 2 for the whole of the flight and may present better capabilities for stretch as the fuel consumption is so low in comparison with the solid rocket motor.[6]

Development time was estimated as four to four and a half years, which would mean coming into service in 1967–8, at a cost of £18–20 million.

The aircraft manufacturers were not slow in coming forward with ideas, although the practicality of many of the proposals was very dubious. One major snag to many of the proposals was that very few were adaptations of existing weapons, and so the project would mean starting from scratch, which inevitably meant that it would be some years before they could come into service; that was rather pointless, given that they were supposed to be stopgaps.

Thorneycroft himself was not convinced about the 'gap', and neither were his officials in the Ministry of Defence. After reading the papers outlining indigenous British options for the deterrent, H. L. Lawrence-Wilson, who had been present at the Nassau talks, commented:

A full examination of the various suggestions for going it alone with alternatives to Skybolt/Polaris would be a lengthy business and one on which we should not, I am sure, embark at present, if ever. I suggested that a minute might go to the Minister from the Secretary on the lines of the attached draft.[7]

The attached draft read:

Although the various proposals in Mr Amery's minute of 15th January for go-it-alone alternatives to Skybolt/Polaris are useful for the record, it would, I am sure, be wrong to devote to the fairly considerable effort needed to evaluate

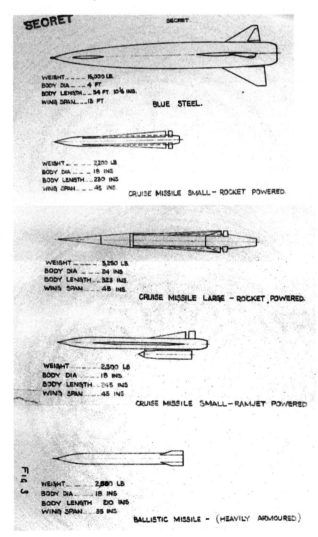

Some of the many stopgaps being considered by the Air Staff. The ramjet-powered cruise missile would have used the ramjet motor from the Bloodhound missile.

them properly. The cost and time scale, even as stated, rule them out except as rather late alternatives to Polaris and this is not what we are looking for.

The Ministry of Aviation have clearly put a good deal of work into the suggestions. Nevertheless, past experience shows that it would be foolish to expect any one of these proposals to prove anything like and quick as suggested, despite the assumption that some American components would be used. We know, for example, that with all their experience behind them, the Americans expect to spend about £500 million in all on developing Polaris A3 missile, whereas Mr Amery opens to do a Polaris A2 equipment for 'not less than £200m' starting from scratch. The fact that the French have made an estimate of £300m as the cost to them of a Polaris type project is not really very useful evidence on likely costs. It is even more difficult to accept that we could take on one or other of the proposed projects without serious destruction of the existing R and D programme. By any standards each of them is very large indeed and we would be superimposing it on an R and D programme there are already laws be overloaded in this decade. As regards industry, Mr Amery was probably right in saying that the necessary capacity is there in general terms: what is not so clear is that the special kind of capacity needed could be found or built up. This would require detailed study with industry.

My feeling is that we should not pursue these proposals any further at present ...[8]

Thorneycroft then wrote to Amery:

I have carefully considered your minute of 15th January about British alternatives to Polaris. Clearly a lot of work has gone into the preparation of these proposals, and they would provide a useful starting point for more detailed study should we have to face a go-it-alone situation.

I entirely agree with you, however, that we cannot consider a British project at this moment in time, nor do I think we should carry out now the further studies in consultation with industry that would be needed to

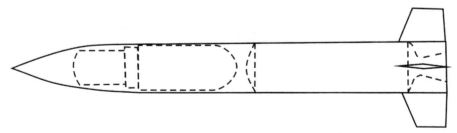

One of the more basic proposals—an unguided missile with the Skybolt warhead and a rocket motor derived from the Skylark missile. Known as 'One Club', it would be cheap and simple, but with very limited range and accuracy.

evaluate the merits and obstacles in the alternatives which you pose. I would prefer to leave these proposals on the record, at least until we are clear how the Polaris plan is going to work out.[9]

Air-Launched Blue Water

English Electric came up with an idea that had some superficial merit, which was to adapt the cancelled Blue Water missile with the TSR 2 aircraft that was due to come into service in the mid- to late '60s. They drew up a brochure illustrating the combination, and described it thus:

> The system is based on the principle of reducing the modifications to both aircraft and missile to a minimum. This has been achieved whilst retaining a simple and effective missile system and a maximum range (from missile launch) of 90 statute miles with a CPE of approximately 2,200 feet. A nuclear warhead is assumed of the type proposed for the surface-to-surface Blue Water system. The readiness time on the ground will not exceed five minutes and it may be possible to reduce this to the 30 seconds readiness time of the aircraft. Each aircraft carries one missile carried in a partially buried position underneath the aircraft fuselage.
>
> The method of operation is simple and a reasonable amount of flexibility is available. In attacking a strategic target there is sufficient time to prepare a plan of attack in detail. The necessary target coordinates and navigation factors can be fed into the aircraft equipment and the missile before the aircraft leaves the ground. This leaves the aircrew with only minor corrections to make in the air just prior to attack. These adjustments need to be made only if the pilot decides, for tactical reasons, to attack from a bearing not previously plotted in the original plan.

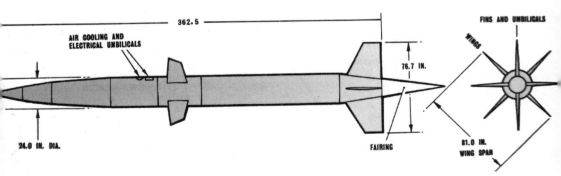

The version of Blue Water proposed as an air-launched missile. For use in this role, it would have needed considerable modification.

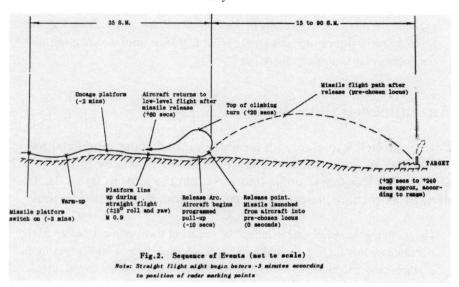

Fig.2. Sequence of Events (not to scale)
Note: Straight flight might begin before -3 minutes according to position of radar marking points

The sequence of events for the launch of a Blue Water missile from the TSR 2.

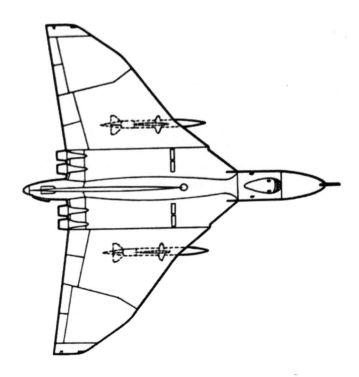

A representation of the Vulcan carrying two Blue Water missiles on the Skybolt pylons.

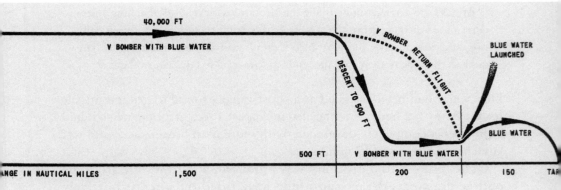

40,000 FT

V BOMBER WITH BLUE WATER

V BOMBER RETURN FLIGHT

BLUE WATER LAUNCHED

DESCENT TO 500 FT

BLUE WATER

500 FT

V BOMBER WITH BLUE WATER

RANGE IN NAUTICAL MILES   1,500   200   150   TAR

SUGGESTED V-BOMBER STRIKE SORTIE.

The proposed flight plan for a Vulcan carrying Blue Water missiles. According to this, the last 300 miles or so would be made at a low level, but even that would be hardly adequate.

SECRET

An artist's impression from the BAC brochure of a Blue Water missile being launched from a Vulcan.

Attacks are carried out by flying the aircraft low-level until reaching a pre-determined distance from the target. At this point the aircraft automatically prepares the missile, pulls up into a climb and releases the missile. The aircraft then turns away and descends to low-level for the return flight.[10]

Blue Water had been designed as a short-range ground to ground missile for the Army but had been cancelled in August 1962, at a time when it had been almost completely developed, with more than fifteen successful test launches at a cost of £17 million.

Quite a substantial brochure was produced, and to be fair, from the outline drawings, the missile would have fitted the aircraft relatively easily. The range of the missile after being released from the aircraft flying at low level was estimated at between 15 and 90 miles.[11]

This was followed by a second brochure in February 1963, obviously in response to the Skybolt cancellation, with a proposal to mount Blue Water on not only the TSR 2 but also on the Vulcan. In both cases, the aircraft could carry two missiles, one under each wing, Skybolt style. The missile was stretched; the motor section would be 4 feet longer to increase the range. The launch weight was given as 6,600 lb, compared with 12,000 lb for Skybolt and 15,000 lb for Blue Steel. The proposal was to launch the missile at a height of 500 feet, which would give a maximum range of 150 miles. However, this did not give it a great advantage over Blue Steel. One interesting feature of the missile was that it would be fitted with a discarding tail cone fairing that would carry decoys.[12]

The brochure was sent to the Minister of Aviation by Lord Caldecote, Deputy Managing Direction of the British Aircraft Corporation (BAC):

Dear Julian,

Not long after the cancellation of Blue Water last summer you asked whether there was any possibility of making use of the Blue Water development work for other purposes such as an air-launched weapon.

We have now considered this in some detail and have submitted brochures to the Ministry and had a number of discussions. As you yourself shown interest in the work I thought you might like to see a copy of the brochure, particularly in light of all that is going on at present.[13]

Naturally, the Minister needed to send a suitable reply. The brochures were forwarded to CGWL's department for comments, which were not very favourable:

The particular proposal referred to in Lord Caldecote's letter is not, in fact, very attractive for the following reasons:—

1. Considerable development of the Blue Water weapon itself would be necessary to make it suitable, and the nature of the inertial navigation table incorporated in Blue Water is such that it would impose fairly severe manoeuvring restrictions on the aircraft that carried it.

2. Fairly extensive airborne trials would be necessary and these are, of course, costly.

3. The range suggested for the missile is of the order of 150–200 miles and this puts it neither in the category of launch range (1,000 miles) of full stand-off weapons which would confer real invulnerability on the launching aircraft, nor in the category of cheap short-range weapons.

4. Cost and time scale suggested by the firm are far too optimistic.

I would advise, therefore, that the Minister simply acknowledges Lord Caldecote's letter and suggestions and, in thanking him for them, assures him that they will be considered along with the several other such proposals we have had from industry.[14]

TSR 2 was already distinctly marginal in terms of reaching Moscow from the UK, and the additional range given by the missile would not help that much. Consideration had already been given to the use of TSR 2 in the strategic role (as described in the next chapter), although it would not have been so much use as a stopgap, given that it would not come into service before about 1968.

Blue Steel Low Level

Avro put various proposals forward to the Chief of Air Staff in January 1963:

1. Blue Steel flying 70 miles at Mach 0.90 and 500 feet. The missile would have to be fitted with a radio altimeter. The estimated time for this project was 30 months;

2. Blue Steel with the rocket motor replaced by a standard Bristol Siddeley Viper turbojet. It would fly at low level in the same way as Proposal I but should reach a range of 500 miles. Estimated time: 42 months.

3. A low-level ballistic unguided rocket capable of 40–50 miles range. It would have a very flat trajectory and reach a speed of Mach 5. It would be powered by two Skylark rocket motors. Development time was estimated at two years.

4. A guided ballistic rocket powered by three Skylark motors and using the inertial guidance from Blue Steel. Development time was estimated at four years.[15]

Avro obviously had some hopes for the version with the Viper turbojet. The brochure gives some impression of being rather hastily produced, but a substantial mock-up of the missile had been produced at the AVRO works. AVRO's brochure stated:

> It has a range of about 600 miles and has a modified version of the present Blue Steel navigator. It cruises at Mach 0.9 at 500 foot altitude. With this missile attacks could be made at low-level targets well inside enemy territory from V-bombers which themselves remained at high level. In this way it enables the attacking force to combine the advantages of the long range and endurance of the high altitude subsonic bomber with the low vulnerability of the terrain following missile. Standing patrols of the type which had been planned with Skybolt would be practicable, thus minimising the risk of being caught on the ground by the enemy's first strike. This missile could be available for Squadron use in about 2½ years, although proving over the full 600 mile range would take longer.
>
> The type has considerable development potential. One possibility would be to fit the smaller Skybolt type warhead and use of volume thus made available for additional fuel. The range with a Viper engine with then be about 850 miles, but a new navigator would have to be fitted to give acceptable accuracy at this range. Alternatively, if a larger turbojet than the Viper were fitted, then with this greater fuel load, a partly subsonic low-level trajectory could be flown giving, say, 450 miles at Mach 0.9 followed by a 100 miles spurt to Mach 1.5; for this trajectory the present navigator would be adequate.[16]

It was proposed to use a radio altimeter to adjust the height of the aircraft; terrain-following radar would obviously be much better but would have taken longer to develop.

None of these proposals were regarded as realistic, except possibly for the low-level Blue Steel, which was also considered by the RAE in a report about releasing Blue Steel from the V bombers at low level. It considered two types of operation.

The first involved launching the missile at the minimum possible height and then allowing it to carry on as in the normal high-level launch. The release altitude would be about 1,000 feet. If the weapon were used without any modifications to the flight rules computer, it would climb at maximum boost to burn out at fifty-seven seconds, a height of 22,000 feet, and a speed of Mach 2.5. Alternatively, it would be possible by a fairly simple modification to the computer to cut the boost motor at twenty-nine seconds and continue to climb on the cruise motor to 45,000 feet. Once the motor had cut out, the missile would then descend in a shallow dive. The time of flight would be 250 seconds and range about 50 miles.

The second method would need some modifications to the missile since the proposal was that it should cruise to the target at a height of about 1,000 feet. The range would be between 20 and 60 miles, depending on whether it was required to fly supersonically or not. After the release manoeuvre, the missile would follow a straight and level flight throughout, reaching a speed of Mach 2 after forty-five seconds with full boost. The missile would then carry on in level flight with a speed dropping to about Mach 0.9 at the target. The time of flight would be about ninety-two seconds and the range 22.5 miles. If the missile was allowed to continue to fly until its speed had dropped to Mach 0.6, time of flight would be increased to 246 seconds and the total range to 30 miles. However, this trajectory would involve considerable modification to the flight rules computer and a radio altimeter to provide height control. Alternatively, the missile could be accelerated to Mach 0.9 at 13.5 seconds with full boost and then maintained at about this speed by the cruise motor until the target was reached. The time of flight would be 330 seconds and the range about 55 miles.

The high-level mode of operation would cost £1 million, whereas the low-level method would cost about £20 million. Given the costs involved and the minor advantages of the low-level flight, there was really no competition.

The idea of low-level release was put to the DRPC, who gave it the go ahead. Zuckerman wrote to the Minister of Defence to recommend low-level release:

> If the proposals were not accepted, it would be necessary to choose between two alternatives:
>
> (a) to abandon BLUE STEEL altogether and equip the whole 'V' bomber force with the laydown bomb. This would cost at least £2m more than the proposed modification of BLUE STEEL, and would not be preferable operationally.
>
> (b) to do nothing. This would mean that half the 'V' bomber force would be of negligible value in the deterrent role after about 1965. The logical course would then be to phase out these 'V' bombers as soon as possible and so save money; but to do this before the POLARIS force was deployed would be open to serious objection on political grounds.[17]

The Treasury, with their usual acute grasp of military matters, was not impressed: 'The Treasury (like some of the Air Staff) are privately sceptical about the new low-flying concept but we cannot very well press this'. In a footnote, they added:

> The Air Staff are reticent about the height and speed envisaged in the new role (?200 feet and up to 400 knots). But they believe that, even if anybody

reaches its target, nobody will return. War Office A.A. gunners don't believe that anybody will reach his target.[18]

Quite where they got that last piece of information is difficult to know since there were very few War Office AA gunners left in 1963.

Low-level release meant a new mission profile for the V bombers. Up until then, it had been very straightforward—twenty minutes to climb to an altitude of 40,000 feet, and then maintain that height for the next three and a quarter hours. Now, it would be something along the lines of the following:

climb to 40,000 feet:	20 minutes
cruise climb 40-50,000 feet:	60 minutes
descend to 500 feet:	45 minutes
low level (500 feet):	30 minutes
high-speed run to launch:	10 minutes

This is effectively what Group Captain Vieille of the Air Staff said about the V bombers fifteen years earlier; sadly, he had been a prophet without honour.

Proposing stopgaps was one thing; persuading Thorneycroft of their necessity was another. It was clear he would not sanction any great expenditure. Converting Blue Steel to low-level release was a cheaper option. Yet Thorneycroft was not alone in this opinion. Soon after the Nassau talks, the defence correspondent of *The Times* wrote two articles with the heading 'BRITAIN WITHOUT SKYBOLT'. He began the first by describing Skybolt as 'a sort of old-age pension for the manned bomber'. In the second, he said:

If the government are determined to have a British controlled nuclear striking force the most logical adjustment in British defence policy to meet the change from Skybolt or Polaris would be in the deterrent itself. Polaris missiles will be available to Britain in 1966... Until then the V-bombers, with the Blue Steel missile, could continue to be the British nuclear striking force. For a year or so at the end of his life Blue Steel would probably be ineffective against Russian anti-aircraft defences without American help.

To accept this marginal risk would enable the Government to stop further production of manned bombers as the Americans have already done, to do without further development of Blue Steel and to dispense with the nuclear weapon which is to be carried by the TSR 2. It might even be possible to take another cool look at the whole expensive TSR 2 project. That the government have evidently decided against this course is probably as much a matter of political expediency as of deep strategic assessment—the uproar from the Conservative right wing and the aircraft lobby would have been deafening. [19]

There was one other stopgap that would not cost a great deal of time and money; this was an adaptation of the laydown bomb already being developed for the TSR 2 (and which the correspondent from *The Times* would have liked to see cancelled).

Thorneycroft put these ideas to the Cabinet Defence Committee on 23 January, as can be seen from the minutes of the meeting:

The Deterrent in the pre-POLARIS Period.

The Committee had before them a memorandum by the Minister of Defence about measures to be taken to improve the effectiveness of British deterrent forces in the period before the effective deployment of POLARIS.

The Minister of Defence said that from about 1965 the capacity of the V-bombers to penetrate Russian anti-aircraft defences will gradually diminish, so that the credibility of the British contributions to the Western nuclear strategic deterrent would fall for a time below that which would have been achieved if the Skybolt missile had been available. He was convinced that any attempt to devise a British weapon to take the place of POLARIS in case the American undertaking to supply POLARIS should not be fulfilled, would be financially and politically unjustifiable. The question was therefore what measures might be taken which could be effective by, say, 1967 for a period of about two years before British POLARIS-firing submarines could mount an adequate deterrent. The Air Staff had concluded that for this purpose it was necessary to enable the V-bombers to deliver their attack at low altitude. This would involve strengthening the airframe of the Victor and fitting both the Victors and the Vulcans with additional navigational and electronic equipment. It would also be necessary to continue the development of the laydown bomb which had been designed for the TSR 2, so that it could be dropped with a warhead in the megaton range from either the V-bombers or the TSR 2. The full cost of the programme on these lines would be between £27-30 million spread over the next five years ...

It was undesirable for security reasons to suggest in public that a low-level bombing capability have been specially developed to compensate for the loss of the SKYBOLT missile. In any public announcement of measures to be taken to fill up the 'missile gap' it would be important to emphasise the wide diversity of methods available to the RAF for the delivery of nuclear missiles. A form of public presentation should be worked out in advance of the debate on the subject in the House of Commons during the following week.

The Committee agreed, subject to all the processes of inter-departmental consultation, to the proposals for modifications to the V-bomber aircraft, and for the development of a high yield version of the laydown bomb.[20]

The phrase 'any attempt to devise a British weapon to take the place of POLARIS in case the American undertaking to supply POLARIS should not be fulfilled would be financially and politically unjustifiable' is interesting. It could imply one of two thing, the first being that it was not worth pursuing any insurance weapons; a more radical interpretation might be that if Britain were let down with Polaris as it had been with Skybolt, then the British independent deterrent would effectively be allowed to wither away.

The Laydown Bomb

'In the case of a thermonuclear exchange the complete return journey would have little point ...'

From a Ministry of Aviation memo, September 1960.[21]

Despite the ban on any public announcement, indirect reference was made to the laydown bomb by Thorneycroft when talking to the Conservative backbenchers: 'It is in fact the mysterious Weapon X with which the Secretary of State comforted the Tory back-benchers after Skybolt's decease'.

The device that would see the longest service of any nuclear weapon in the RAF had its origin, at least in part, in an RAE report of December 1960 when investigations were being made on the possible use of TSR 2 in the strategic role. The report was entitled 'A Survey of the Problems in Design of a Megaton Laydown Weapon for TSR 2'.

... if a weapon is released from a high-speed aircraft at 50 feet above a level
    surface such as a runway, then: -
(i) the time of fall will be short;
(ii) the vertical velocity of the weapon will be low;
(iii) even with the best techniques for rapid opening of single stage parachutes,
    the horizontal velocity on impact will still be high, say 150-250 feet/second;
(iv) the angle between weapon axis and the ground will be small;
(v) variations in wind speed will be considerably smaller than horizontal
    impact velocities.[22]

The memorandum then went on to describe what happens when the bomb hits the ground:

Because of the small angle on impact, the nose is unable to give any substantial axial deceleration before the lower forward lip of the warhead case receives a glancing blow from the ground. This is a shock load which, without substantially checking forward speed, applies a rapid nose-up pitching rotation to the weapon. This in turn causes a heavy 'slap down' of the tail followed by a skid along the ground until the parachute and friction bring the weapon to rest. [23]

Three warheads were considered: a British warhead similar to the American Mark 43 laydown weapon; the Red Snow warhead, which was then being developed for the Blue Steel missile and the Yellow Sun free-fall bomb; and the Skybolt warhead.

The nose section has an outer metal skin which will crumple without fracture and it is proposed tentatively that all the available internal space should be packed with hexagonal aluminium foil honeycomb possibly with a foamed plastic filler.

Two design features in the tail are thought to be important in reducing warhead shock loads during 'slap down'. After the first nose impact the weapon pitches rapidly nose up and the forward parts of the tail fins which are retained after parachute deployment take the initial blow in the second ground contact. The deformation of the lower fins followed by buckling of the tail cone provides a useful shock absorption before the rear flange of the warhead makes its impact and is itself deformed to give further attenuation. The tail cone has been shown here as a sandwich construction but this would not necessarily be the final selection.[24]

Meanwhile, the services had been looking for a replacement for the first-generation Red Beard weapon, which had considerable limitations on its use:

R.B. cannot withstand the low-level flight environment, is limited in method of fuzing and delivery and possesses some undesirable safety restrictions when held at readiness in an operational state. Early replacement is essential.[25]

These ideas evolved into Operational Requirement 1177 for what was described as an improved kiloton weapon, which would emerge as WE177 (the old system of the rainbow codes had gone, to be replaced by a two-letter, three-number code—no more Violet Clubs or Blue Danubes, but now more boring and less colourful designations such as WE177 or KH973). It was often described as a tactical nuclear weapon, but the only distinction between tactical and strategic nuclear weapons seems to be that strategic nuclear weapons were designed solely to wipe out cities. However, British ministers were not happy with the idea of using large warheads on such targets as Warsaw Pact airfields, and so they decreed that tactical nuclear warheads should have a maximum yield of 10 kilotons.

The warhead that was to be used in WE177 was effectively the primary of the Skybolt warhead—in other words, the fission trigger. To produce a version with a much larger yield was very simple—put the fusion stage back in. This merely meant putting an extra section into the centre of the bomb. The new variety was referred to as WE177B. The kiloton version was now WE177A.

The megaton variety was needed urgently as a stopgap, and its production took precedence over the 'A' version. Deliveries to the RAF began in September 1966, and fifty-three weapons later, they were complete by October 1967; although, as the TSR 2 had been cancelled by then, it was left to the Vulcans to try to fly at a few hundred feet across Russia to Moscow to release their weapon. How successful they would have been is a matter for debate.

There is a somewhat acid memo written on Admiralty notepaper, but unfortunately unsigned, commenting on the military value of the low flying V force:

> I take it that we are all entirely agreed that the object must be to spend the very minimum that HMG can get away with politically of measures to fill the deterrent; and also, that we must at all costs avoid encouraging Ministers to commit themselves in public statements to any shaky steps or projects.
>
> It must be obvious to everyone that the credibility of a low-level V bomber deterrent force will be challenged in many quarters because the bombers will be incapable of mounting any standing air patrol. Hence they could all be destroyed on the ground by an enemy first strike.
>
> There are a number of supplementary questions to this one which occurred to me, and which therefore I am sure will occur to better informed critics; but I believe there is reason to hope that time will now allow the Chiefs of Staff to advise on technical military points of this kind. I have in mind particularly:—
>
> (a) Whether the radius of action of the V bombers can be categorically stated to be adequate when they are flying at low level, having regard to the greater fuel consumption.
>
> (b) How much practice flying at low level would be required and where this will be done.
>
> (c) Whether the fatigue life of the aircraft would be adequate.[26]

These were all very good questions, to which no real adequate responses were produced. It might be fair to say that the military value of Britain's deterrent, particularly in the latter part of the 1960s, was woefully inadequate. Fortunately, in many ways, it was never put to the test.

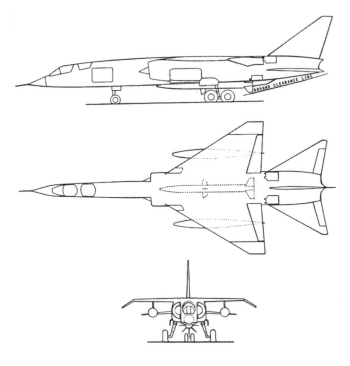

TSR 2 carrying a
Blue Water missile
in the bomb bay.

Fig. 1. Blue Water on T.S.R. 2 Aircraft

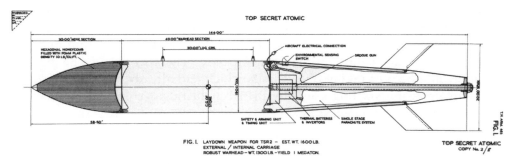

FIG. I. LAYDOWN WEAPON FOR TSR2 — EST. WT. 1600 LB.
EXTERNAL / INTERNAL CARRIAGE
ROBUST WARHEAD — WT. 1300 LB. — YIELD 1 MEGATON.

The proposed lay-down bomb for TSR 2, which is a clear forerunner of the WE177
lay-down bomb.

What If ... ?

What if Macmillan had failed to get Polaris on acceptable terms? Leaving aside for the moment the political consequences, what options for a home-grown British deterrent would have been open to the Government? The answer is very few.

Polaris itself was a remarkable technical achievement, and there was no way in which Britain could have replicated such a system except at tremendous cost, both in time and money. Completing Skybolt in the UK was a non-starter, as was asking Douglas to finish the project off. Apart from anything else, given the relatively few missiles needed by the UK, the unit cost would be prohibitive, and there would be the problem of where to conduct the test flights. Would the US allow the British to continue using the range facilities at the Eglin Air Base? There would also be the political odium of taking on a missile which had already been spurned by its creators. Starting a wholly British ballistic air-launched missile from scratch would be just as expensive, and could easily have taken ten years or so.

Even as the Nassau conference was getting underway, ideas for alternatives were already surfacing, and even after Macmillan had secured Kennedy's agreement to supply Polaris to the UK, there was still obviously a lot of nervousness in the air—in the old saying, once bitten twice shy. Indeed, even as late as March, when the negotiations for Polaris had been wrapped up, the Prime Minister was still asking the Ministry of Aviation 'to consider further the possibility of making a British deterrent which might in certain circumstances replace Polaris'. A draft memo written for Thorneycroft immediately after the Nassau talks shows Macmillan was still worried about the possibility of the Polaris deal falling through:

TSR 2 launching a Blue Water missile.

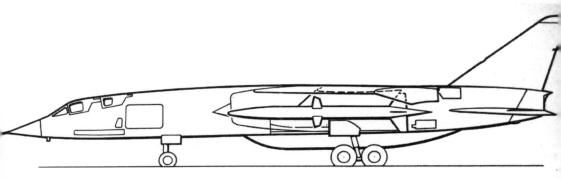

TSR 2 carrying two Blue Water missiles, one under each wing, with a rather large bomb bay fuel tank.

In his minute to you of 26th December the Prime Minister asked whether, if
we were driven into a corner, we could either as a bluff or as a reality make
a Polaris missile from UK designs. Subsequently at a meeting with Secretary
of State for Air and myself on 31st of December, you concluded that while
we could not afford at the same time to build and buy the Polaris system as
well as to develop our own alternative, it would be open to my Department
to make a case for limited expenditure on studying re-insurance schemes. I
thought that as a first step it might be helpful if a quick examination were
made of the possible alternative systems we might adopt should for any
reason Polaris not become available.[1]

The memo outlines the possible alternative systems with true Civil Service
clarity:

We have examined four types of systems: an air-launched ballistic missile,
an air-launched cruise missile, a submarine-launched ballistic missile and,
based on our Black Knight work, a ground-launched ballistic missile ...
Our conclusion is that all four systems could be developed within time
scales varying from seven to ten years. All can, therefore, be considered as
providing an independent deterrent from the early 1970s. We have assumed
virtually no American help in arriving at these figures; if we could, in the
circumstances of a collapse of the Polaris negotiations, continue to rely on
ready American assistance, the timescale undoubtedly and cost possibly
could be cut.[2]

It comments on the cruise type missile:

An air-launched cruise type missile should also be ruled out, for the time
being. The present indications are that it would be more vulnerable to enemy
defences and have less target coverage than an air-launched ballistic missile
fitted with decoys.[3]

That left either a ground-based, air-launched, or submarine-launched
ballistic missile. Starting again to produce a Skybolt-type missile would
rather smack of reinventing the wheel, although Avro had made a brief
and sketchy study of an ALBM in January 1960, presumably as a reaction
to Skybolt. However, the papers that still exist show that little or no
detailed design work had been done. The missile was described as a two-
stage booster and the warhead, structural weight, and guidance of the
payload were assumed to weigh 1,550 lb (guidance, power unit, etc. 300
lb; warhead 750 lb; and structure 500 lb). The design assumptions made
were as follows:

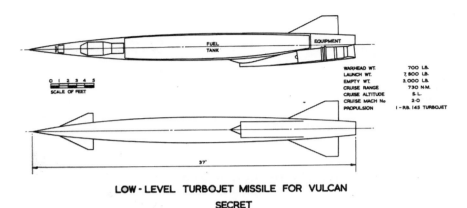

Launch weight 7,800 lb, empty weight 3,000 lb, and warhead weight 700 lb. This was a post-cancellation proposal from Avro. It has the merit of simplicity: just one turbojet. In front of the fuel tank is the Skybolt warhead and then a radar for terrain following. It had a claimed range of 700 miles at a low level, although this was probably more of a guesstimate than anything else. However, the devil lies in the detail; producing a navigation system capable of navigating 700 miles at Mach 2 and low level would have been extremely challenging.

      solid propellant rocket booster with specific impulse—250 seconds

      air-launched from a Vulcan at 800 feet/sec at 40,000 feet

      the launch weight of the missile to be not greater than 20,000 lb. [4]

Starting from that basis, calculations were made of the final velocity of the missile for a range of values of launch weight between 10,000 and 20,000 lb and four solid rocket booster case weights of 10, 20, and 30 per cent of the total booster weight. Then range calculations were made, assuming the final angle of climb to be 35 degrees, and the booster thrust was assumed to be a constant at five times the appropriate stage weight. The conclusion was: 'With the assumptions made in this study it seems certain that the Vulcan could be used to launch a 15,000 lb ALBM over a range of 1,000 miles'.

    There is a diagram of the missile in AVRO's master list of projects. This is dated February 1960, and so presumably there has been some refinement of the design, although the illustration is, to put it politely, merely schematic.

    The launch weight is given as 16,000 lb; the first stage boost is 11,020 lb, second stage is 3,430 lb, and what is referred to as the third stage, which contains the equipment and warhead, is 1,550 lb.

    Making estimates about range and rocket motors are only scratching the surface. The concept of such a missile was very novel in 1960, but the

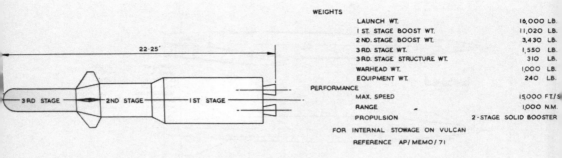

WEIGHTS	
LAUNCH WT.	16,000 LB.
I ST. STAGE BOOST WT.	11,020 LB.
2 ND. STAGE BOOST WT.	3,430 LB.
3 RD. STAGE WT.	1,550 LB.
3 RD. STAGE STRUCTURE WT.	310 LB.
WARHEAD WT.	1,000 LB.
EQUIPMENT WT.	240 LB.
PERFORMANCE	
MAX. SPEED	15,000 FT/S
RANGE	1,000 N.M.
PROPULSION	2 - STAGE SOLID BOOSTER
FOR INTERNAL STOWAGE ON VULCAN	
REFERENCE AP/ MEMO/ 71	

AIR-LAUNCHED BALLISTIC MISSILE PROPOSAL.
SECRET

AVRO's design for an air-launched ballistic missile to be carried by the Vulcan. There seems to be little other design analysis other than this very sketchy outline.

difficult part is not in getting the rocket motors to work but in devising an accurate guidance system. The Skybolt guidance system required a computer that was pushing the boundaries of current technology, and it is very unlikely that such a computer could easily have been built from scratch in the UK. It would probably have been possible to buy the Skybolt system 'off-the-shelf', so to speak, but there were political implications to that. McNamara and Rubel had done all they could to damage the reputation of the missile, and it might have appeared that the UK was buying tainted goods.

The only other British attempt at a strategic ALBM came from de Havilland; the only apparently surviving reference to it is in Handley Page's brochure for the Victor carrying missiles to OR 1182. There is no reference to a star seeker in the drawings.

Attempting an indigenous Polaris programme would be equally difficult. The American Polaris missile was extremely sophisticated in construction, and a very great deal of time, money, and effort would have been needed to produce a British equivalent.

Ground-based missiles had been ruled out by the Powell Report when it recommended the cancellation of Blue Streak, and reversing that decision would have made for some rather awkward political moments. Indeed, when Skybolt was in the throes of cancellation, an Air Ministry official noted that 'Polaris is preferable to Minuteman. We would be bound to admit that Minuteman was open to all the objections which we advanced in order to justify the cancellation of Blue Streak as a weapon.' On the other hand, one wonders why America was spending so much money on something so apparently vulnerable—indeed, not just America. Russia was building missiles in silos, as would France. It is certainly true that submarines offer the most invulnerable option, but if submarines are not available, then a land-based system would seem to be the next best option. Having said that, the UK has a problem that America and Russia do not, in that it is a small and densely populated island, and, geologically, the areas in which silos can be built are relatively few.

However, Boeing thought they might try putting the idea forward:

On his own initiative Mister Clayman, European Manager of Boeing, came to see me today to disclose the attractions of the firm's Minuteman as a British deterrent weapon system instead of submarine-borne Polaris.

The main points of his submission were as follows:—

(a) Minuteman could be available to the British from 1965 onwards in its 1500 mile range version (which uses only the upper two stages of the three stage missile and offers a 1000 foot CEP).

(b) It is already in its silo stored form capable of standing 300 psi and could, with only trivial alterations to the silo design, been made to stand up to 500 psi.

(c) Costed over five years Boeing claim that per effective missile the cost ratio is 6.6 to 1 in favour of their Minuteman. Much of this depends on a 12 to 1 ratio in capital cost of the ground system, i.e. submarine versus silo, and spread over ten years this ratio would be reduced to something nearer 5 to 1.

(d) The claimed CEP (1000 feet) is so much better than that claimed for Polaris that if achieved it would mean Minuteman could deal effectively with the hard targets as well as the soft ones.

I pointed out to him the political difficulties associated with this country's reverting to a weapon based on holes in the ground having discarded Blue Streak for that reason some three years ago, and the length to which the Nassau agreements had gone in respect of Polaris. Not unnaturally he regards the first argument as one being based on unsound technical grounds and as regards the second he quoted the President of the US are saying after the Nassau talks that 'if the UK had any different suggestions to offer they would be considered'. Pretty clearly, Mister Clayman was merely discharging a duty imposed on him from Seattle and I cannot believe that he has any real hope that British policy could, at this late stage in the discussions, be changed. I undertook however to report his message.[5]

Rather surprisingly, the idea took root in the Air Ministry, or certainly with the Scientific Adviser. This was a result of a Boeing presentation in January 1963. A paper written by the Assistant Scientific Adviser (Operations) discussed the possibilities.

The issue with the land-based missiles in the UK was that of pre-emption since that was the basis on which Blue Streak had been cancelled. The Minuteman silo was claimed to be hardened to a blast of 500 psi and was certainly less vulnerable than the Blue Streak silo, and the missile was a good deal more robust. It was fitted with a 1-megaton warhead, with a range of up to 5,000 miles, which was far more than the UK required, but it did give the option of fitting a heavier warhead, or perhaps a cluster of warheads.

Certain assumptions were made in the memo. Moscow and Leningrad were treated as multiple targets, and so the total requirement was for nineteen missiles to arrive for a fifteen-city deterrent, and twenty-four to arrive for a twenty-city deterrent. The question then was how many missiles altogether would be needed if twenty-four were to survive a pre-emptive attack. A further assumption was then made that if the Russians attacked with 500 3-megaton weapons, 125 Minutemen would be needed to pose a fifteen-city deterrent, and 135 sites needed for a twenty-city deterrent. Again, the idea of a Russian attack using 500 warheads of that size is fairly ludicrous. The paper even went on to consider the consequences of the Russians using 70-megaton warheads.

Boeing provided comparative costs for the Polaris and Minutemen weapon system, which they claimed to be official DOD costs. Apparently, 135 Minutemen silos would cost £230 million over ten years, and four Polaris submarines would cost just over £400 million. However, by now, this was all academic; Polaris was going ahead at full speed, and no one would want to upset that particular apple cart.[6]

During the Nassau talks, James Lighthill, then the Director of the RAE, wrote to Thorneycroft to suggest a missile based on Black Knight:

> The Prime Minister may wish to note that he has the following position to fall back upon, should the POLARIS negotiation break down.
>
> Advances in technology make it possible, today, to do BLUE STREAK's job with a rocket at one tenth of BLUE STREAK's weight. The main advances have been in reduction of weight of warhead, and in perfection of the technique of the two-stage rocket, whose first stage is shed after it has burnt itself out.
>
> Consequently, the very successful research vehicle BLACK KNIGHT (an entirely British development began in 1956 as a 'lead into' BLUE STREAK and first fired 2½ years later) could now do the job with a small second stage. Several two stage rockets with BLACK KNIGHT as first stage have actually been fired. In the last three firings, all systems (including first and second stage separation, and complex data processing and transmission systems) worked as planned. In all 14 firings of BLACK KNIGHT, the first stage flew successfully.

For delivery of nuclear warheads over 1,500 nautical miles (the London/ Moscow distance), a suitable second stage would be one using extremely well tried Gamma 201 engine (of 4,000 pound thrust). Guidance would be based on the Ferranti miniature stable platform, of which the prototype has already been satisfactorily tested.

The fuels would be kerosene and hydrogen peroxide (which can be stored at room temperature for a whole month). The missiles be fired from small hardened sites (a tenth of the size contemplated for BLUE STREAK), and would be vulnerable to a megaton explosion only if it took place less than half a mile away.

The system suggested would use proven components that started development in 1956. It would probably reach the first flight after two years of further development (at high priority), and begin to come into service after another two years (and some 30 test flights).

A tentative estimate of research and development cost includes £15m. spent on the missiles plus £20m. on the Woomera range, which I add together and round up to £50m. The cost of operational missiles and launch sites is estimated at £200,000 and £500,000 respectively, which I add together and round up to £1m. per missile. These figures suggest that for £100m. (essentially what remained to be spent by us on SKYBOLT) we could have 50 of these rockets. (They would be simpler and cheaper than the US rocket Minuteman because of the much shorter range required).

Such a deterrent will be more vulnerable to possible massive simultaneous attack than POLARIS, but would have a compensating advantage of being entirely British in design, construction and control.[7]

Black Knight was a small rocket built in order to test the design of the re-entry vehicle for Blue Streak. A re-entry vehicle is designed to protect the warhead (the 'physics package') during its re-entry into the Earth's atmosphere. In 1955, no one knew what would happen when the re-entry vehicle hit the top of the atmosphere travelling at around 4 km/s. The only way to find out was to fire something up into space and see what happened when it came back again. That was the function of Black Knight. The original rocket had been a slim cylinder that was 36 inches in diameter; a larger version was under development, being 54 inches in diameter. The proposed missile would use the inertial navigation system developed for the Buccaneer aircraft, carry a warhead of 450 kilotons, and have a range of 1,650 nautical miles. Mention was made of a larger vehicle, 49 feet long, 5.5 feet in diameter, and weighing 40,000 lb with a range of 3,000 nautical miles. No further details of the design were, however, given.[8]

Black Knight was built by the firm of Saunders-Roe on the Isle of Wight, using rocket motors designed and built by Bristol Siddeley Engines.

Like Blue Steel, the rocket motors used kerosene and HTP (85 per cent hydrogen peroxide and 15 per cent water). From the point of view of a missile in a silo, this was an excellent combination since the fuels could be left in the rocket for long periods of time. This would mean that there would be no delay in the event of a sudden order to launch.

The other possible liquid-fuel combination was nitrogen dioxide (strictly speaking, dinitrogen tetroxide or N_2O_4) as the oxidiser and a 50-50 mix of hydrazine (N_2H_4) and UDMH (a derivative of hydrazine, $(CH_3)_2N.NH_2$). Both of these are extremely toxic. They are also volatile, which means they vaporise easily. If the two vapours come into contact, they can explode. The American Titan II missile used this combination and did indeed suffer a silo explosion. It was a combination widely used in Russia. By comparison, HTP/kerosene might not have been as energetic, but it was far safer, non-volatile, and gave off no toxic vapours.

Black Knight was minuscule in comparison to Blue Streak, but warhead sizes had shrunk considerably since Blue Streak had first been designed. Blue Streak had been designed for a warhead of 2,200 lb, but the Skybolt warhead was a mere 700 lb. The original Black Knight would have been far too small to launch a warhead to Moscow, but a larger version was already being evaluated, and there was a great deal of potential in the design. Indeed, in 1963–64, studies were underway to produce a satellite launcher based on Black Knight technology, which would materialise as the Black Arrow satellite launcher. This was given the go-ahead at the end of 1964 and had its first test launch in June 1969. Four Black Arrow launches were made, the final one being in October 1971 when it launched a small satellite into orbit. The first two stages of the launcher would have made an excellent small and compact IRBM. The complete development costs were £10 million.

The original Black Knight had four rocket motors produced from a design by the Rocket Propulsion Establishment, and these were later replaced by a version which used the small chamber from the Stentor motor of Blue Steel which was capable of a greater thrust. A small solid-fuel motor was added as a second stage. An enlarged version, with a diameter of 54 inches compared with the original 36 inches and a new solid-fuel second stage, had been under construction when it was dropped in favour of building the Black Arrow satellite launcher. The first stage motor of Black Arrow replaced each single chamber of Black Knight with two chambers, making eight in total. There was a second stage using two rocket chambers also burning kerosene and HTP, and finally a small solid-fuel first stage. Black Arrow would have been quite capable of launching a Skybolt-sized warhead to Moscow.

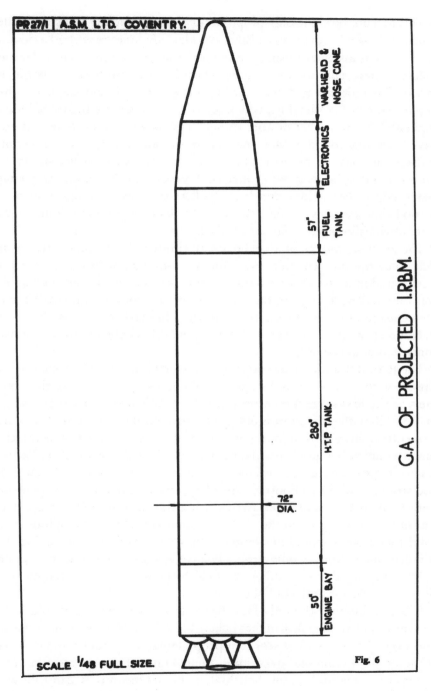

PR 27/1 | A.S.M. LTD. COVENTRY.

WARHEAD & NOSE CONE

ELECTRONICS

5'1" FUEL TANK

280" H.T.P. TANK.

72" DIA.

50" ENGINE BAY

SCALE 1/48 FULL SIZE.

Fig. 6

G.A. OF PROJECTED I.R.B.M.

The design for an IRBM produced by Bristol Siddeley Engines. This would be powered by the large chamber of the rocket motor used in the Blue Steel missile and have the advantage of using storable propellants.

This had not been the only proposal for a medium-range ballistic missile using HTP. David Andrews of Bristol Siddeley Engines produced a design in 1958 that, instead of using the small chamber from the Stentor motor, used the large chamber. This gave approximately four times as much thrust. The motor was drawn out in great detail, although details of the missile were rather sketchier, which is not surprising since Bristol Siddeley concentrated on rocket motors rather than rocket bodies. It would not have been able to make Moscow as it stood, but adding a small second stage would have done the trick. No official interest was ever shown in this design despite its obvious merits. A version of this design was later proposed for the satellite launcher. The RAE did some costings of its own version (Black Arrow) against the Bristol Siddeley Engines version, which were obviously rigged in favour of Black Arrow.

The great advantage of an HTP design compared with Blue Streak was that since the fuel was not cryogenic, it could be left in the missile for weeks, and in addition, new lightweight warheads meant that the missile was far smaller; this meant that, in turn, the silo could be far smaller and thus cheaper. One of the problems of the Blue Streak silo was its sheer size, which would have presented a formidable challenge to the British construction industry.

The RAE did some calculations on a missile based on the 54-inch Black Knight with a small second stage. The second stage would use the same fuels as the first stage, kerosene and HTP, and it was found that a stage of 3,500 lb with a thrust of 6,000 lb was around the optimum. Assuming a re-entry vehicle of 800 lb (the weight of the Skybolt re-entry head), the range would be around 1,100 nautical miles. There is one 'quick and dirty' way of improving the performance of a launcher or missile, and that is to add strap-on solid-fuel boosters. As it happens, calculations were done on both Black Knight and Black Arrow using Raven solid-fuel rockets. The Raven motor was used in the Skylark sounding rocket. Adding four such solid-fuel motors would be comparatively easy, and, without doing the detailed calculations, would probably have increased the range to around 2,000 miles; in addition, adding the solid-fuel boosters means that the first or second stage or both could be 'stretched'.

It is notable that the only land-based missiles to be considered were derivatives of the Black Knight rocket. Black Knight was liquid-fuelled, and even though it used storable propellants, solid-fuel missiles have considerable advantages over liquid-fuelled ones. They are more robust, far easier to maintain, and their higher thrusts mean they can follow a more efficient trajectory. Indeed, back in 1955, when the design of Blue Streak was beginning to crystallise, sketches were made for a solid-fuelled version, but the best that could be said of them is that they remained

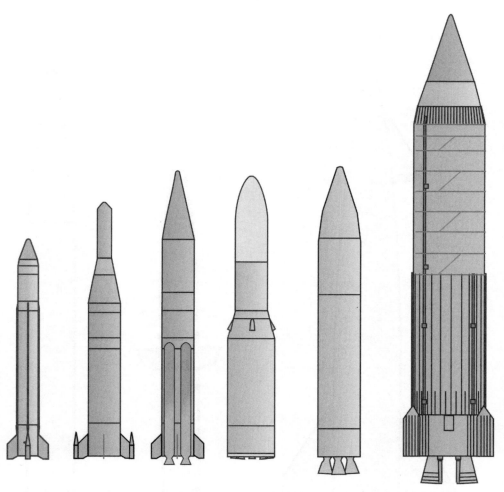

British ballistic rockets. *Left to right*: Original 36-inch Black Knight; 54-inch Black Knight (under development before being cancelled in favour of Black Arrow); possible MRBM based on the 54-inch Black Knight; Black Arrow satellite launcher developed for £10 million; Bristol Siddeley suggestion for an HTP/kerosene missile; and Blue Streak. The major problem with Blue Streak was its use of liquid oxygen, which boils at -183°C. All the others used storable propellants (HTP and kerosene).

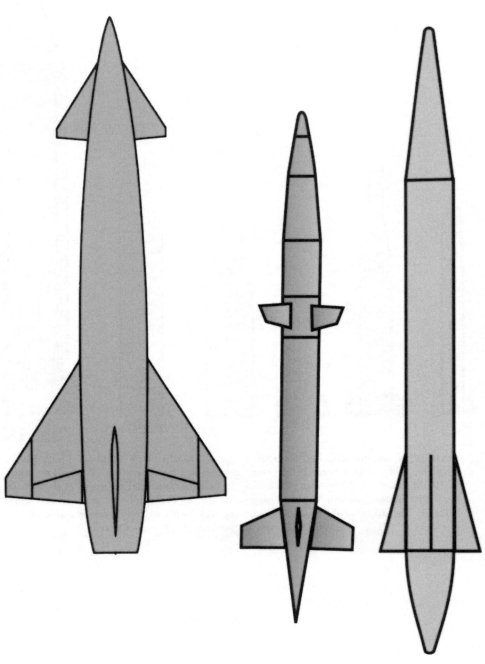

A comparison of the Blue Steel, Blue Water, and Skybolt missiles.

sketches. British solid-fuel rocket motors of the time were relatively small and inefficient.

The largest solid-fuel rocket motor produced in the UK was the Stonechat motor, which was 36 inches in diameter, although some 54-inch motors were tested at the Rocket Propulsion Establishment at Westcott. Stonechat was used in the 1970s as a launcher for test vehicles for the Chevaline programme (Chevaline was a Polaris improvement programme). As a comparison, the first stage of Skybolt, including the eight fins and control mechanism, weighed 6,435 lb, of which 5,425 lb was fuel. The SI was 245.

	Thrust	Burn time	Initial mass	Final mass	mass ratio	SI
Stonechat	32,000 lb	53 seconds	10,300 lb	1,800 lb	5.72	200s
Skybolt	25,000 lb	41 seconds	6,435 lb	1,010 lb	6.37	245s

Notes: mass ratio is the (initial mass/final mass). SI is the specific impulse, which can be thought of as the (thrust × burn time)/mass of fuel.

At first glance, these look very comparable. However, the Skybolt stage is not only more efficient structurally, but also uses a much more powerful rocket fuel. There is an equation that gives the velocity obtained by a rocket (assumed to be in a vacuum with no other external forces): $v = v_{exhaust} \times \ln$ (mass ratio), where ln refers to the natural logarithm. $v_{exhaust}$ can be obtained by multiplying the specific impulse by the acceleration due to gravity, g.

For the Skybolt stage, this gives a velocity of 4,450 m/s, and for the Stonechat, 3,500 m/s. This shows a very clear disparity. To be fair, they were designed for different purposes, but even so, it would have taken some considerable time and money to develop a British equivalent.

Zuckerman—not an entirely impartial observer—made some comments about this in a memo written soon after the cancellation. The question was whether the UK could, using its own resources, produce its own version of Polaris and Skybolt. He remarked:

> The essential problem here is solid fuel technology. We have made the start in this field, but in the light of what is required for both Polaris and Skybolt, we could not claim that we are in anything but a primitive stage of development.[9]

UNDER THE RADAR SCREEN

TSR 2

TACTICAL · STRIKE · RECONNAISSANCE

*Powered by Bristol Siddeley **Olympus** Turbo-jets*

BRITISH AIRCRAFT CORPORATION ONE HUNDRED PALL MALL LONDON SW1

An advert in the aviation press extolling the virtues of TSR 2—'Under the Radar Screen'. (*aviationancestry.co.uk*)

However, the problem with this idea was neither technical nor financial; from these points of view, a ground-based missile would probably have been the best solution. The problem was political; first of all, finding sites for the silos, and secondly, trying to explain why 'fixed sites' had been such a bad idea for Blue Streak, but which now were suddenly a good idea for this new missile.

There was one other possibility which might have become available in the late '60s: the TSR 2.

TSR 2

The TSR 2 was an incredibly ambitious requirement. It is quite likely that the Air Staff were smarting under 'no more manned aircraft' philosophy of the days of Sandys and the 1957 Defence White Paper, seeing the TSR 2 as a way of covering a multiplicity of roles, none of which were very clearly defined. On the industrial front, it was used as a way of forcing amalgamation on to the aircraft industry, forcing bitter rivals with very different cultures into partnership. Whether this was the best way to rationalise the industry is debatable.

It would not have been suitable as a stopgap weapon since it would have been likely to reach operational service before about 1968. However, in the absence of Polaris, it would have probably played a much more important role in the UK deterrent.

Although it was supposedly a tactical strike aircraft (TSR apparently stood for Tactical Strike and Reconnaissance, although the meaning of the numeral '2' is more obscure), its strategic role was considered very early in its career. A long memorandum was drafted in July 1960, which said that 'A strategic capability must be interpreted as the ability to drop a megaton warhead on major Russian cities from this country'. Could TSR 2 do this? The paper went on to say, 'Some superficial consideration has been given to the carriage of the following weapons and to the performance of the resulting system'. Four systems were considered: Skybolt, Blue Steel, a new ballistic weapon proposed by Vickers, and a scaled down version of Blue Steel:

> Vickers have done a brief investigation of the problem of finding a suitable new propelled weapon to be carried by the TSR 2 for strategic purposes and have produced a very brief brochure. This has been discussed with the firm. Having considered missiles flying at low level at about M = 2.5 they dismissed these in favour of a rocket boosted ballistic missile and this seems to us a sound conclusion because a missile flying at low level at M = 2.5 would be either an inconveniently large missile or have a very short range.

Vickers subsequently concentrated most of their brief investigation on ballistic missiles and produced three paper versions giving 20 nautical miles range for a missile of weight 2500 lb, 350 nautical miles range for 7250 lb, and 700 nautical miles range for a weight of 10,000 lb, all with the possibility of a warhead with a yield of something over ½ megaton ...

It was concluded, therefore, that if a new design of strategic missile for the TSR 2 were to go ahead, a range of 100 to 200 miles, with a terminal accuracy of 1 to 2 miles, should be aimed at. This would make the weapon somewhat smaller and ease the problem of installation, and Vickers have now turned their thoughts towards using as much of Blue Water as possible, probably the inertia platform and perhaps a developed Blue Water motor, but the missile would be purely ballistic, and Blue Water wings not be used and, indeed, the structure would be new. They are to have discussions with English Electric and will then put forward a definite design proposal. Until this is seen it would be unwise to attempt a realistic cost or time scale.

It is proposed to carry the weapon below the fuselage with extra fuel tanks in the bomb bay and two 450 gallon tanks on the wings ... The firm feel confident that when the aircraft is flying at no more than 500 feet altitude the weapon could be launched from underneath by first putting the aircraft into a shallow climb of perhaps 5 degrees.[10]

The report then went on to consider the somewhat unlikely idea of the carriage of Skybolt.

There are three possible ways of carrying the Skybolt—on top, under the body and under the wing.

There are three serious objections to carrying it under the body and these are:—

(a) The star tracker cannot be used.

(b) The aircraft Doppler cannot function as it would be masked by Skybolt.

(c) The ground clearance would be a minus quantity and a redesign of Skybolt fins would be necessary to overcome this.

Aircraft longitudinal and lateral stability would also be a matter of some doubt...

The objections to the underwing position are the rolling moment due to lateral c.g. shift and buffeting of the tailplane which is directly in line with the rear of the missile; in addition there is likely to be some loss of wing lift and the combination is likely to have a low drag critical Mach number. Wind tunnel tests are essential to confirm the severity of buffeting and the drag critical Mach number, but it is considered that this position is the least attractive.

The overwing position has less aerodynamic objection than the underwing position and has to recommend it that the star tracker can be used, the missile does not need modifying and Doppler is not obscured. The objections to it are fin buffeting and shielding and longitudinal and lateral stability. Wind tunnel tests would be required before it could be said just how severe these problems are. An additional difficulty would be the positioning of the missile on the aircraft.

This seems to boil down to the positioning of the Skybolt on top of the TSR 2 as being the least unlikely solution. This solution, however, presents launching problems of its own. If attempts were made to take advantage of the TSR 2's low altitude capability by launching from low altitude with perhaps a shallow angle of climb to get Skybolt off without hitting the ground, this would entail also the TSR 2 rolling over onto its back. The minimum altitude at which this manoeuvre could be started would be greater than the minimum cruising altitude. It would also be necessary to ensure that Skybolt could be operated this way through 180° without redesign of its inertia platform. An alternative way of employing TSR 2 with Skybolt mounted on top would be to forget any attempt to use TSR 2's low altitude capability and make full use of the Skybolt's range. The TSR 2 would have a cruising height of 25,000 feet from which Skybolt could be launched, together with a radius of 1090nm. This may provide a reasonable way of employing the combination, in that the Skybolt could be launched out of range of enemy defences. The mechanics of launching still present very great difficulties ...

Blue Steel suffers to an even greater extent from all the disadvantages of Skybolt when installing it on TSR 2, except that it does not lose any accuracy when mounted underneath the body and there is a reasonable hope that it can be mounted underneath with some ground clearance ... The aircraft Doppler however, would be obscured and only if a suitable position be found for this could be the under fuselage mounting of Blue Steel be possible. There would, of course, be a loss of range of Blue Steel when launched from low altitude.[11]

The main problem with the TSR 2 was its range, or lack of. There does exist a map showing how the TSR 2 could reach Moscow and return, but the major problem is that it would need to be refuelled both on the way out and the way back by tanker aircraft operating close to Soviet air defences. There was an alternative which several brochures from the aircraft manufacturers made mention of, which was not to start and end the mission in the UK, but using European NATO bases in such countries as Norway or Turkey, or even bases in Cyprus.

As part of the studies, two questions were posed—firstly, what would be the maximum range of an internally stowed low level all the way strategic

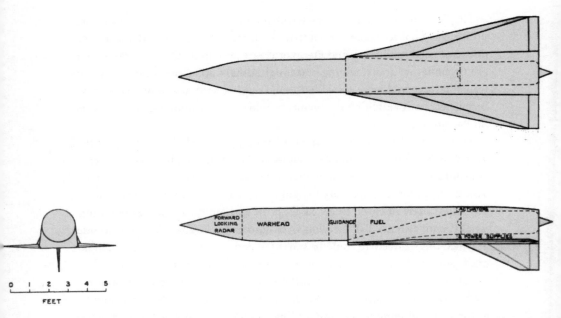

FEET

FIG. I. LOW ALTITUDE SUBSONIC STRATEGIC MISSILE (SINGLE JET ENGINED)

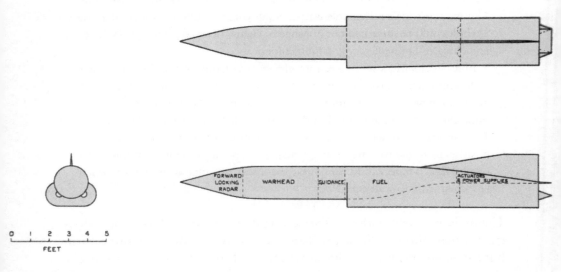

G. 3. LOW ALTITUDE SUPERSONIC STRATEGIC MISSILE (TWIN JET ENGINED).

The RAE's proposal for stand-off missiles for the TSR 2. Their dimensions were carefully chosen so that the missiles could fit inside the bomb bay of the aircraft without any wasted space.

weapon for the aircraft, and secondly, what would be the combined performance of the aircraft/weapon system? The RAE took a rather novel approach to the question: it considered what equipment was necessary for payload, structure, and so on, then designed a missile that would be an exact fit for the bomb bay. The rest of the missile would simply be fuel. A rocket-powered version was considered, but a jet-propelled missile would give a better performance. One missile design was subsonic and the other supersonic; the subsonic missile would have wings that would be folded when the missile was stowed in the bomb bay, while the other would not need wings since the body itself could generate sufficient lift.

The calculations showed that the single jet engine subsonic missile would have a range of about 225 nautical miles with a 500-kiloton warhead and up to 255 miles with a lighter 300-kiloton warhead. The twinjet supersonic missile would have a range of around 140 nautical miles.

The question then was how many targets could be covered. Considering fourteen major strategic targets in the USSR, more than half of them were within 1,400 miles from the UK, and that nearly three-quarters of the targets were within 300 miles of a perimeter around the USSR and satellite countries. If the aircraft flew at a high level to within 200 miles of its target, then the radius of action would be about 1,150 miles. Adding on the extra 250-mile range of the missile brought it up to the figure of 1,400 miles.

However, it was thought that the development time of the missile would be seven–eight years, and one of the snags was that it would be another four years until the first flight of the TSR 2. This would have ruled it out as a stopgap, but it might have made a useful strategic weapon if the UK had been forced to go it alone. However, many sensible ideas are often never followed up, and this would probably have fallen into that category.

At the same time, a rather less convincing proposal was produced. This was to fit an ordinary bomb with wings that would be folded away while in the bomb bay. The aircraft would pull up into a climb, the bomb would be released, the wings would open out, and then the bomb would glide forward. Ranges of up to 10 miles were predicted, although from the strategic view, it made little sense since a range of a few miles was not worthwhile.

It is considered essential ... to fly low if it is to penetrate defences likely to be in operation against it when attacking important targets as it is believed that the only good chance of survival will be to fly below the radar horizon. A suggested operating height of the aircraft while over enemy territory is no more than 200 ft, and it is thought when in a well defended locality (such as the target area is likely to be) even a brief climb to a few hundred feet will be extremely hazardous. This makes the delivery of any ordinary nuclear bomb very difficult and dangerous. Low altitude level flight bombing at high speed with a free-fall bomb is impossible because an instantaneous impact fuze on the bomb would lead to the aircraft being destroyed by its own weapon and no nuclear bomb is robust enough to withstand the ground impact so a time fuse cannot be used to delay the explosion until the aircraft reaches a safe distance. The very low release height and high release speed makes it very difficult to retard the bomb sufficiently by parachute or any other means so that it can stand the ground impact shock and still function properly later. An additional disadvantage of all these methods of delivery is that the aircraft has to pass over the target, and knowledge that it has to pass over a given point makes it vulnerable to fixed defences such as balloon barrages, gun barrages etc. Toss bombing will also be very dangerous for if the aircraft is to throw the bomb forward far enough for it to escape from the explosion,

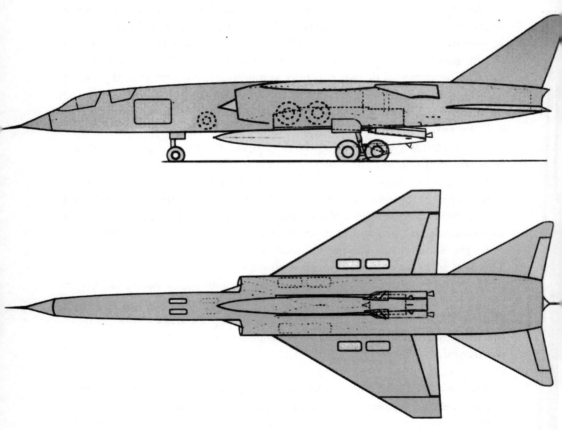

TSR 2 carrying an Avro W170 stand-off missile.

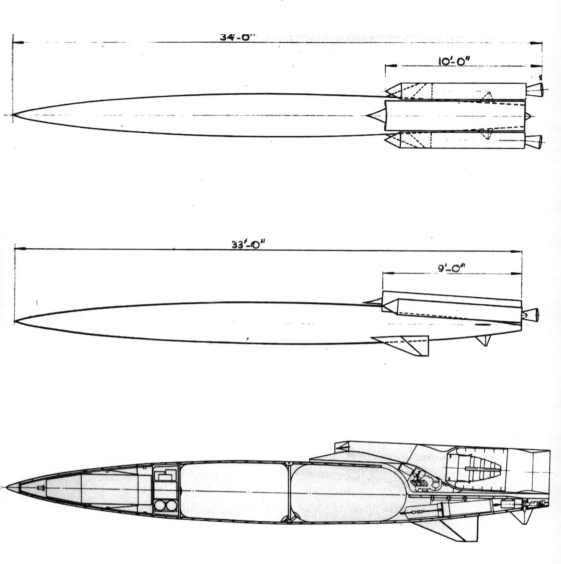

The layout of the Avro W170 missile intended for TSR 2.

then it has to rise a minimum of several hundred feet during the manoeuvre and becomes vulnerable to the defences even before it has time to release its weapon.

One possibility which overcomes many of the difficulties of delivering the barn is to fixed wings to it so that after release the bomb continues to fly forward while the aircraft turns away and escapes without climbing. If the bomb is powered by a rocket or other motor there is obviously no difficulty in sustaining flight long enough for the attacking aircraft to be able to release the bomb well clear of the target and escape the effects of the explosion. If the bomb is unpowered and is gradually slowed down by drag, the wings can only sustain it until stalling speed is reached and it is no longer obvious whether it will have sufficient range ...

The intention is that the weapon would have wings and control surfaces and autopilot system would trim the aircraft to fly at constant height ...

The best configuration and weight combination seems capable of keeping the aircraft a minimum distance of seven or eight miles from the target ... [12]

All these speculations were brought to an end by a decision of the BNDSG in September 1960:

The possible stand-off weapon systems for the TSR 2 was so unattractive on technical, financial and development time considerations that they were not worthy of further study. This conclusion was applicable to all stand-off weapon proposals, including those put forward for modifying BLUE WATER for the air-launched role. The claims which have been made for this development were considered to underestimate the R and D costs and to exaggerate the attainable performance. [13]

Yet, later on in the minutes came the interesting statement: 'On the other hand, if the SKYBOLT development project failed, the development of the TSR 2 weapons system could represent a real insurance'.

Inevitably, in March 1963, Avro produced a brochure for a missile designed specifically for the TSR 2. This, too, must have been put together in the light of the Skybolt cancellation. There is an attempt to broaden out the interest in the missile by suggesting that it could also be carried by the Buccaneer.

The development of a long-range missile should be preceded by the design and development of a smaller vehicle which operates at the same speed but has slightly less sophisticated guidance and terrain clearance equipment. This policy matches the present timescale of the TSR 2 aircraft and, in addition, provides an interim missile in a very short time to operate from the Buccaneer.

Accordingly, this brochure describes two missiles designated Type W.170A and W.170B. The former has a length of only 20 feet and a range of 115 nautical miles if fuelled with kerosene or 140 nautical miles if fuelled with a high density hydrocarbon fuel. The latter is 33 feet long with a range of 360 miles on kerosene fuel or 450 miles on high-density hydrocarbon. Each cruises at M = 2.4 at low altitude.[14]

If the missile had been able to achieve the ranges claimed for it, it would seem to be a worthwhile proposition. On the other hand, there was no attempt to evaluate the impact of the carriage of the missile on the range of the aircraft itself.

Of all the suggestions, the idea put forward by the RAE seems the most sensible—design a missile that would fit closely as possible into the bomb bay of the aircraft, which would mean that there would be no extra drag due to the external carriage of a missile.

Yet would TSR 2 have been a credible deterrent? By 1970, bombers on airfields would have looked appallingly vulnerable. Some sort of standing patrol, as proposed for the VC 10, would have been needed. Whether this would represent a long-term solution is another matter. Perhaps governments in the 1970s or '80s might have seen the deterrent as being increasingly obsolescent and so would not have been prepared to face the cost and challenge of a replacement. Perhaps the deterrent might finally have been abandoned.

Policy Options, or What Could Be Achieved for the Same Price as Polaris?

The capital cost of Polaris from 1963 to 1971 came to £345 million with running costs of about £95 million in the same period. What could the UK have done for the same amount of money?

Watkinson once referred to 'a mixed bag of clubs', a golfing metaphor meaning, in this context, several different types of weapon. An IRBM based on a design similar to the Black Arrow satellite launcher housed in silos (perhaps twenty-five or so) could be accomplished for about £100 million; Black Arrow itself cost £10 million to develop. There was the usual 'fixed site' problem, but it could be presented as only one part of a mixed bag. A weapon similar to the AVRO W140, as proposed for OR 1182, would also cost around £100 million to develop. This could be carried by Victor aircraft on an air alert system—that is, making sure that some aircraft are always airborne and carrying the missile. Then, there was the possibility of the TSR 2, carrying either a stand-off missile (perhaps another £50 million) or a laydown bomb. All this could have been done for the price of Polaris, but what may seem obvious now might not have been seen as obvious then.

Maybe, there was another option altogether—let the independent deterrent wither on the vine as the bomber force slowly became obsolete.

Journey's End?

In this context, there are some interesting comments in Neustadt's account. He quotes Tim Bligh, Macmillan's principal private secretary:

> For several months I think there had been going an uncrystallised, uncanvassed, latent Cabinet sentiment against prolonging the effort to sustain the independent deterrent. Butler, our 'Prince of Wales for 37 years,' had never shared the PM's sense of its electoral importance; Maudling had little to complain of, so long as the deterrent didn't rise in cost, but looking ahead to obsolescing V bombers ... MacLeod had been impressed by McNamara's logic ... and probably at heart was for dismantling all deterrents except yours. Boyle and Joseph wanted all the money and attention they could get for 'welfare'.
>
> But if a change had been put to the Cabinet in November, especially if it involved more money, all those latent feelings might have crystallised against going on ...[15]

Michael Cary had been temporary cabinet secretary during the absence through illness of Norman Brook; he recalls:

> ... left their own devices, the Cabinet at home would rather have seen Nassau conclude with a joint-study of what should be done after Skybolt cancellation—and then another meeting ...
> Butler and MacLeod weren't sold on the deterrent; Maudling was concerned about the money; so was Boyle ... Mountbatten, whose views would have been heard had time allowed, was scornful about going on with Skybolt, but he was also unprepared for and unhappy about Polaris.[16]

It was not only Westminster but also Whitehall that was sceptical about the 'independent deterrent', particularly (perhaps inevitably) the Treasury. This is shown very clearly in a Treasury memo a few years later in the context of the Polaris improvement programme.

> Our best line seems to be that, since our nuclear capability was never a credible weapon, its abolition could not leave a gap in our defences. We

cannot see how the Ministry of Defence can claim that their requirements of conventional forces would have to be different if they thought that they were not going to have a nuclear capability as well. We have to stick to our view that in terms of Russia a UK nuclear capability is a nonsense because we should never use it alone and if we used it in conjunction with the USA it would be an insignificant addition. If the Ministry of Defence claim that over the rest of the world the 'other nuclear weapons' would make a considerable difference to our ability to influence events then this only goes to show that they have not yet abandoned the delusion that we can still be a worldwide power at all. If they attach much importance to the retention of these 'other nuclear weapons' then they have not accepted the decision which is implicit in the Supplementary Statement on Defence Policy 1967, namely that we are in process of withdrawing as far as we possibly can to the status of a country concerned with its own defence in Europe.[17]

Ian Bancroft (who was then an Under-Secretary to the Treasury and went on to have a very distinguished career in the Civil Service, culminating in a life peerage in 1982) wholeheartedly endorsed the memo. Those who wanted to get rid of the deterrent were usually referred to as 'abolitionists'. Bancroft reversed this conventional usage by referring those who wanted to keep the deterrent as 'retentionists':

Note the reluctance (query inability) of the retentionist Departments to produce convincing scenarios for the UK as a first division or second division nuclear power; and a similar reluctance to define the increased conventional contributions which they claim would have to be substituted for nuclear abandonment. This plays straight into our hands ...

One way or the other, life will never be the same for the retentionists after the inroads which we have been able to make (rather to our astonishment) on the sanctity of this subject.[18]

So perhaps Skybolt might not have had any replacement after all, and the deterrent left to wither on the vine as Blue Steel became increasing obsolescent and the V bombers gradually went out of service.

16

Tidying Up

There were still some loose ends to be tied up after the cancellation.

Up to the end of 1962, the Skybolt programme had cost the US $356 million (£127 million) in research and development. The official estimate of the cost to completion still stood at $492 million, but it is probable that both the contractor and the USAF would have asked for more money had the Department of Defense's attitude to the project been less forbidding. One estimate is that the project could have been completed at a cost of about $550 million, a figure about 12 per cent above the estimate made over two years earlier. This is certainly not unreasonable for a project that was breaking new ground, and certainly puts the UK's budget analysis to shame.

The estimated procurement costs for 1,000 missiles and associated equipment for the B-52 still stood at $1.8 billion, the figure accepted by McNamara in August 1962. Again, the probable cost would probably have been somewhat higher.

UK participation in the project was on terms which were highly favourable in that under the Skybolt agreement of September 1960, the UK made no contribution to the development costs of the weapon system. The UK was merely required to pay the costs arising from its application to the Vulcan; these were estimated at £10 million in June 1962. Up to the end of 1962, the UK had spent just over $21 million on US contracts; if the project had been allowed to continue to completion, a further contribution of about $30 million would have been required. No procurement arrangement had been negotiated before the contract was cancelled, but there were indications that the UK would have been called upon to pay a proportionate share of the production tooling costs.

At the end of 1962, the UK had eighty-seven full-time staff based in the US for Skybolt duties, of which seventeen were on Ministry of Aviation and seventy on Air Ministry strength. As a result of the cancellation of Skybolt, approximately 250 (including dependents) were repatriated. Apart from those who were permanently based in the United States at Dayton, Santa Monica, and Eglin, over 250 staff from the Ministry of Aviation made short visits to review particular aspects of the Skybolt programme between September 1960 and December 1962.[1]

Skybolt having gone, there were then various contracts that would need to be cancelled. Those which were to be terminated immediately included:

DEVELOPMENT:

Main contract with USAF for missiles and equipment for R and D trials of Skybolt/Vulcan: value £6.4M;

Supporting contracts with the USAF (spares and services): value £0.3M;

Main development contract with Avro for adaptation of Vulcan to Skybolt role: value £3.8M;

Supporting contracts with Elliott, AEI, and Microcell: value £0.05 million.

Contracts which would be continued pending decision about each:

With the USAF: nil;

With Avro for trial installation of improved Heading Reference System: value £0.1M (almost complete);

With Avro for improvements to Vulcan Electrical System: value £0.05 million (spending at rate of about £2000 per month);

With Kollsman (UK), Sperry, Smiths and Elliott for improved Heading Reference System: value £0.5 million (almost complete);

With English Electric for Voltage Regulator in Vulcan: value £0.04M (almost complete);

With AEI for Converter Unit for Vulcan: value £0.2 million (almost complete);

In addition, the UK would be sent small 'housekeeping' contracts with the USAF for the maintenance of RAF staff at Eglin, which would have to be continued until the staff were withdrawn. Value less than £10,000.

PRODUCTION:

Contracts that were terminated immediately:

Contracts with USAF for ground training equipment: value £3.3 million;

Contracts with Avro for Skybolt modifications in the Vulcan: value £15 million (subject to reinstatement of some of the modifications if found to be required for aircraft without Skybolt)

Contracts to be continued pending decision about each:

Contracts with the USAF: nil; contract with firms for improved Heading Reference System and with Avro for improved electrical system: total value £6/7 million (spending at rate of £250,000 per month).

AVRO and the RAF had been supplied with dummy test missiles to be fitted the Vulcans to ensure aerodynamic and electronic compatibility. Some of these were also dropped over the range at West Freugh, to ensure that they fell away cleanly. Testing live missiles would be a different proposition due to the high density of shipping around the UK. The UK test site at Woomera was also ruled out since it would mean testing an American missile on Australian territory. The obvious answer was to use the same test base as the USAF, which was at Eglin in Florida.

This meant sending a large number of servicemen over to support the programme, not only aircrew, but ground crew and other for training in the handling of the missile. Around twenty-four officers and 114 airmen were involved initially. Air Ministry policy stated that any personnel who were to be posted away for more than six months were entitled to take their family with them. Unfortunately, there was no suitable accommodation available at Eglin itself, and so some other expedient had to be found fairly rapidly. The answer was to provide trailer homes. The rent for each home would be $130 plus $25 for air conditioning per month. This was agreed with the Treasury, and in October 1962, families began to arrive in Florida. A report in *The Daily Express* headlined 'Little Britain' read:

> RAF families gasp as they fly to luxury at Florida airbase
>
> Sixty-six British wives and children stepped out of a plane into the Florida sunshine today on their way to America's first 'Little Britain'.
>
> They had flown from London to join their husbands at the giant Eglin air base, where 250 British servicemen, mostly from the R.A.F., are being trained in the use of the Skybolt missile, using Vulcan bombers.
>
> Eventually there will be nearly 1,000 British men, women and children living on the caravan site set aside for them.
>
> A cheer went up from husbands waiting on the landing strip as the plane carrying the wives taxied to a halt ...
>
> Gillian and all the other wives gasped with delight when they saw their new caravan homes, which have air-conditioning, television and fitted kitchens ...
>
> Wing Commander Charles Ness, commander of the British force, said: 'I think everyone is going to have a very good time.'[2]

The Treasury must have winced when they saw the word 'luxury'. Yet not only did the wives have fitted kitchens, but all the pots, pans, and utensils to go with it.

This was in October, and by December, Skybolt had been cancelled, and all the servicemen and their families would have to come back to the UK, which presented certain financial problems, as a letter from the Treasury noted:

The abandonment of Skybolt has caused problems against which the following might be thought to be a little one. Nevertheless it is tricky enough and I thought it wise to forewarn you of what you may be about to receive from the Air Ministry.

The decision on Skybolt has, of course, resulted in the disbandment of the British Joint Trials Force at Eglin Air Base and other centres of operation. Sixty Servicemen have already arrived at Eglin with the definite understanding that their tour in the United States would be from two to two and a half years, depending on their arrival date. Acting on this assumption these officers and men bought themselves cars and semi-durables which they expected to enjoy for the period of duty and then either sell or bring back to England. (Electrical appliances are, of course, the wrong voltage for the U.K.) These men will all be returning during the period from March to the end of May and will, therefore, be faced with the problem of the forced sale of these purchases. This will involve them in heavy loss and the question is what, if any, compensation should be paid to them.

It is clear that if the men had served their expected tour of duty the Government would have been under no responsibility to meet the losses incurred on their expenditure on capital items and one must assume that the prudent man would have taken into account the amount of C.L.O.A. he would need to set aside to meet the difference between their original price and their residual value. They are now faced with the fact that their C.L.O.A. will cease on their departure and the goods or equipment would have to be disposed of at a far greater rate of depreciation ...

Before making any concrete suggestions I would like to point out that what in the UK might seem to be rash extravagance does not appear quite the same over here. Take the question of a car. Eglin Air Base is 600 square miles in extent. No public transportation is provided and the distance from living quarters to the shopping centre and other amenities may be 4 miles or more. This ignores the necessity for occasional escape from the base. Practically every American, from the Negro who mows your lawn upwards, owns a car of some sort with the consequence that public transport is seldom provided. Consequently the first thing that anyone, officer or airmen, does when posted to such a place is to buy a car ...[3]

'From the Negro who mows your lawn upwards' is not a phrase you would expect to see in a memorandum today.

The result has been that nearly all members of the Force have spent money on cars and their price has ranged from $3373 downwards. The total outlay including semi-durables has varied from $7208 by the Wing Commander in charge down to $98.50 by a corporal ... Some of this expenditure has been financed from loans from the local banks, most of it by hire purchase arrangements. Clearly the Trials Force cannot depart from Eglin leaving a litter of local debts behind them, and if the men have not got the money to meet their losses these will have to be paid and some arrangement whereby the debt is met from future pay will have to be made. I am convinced, however, that the men should receive some compensation for the unexpected losses to which they have been subjected by the abandonment of Skybolt, and I do not feel that the man who has paid out a good deal on semi-durables should carry away with him a load of debt which will take years to pay off. On the other hand, I would not suggest that HMG should stand the whole of the loss because (a) the man has had some use of the equipment and (b) he must have an incentive to sell at the best possible price. Admittedly sales will be difficult since the area contains no large towns or wealthy centres of population and there may be a certain ganging up amongst dealers to limit bidding against each other ... Consequently I would favour a rough and ready type of settlement. The kind of thing that I have in mind is that H.M.G. should meet a percentage of the cost.

I can see difficulties for you in any such arrangement because, obviously, when a Serviceman is sent overseas there can be no guarantee of the period he would serve and he must take some risk. I would have thought, however, that this was an exceptional situation and that any arrangement finally agreed to would be on a purely ad hoc basis and it would have to be strictly understood that it set no precedent for the future.[4]

A list of goods purchased included a mink stole at $350, a watch at $60, a boat at $1,500 and a canoe at $129. There was a note to the effect that 'no compensation is proposed for these items'. The total compensation paid out to members of the force was £3,187 5s 2d.

In addition, of course, the Treasury had to arrange for the sale of all the pots and pans and knives and forks that had been provided in the caravans. The life of luxury for the airmen and their families was over.

17

So What Went Wrong?

Harold Brown was Director of Defense Research Engineering in the Department of Defense from 1961 to 1965. In an oral history interview in 1964, he remarked that 'The British could not believe that we would cancel it, and we could not believe that they would not believe that we meant to cancel it'.

After it was all over, President Kennedy demanded an inquest into what went wrong. The historian Richard Neustadt seized the opportunity with both hands. One limitation from Neustadt's point of view was that the report would remain completely confidential, and he had to assure all those people he had interviewed that what they told him would remain confidential. Not everyone was convinced by this assurance; Macmillan wrote on a letter from Thorneycroft, in spiky semi-legible handwriting, 'I do not like this. There is nothing to enquire into,' and on a later memorandum, 'It will all be in *Newsweek* before you can say McNamara'.

So what went wrong? A whole number of things, but rightly or wrongly, there was a strong feeling of anger on the British side. This comes out very clearly in a memorandum that the Permanent Secretary at the Ministry of Defence, Sir Robert Scott, was asked to write for Neustadt. It begins with a short preamble, and then goes on to say:

There followed Mr McNamara's visit to London when, on 11th December, he left with Mr Thorneycroft a detailed memorandum on the SKYBOLT situation. The gist of this was that, while there was not much doubt that Skybolt could be made to work, it would take considerably longer and cost much more to develop the weapon system than had been foreseen, and it was by no means certain that, when developed, it would be able to achieve its planned performance. The US government had other deterrent weapons available to them which were more promising and, in the circumstances, it was not worthwhile from their point of view to continue with SKYBOLT. They recognised the difficulties in which this would place the British government and to meet them they suggested three alternative propositions. The British could continue to develop SKYBOLT themselves; or they could buy the air-breathing stand-off weapon HOUND DOG; or they might participate in a sea-based MRBM force under unilateral manning. There was no mention of POLARIS. In fact none of these three propositions could hold any interest for the British in this context. To continue the development of Skybolt on their own in the face of elaborately expressed doubts of the American Administration and after all prospect of US government orders had been removed would be so risky of course, both financially and technically, that it could not have been defended in Parliament. (It must be remembered that under the original SKYBOLT Agreement none of the development costs were to be borne by the British Government. It was only at Nassau that the US government offered to take over half the cost of development if Britain decided to continue with SKYBOLT.) HOUND DOG is a weapon in the same category as the British BLUE STEEL, of longer range than BLUE STEEL but slower. It suffers from the same basic limitation that, though it is a sound weapon for the middle sixties, it cannot be regarded as viable beyond the next few years against likely Russian defences. Moreover, it could not be used by British V-bombers without major modification to the aircraft. Finally participation in a multilateral force, however an interesting proposition in itself, could not be presented, above all in circumstances such as these, as any kind of substitute for an independent British deterrent.

It was clear to the British, and has been so since the signing of the original SKYBOLT Agreement, that the only serious alternative to SKYBOLT was POLARIS. While the SKYBOLT project was still alive, they naturally could not do anything to prejudice its chances by canvassing an alternative to it. But there can have been no doubt from the outset in American minds that what the British would want would be POLARIS—and on equivalent terms to those of which they would have had SKYBOLT. This was made plain by Mr Thorneycroft to Mr McNamara on 11th December, 1962. But the initial American offer was much less than this; and the fact inevitably became known. Instead of a simultaneous announcement that SKYBOLT had been cancelled and that the British would get something equally good in replacement, it became clear to the world that the British were not getting something equally good and that an attempt was being made to screw them down to an arrangement much inferior to what they had had before. The British Minister of Defence had to face a highly critical House of Commons empty-handed on 17th December before the Prime Minister went to

Nassau to meet President Kennedy. Eventually at Nassau, after what was evident to the world as an extremely intensive negotiation, agreement was reached on the provision of POLARIS on terms which the Prime Minister was able to defend as preserving the independent British deterrent. But by then the damage had been done. Supporters of the government who might have welcomed the agreement if it had been freely offered at the outset were embittered by the feeling that America's position of strength had been used in an attempt to force Britain to accept a diminished deterrent or a less independent one. Critics of the Government felt that their long sustained attack on the whole policy of relying on the Americans had been justified. The French appear to have drawn the moral that the British had accepted satellite status and as such were no more worthy to be accepted as genuine Europeans.

From the American point of view, all this seemed quite unjust. The US government had accepted that they had a continuing obligation following the cancellation of SKYBOLT; they have made an opening offer which seemed to them reasonably generous and after a process of bargaining (which is after all not unusual in international negotiations) they had accepted a settlement which allowed the British to have what was generally considered to be a better weapon system than SKYBOLT, and certainly a better proved one, on terms which conceded Britain's right to use it independently in extreme national emergency.

What went wrong? The crucial fact seems to be that the US government for all its general goodwill and in spite of various attempts at explanation on the British side, failed to appreciate the magnitude of the political implications of this affair for the British Government. This was not a new situation in which the advantages or disadvantages of various courses could be considered coolly afresh on their abstract merits. It was a political disaster for the British government, precipitated directly by the US government. The question could be asked with the advantage of hindsight, whether an arrangement which linked British defence policy so closely with the fate of one among a number of American weapons had been wise from the point of view of either government. But at this stage such a question was irrelevant. The situation existed and the SKYBOLT arrangement was inevitably the background against which everything had to be judged. From the British point of view, prompt action to show their rights in relation to Skybolt would simply be transferred without reservation to POLARIS could have restored the situation and could have been presented as an admirable example of the smooth working of the Anglo-American alliance. But at that stage to import such considerations as the possibility of Britain accepting a much more limited weapon such as HOUND DOG of her agreeing to some restrictions on the independence of the British deterrent was inevitably to invite the accusation that an American hold on Britain was being used to exact subservience. Even to adopt a bargaining approach, making an initial low offer with something more generous kept in reserve, however natural this might seem in normal negotiation, was here inevitably to reinforce this effect. The SKYBOLT Agreement had been under frequent heavy fire in Parliament for nearly 3 years on the grounds that SKYBOLT would never materialise. The British Government had steadily defended it as something over which they would not be let down, a prime example of the fruits of their policy of close friendship and interdependence with the United States. The collapse of the SKYBOLT Agreement followed by a prolonged struggle to find some adequate replacement for it was bound, whatever the rights and wrongs, to bring discredit on this policy, to weaken seriously the Government which was identified with it, and cause a certain amount of resentment among the public against the United States.[1]

This sounds as good a summary as any.

The Memorandum of Understanding

The text of the memorandum of understanding signed by Thomas Gates of the United States and Harold Watkinson.

SKYBOLT

MEMORANDUM OF UNDERSTANDING

The United States Secretary of Defense and the Minister of Defense [*sic*.] of Her Majesty's Government in the United Kingdom of Great Britain and Northern Ireland expressed their determination that the two countries shall cooperate in the development of the SKYBOLT missile to permit it to be adopted both by the United States Air Force and the Royal Air Force.

Mr. Gates affirms the intention of the United States Government to make every reasonable effort to ensure the successful and timely completion of SKYBOLT development and compatibility of the missile with Royal Air Force Mark II V-bombers; and agrees that Her Majesty's Government should have full access to all the necessary information on the project. Mr. Watkinson states that if the missile is successfully developed and is compatible with Mark II V-bombers Her Majesty's Government intends to place an order with United States Government for about one hundred missiles and their associated equipment. The warheads would be provided by Her Majesty's Government.

Mr. Gates reaffirms on behalf of the Government of the United States the sale of the SKYBOLT missile, minus warheads, to Her Majesty's Government shall be as outlined by President Eisenhower in his memorandum to Prime Minister Macmillan on 29 March 1960, as amended.

Mr. Gates welcomes Mr. Watkinson's offer to provide services on selected scientific staff to maintain liaison with the U.S. development agency and who operate in the development program.

Mr. Gates and Mr. Watkinson authorize their staffs to proceed with the negotiations on a technical and financial agreement in accordance with the foregoing.

(Signed) Harold Watkinson.

Minister of Defence of the United Kingdom.

(Signed) Thomas S. Gates, Jr.

Secretary of Defense of the United States.

Washington, D.C.

6 June, 1960.

Brief History of Skybolt from the British Perspective

1957	
September	RAF and USAF meet to consider a joint air-to-surface missile project.
1958	
17 November	First successful flight of Bold Orion test vehicle, launched from a B-47.
16 December	Second successful two-stage Bold Orion test flight.
1959	
30 January	A joint USAF/RAF requirement for a 1,000-mile missile of maximum all up weight 10,000 lb and a CEP of 3,000 feet was put to American industry. Twenty-four contractors were invited to reply.
16 March	Evaluation of proposals begins.
May	Douglas Aircraft Company selected as prime contractor for advanced design studies. XGAM-87A Weapon System Project Office [WSOP] set up.
December	Joint Chiefs of Staff recommended the development of advanced air-to-surface missile to DOD.

30 December	George Ward, Secretary of State for Air, writes to Watkinson, Minister of Defence proposing that WS.138A (the initial designation of Skybolt) should be obtained for the V-force in place of Blue Steel Mark 2, which was running into technical difficulties and delays.
1960	
15 January	In-house evaluation completed and results presented to Fletcher Committee, Department of Defense. Delta II configuration for missile adopted in preference to Able III.
4 February	Air Force headquarters authorizes immediate initiation of development, releasing $32 million in FY60 funds to carry programme through 30 September 1960.
29 March	The Prime Minister reaches agreement in principle with President Eisenhower for the sale of Skybolt missiles (minus warheads) to the UK if they were successfully developed. In a memorandum handed to the Prime Minister, the Americans: (i) said they wished to assist in improving and extending the effective life of the V-force; (ii) stated there would be no conditions as to they use other than those usually attaching to the supply of US weapons. In a reply to a Parliamentary Question on 26 April 1960, the Prime Minister announced this as meaning that the missiles would be completely under British control, except that we could not sell them without American consent or use them for aggressive purposes.[1]
4 June	British Joint Project Office formed at Wright Field.
6 June	The Minister of Defence and the Secretary of Defense signed a Memorandum of Understanding in which: (i) they express their determination that the two countries shall cooperate in the development of the Skybolt missile to permit its adaption by the RAF and USAF; (ii) the Secretary of Defense affirms his government's intention to make every reasonable effort to ensure the successful and timely completion of Skybolt's development and its compatibility with the V-bombers; (iii) the Minister of Defence undertakes to buy about 100 missiles and their equipment if they were successful.[2]

20 June	These arrangements reached by the Minister of Defence are endorsed by the Cabinet. In making his case to the Cabinet, the minister states that while there was at that stage no certainty that Skybolt would be successful, the United States was confident that it would be effective and that it would be in our interest to join with the Americans in the joint development of the weapon.
29 July	Full-scale motor testing began with first firing of a test weight first-stage motor.
August	Revised system programme budget presented to Air Force headquarters estimating total research and development cost at $372 million.
September	A technical and financial agreement on Skybolt is signed between the two countries. It amplified but did not basically extend the agreements previously concluded. One significant provision of the formal recognition that either party can terminate its interest in the project, although not without prior consultation. The Americans promised to use their best endeavours (though not to spend money) to get Skybolt developed independently for the British if they withdrew from it. Requirement for heavy (1-MT) warhead dropped. First full-scale, second-stage test weight motor fired successfully at Aerojet-General.
1961	
13 January	Group Captain Fryer of the Skybolt Progress Office in Washington makes his first progress report to the Ministry of Defence. He said that up till December 1960, the progress of Skybolt had been satisfactory although more expensive than expected. Headquarters USAF have, therefore, ordered that a new development plan should be produced and Fryer concluded: 'There is no reason to suppose that the Skybolt weapon system will not continue in development. It has suffered a setback in the last months but it still enjoys solid support from the Research and Engineering Directorate and the principal figures of the USAF'.[3]

29 March	Group Captain Fryer makes his second progress report to the Ministry of Defence. He concluded: 'After some uncertainty the future of Skybolt is virtually assured—though Congress's approval of the additional funding recommended by President Kennedy has not yet been enacted—at least until the middle of 1962. Its long-term prospects also appear to be sound'.[4]
19 April	First powered flight of a GAM-87A missile. Second stage motor failed to ignite.
31 May	Group Captain Fryer makes his third progress report to the Ministry of Defence. He reports rising costs, but he also produces evidence to show that congressional support was strong for the project and concludes, 'In all, therefore, a long life for the B-52/Skybolt combination now seems to be reasonably assured'.[5]
June	Second powered flight of a GAM-87A missile. First stage motor failed to ignite.
September	Third programmed launch. Failure in programmer timer circuitry. Fourth programmed launch. Telemetry data was lost at time of second stage ignition.
3 October	Mr Zuckert, US Secretary of the Air Force, visits the Secretary of State for Air and says that the Skybolt programme was going well.
1 December	Skybolt instrumented dummy drop programme initiated by United Kingdom with drop from a Vulcan at West Freugh, Scotland.
20 December	During his visit to London early in December, Mr McNamara tells Mr Watkinson that the United States was pushing ahead with Skybolt in spite of cost increases because of its importance to the bomber forces of the United States as well as the United Kingdom. McNamara added, however, that there were considerable doubts as to whether the missile would prove sufficiently reliable even if the required limits of accuracy could be achieved.

1962	
30 March	Group Captain Fryer made his fourth progress teport to the Ministry of Defence. He reported that Mr McNamara was having doubts about the cost and reliability of Skybolt. He suggested these were due to misconceptions about the true state of affairs and said that, in any case, Mr McNamara was continuing to release the necessary funds.
April	Mr McNamara gave evidence to the Congressional Committee hearings where he said: 'The contractor and the Air Force are quite confident that they can complete the development satisfactorily but at best it will be a highly complex system operating in a new environment … I personally believe, my belief is shared by my own scientific advisers, that we have a number of unresolved issues. I am hopeful that we can solve them successfully'.[6]
June	Second guided launch made. First stage motor failed to ignite.
October	British Service personnel begin arriving at Eglin Air Force Base to establish a Vulcan trials unit.
November	McNamara visits UK Ambassador in Washington, Ormsby Gore, to tell him Skybolt is to be cancelled. First guided launch marred by malfunction in gas generator/hydraulic subsystem causing flight to end prematurely.
December	McNamara visits London and confirms cancellation to Thorneycroft. Macmillan and Kennedy meet in Nassau in the Bahamas and an agreement for the UK to purchase Polaris is reached. Second guided launch. All test objectives were achieved.

Endnotes

Introduction

1. PREM 11/4737. Discussions on intermediate-range ballistic missiles (IRBMs): cancellation of Skybolt; Polaris sales agreement; part 9.
2. AVIA 65/1193. Warhead for a medium-range missile: Air Staff requirement OR 1142 Orange Herald (DAW plans action). D. Cameron, DAW (Plans), 10 Nov. 1955.
3. *Royal Air Force Historical Society Journal* 24.
4. DEFE 7/2161. Air-to-surface missiles: SKYBOLT. Gp. Capt. Fryer, 9 Dec. 1962.
5. Rubel, J., *Time and Chance* (Santa Fe: Key Say Publications, 2006); *Reflections* (Santa Fe: Sunstone Press, 2009)
6. Heclo H. and Wildavsky A., *The Private Government of Public Money* (London: Macmillan, 1974), p. 70.
7. ADM 205/202. The British nuclear deterrent. Draft Reply to Vice Admiral Sir Geoffrey Twistleton Smith, 22 Apr. 1960.
8. *Ibid.*
9. AIR 20/11493. Long-range powered guided bomb: future of SKYBOLT (DCAS folder). Air Commodore S. W. R. Hughes DRPS (Air) to DCAS, 16 Dec.1960.
10. T 225/1949. Skybolt missile: development in aid of the Vulcan/Skybolt installations. J. Marshall, 22 Jun. 1961.
11. *Ibid.*
12. *Ibid.*
13. DEFE 7/301. Defence Research Policy Committee: basic research.
14. Ibid. Watkinson to Prime Minister, 4 Jun. 1960.
15. TSR 2 with Hindsight. Royal Air Force Historical Society, 1998.
16. *Ibid.*

Chapter 1

1. DEFE 7/1338. RAF production programme for guided weapons: BLOODHOUND.

Chapter 2

1. AVIA 65/1687. Air Vice-Marshal Blockley, 5 November 1958.

Chapter 3

1. TNA T 225/1775. Guided weapons development contracts: Blue Streak and Black Knight.
2. *Ibid.*
3. Neustadt, R., *Report to JFK: The Skybolt Crisis in Perspective* (Ithaca and London: Cornell University Press, 1999)
4. DEFE 10/665 British Nuclear Deterrent Study Group (BNDSG): minutes of meetings and memoranda.
5. *Ibid.*
6. AVIA 66/1. Guided weapons and electronics: BLUE STREAK. Memorandum by CGWL.
7. *Ibid.*
8. AIR 20/10697. SKYBOLT guided missile: papers. Sandys, 30 March 1960.
9. ADM1/31023. The nuclear deterrent. K. T. Nash Head of Military Branch, 1 April 1960.
10. T 225/1952. Memorandum by R. W. B. Clarke, 21 April, 1960.
11. AIR 2/13767. Defence against the guided bomb. J. E. Henderson, 1 December 1958.

Chapter 4

1. AVIA 65/1661. Operational requirement 1159: USAF proposals. RHE Empson, D. A. Arm, 1 April 1959.
2. *Ibid.*

Chapter 5

1. AIR 2/15262. Strategic air-to-surface missiles: interdependence with the USA. Note by Controller of Aircraft.
2. AVIA 65/1661.
3. AVIA 65/1661. Operational requirement 1159: USAF proposals. R. H. E. Empson, D. A. Arm, 1 April 1959.
4. *Ibid.*
5. AIR 20/11493. Long-range powered guided bomb: future of SKYBOLT (DCAS folder).
6. AIR 2/15262. Strategic air-to-surface missiles: interdependence with the USA. Some Notes Taken during the Contractors' Presentation of W.S.138A at W.A.D.C., March 18th to 20th 1959.
7. AIR 2/15261. Strategic air-to-surface missiles: interdependence with the USA.
8. Rubel, J., *Time and Chance* (Santa Fe: Key Say Publications, 2006); *Reflections* (Santa Fe: Sunstone Press, 2009)
9. *Ibid.*
10. DEFE 19/75. SKYBOLT: Anglo/US air-to-surface guided missile. A Report on the Background and Status of Office of Director of Defense Research & Engineering Activities relating to the Air-Launched Ballistic Missile (GAM-87A). 2 February 1960.
11. DEFE 19/75. Memorandum, 1 February 1960.

12. DEFE 19/75. SKYBOLT: Anglo/US air-to-surface guided missile. A Report on the Background and Status of Office of Director of Defense Research & Engineering Activities relating to the Air-Launched Ballistic Missile (GAM-87A), 2 Feb. 1960.
13. *Ibid.*
14. AIR 2/17113. SKYBOLT ASGW: policy. Weapons System WS. 138A or GAM 87—Air-Launched Ballistic Missile (Status as of 1 May 1960). Grp Capt. S.H. Bonser, 26 May 1960.
15. DEFE 19/75, 16 March 1960.

Chapter 6

1. AB 16/2438. Anglo-United States atomic weapons discussions, 1958: Sir Edwin Plowden's papers (Chairman of UKAEA). Report from Sir William Cook, 19 September 1958.
2. AB 16/2438. Anglo-United States atomic weapons discussions, 1958: Sir Edwin Plowden's papers (Chairman of UKAEA). Report from Sir William Cook, 17 September 1958.
3. AIR 20/10808. BLUE STEEL: nuclear warheads. F. Brundrett to Air Marshal Sir Geoffrey Tuttle, 1 May 1959.
4. AVIA 65/912. Use of American Missiles (especially Skybolt) for the British deterrent: CGWL's actions. Notes of meeting with Air Ministry to discuss warheads for Skybolt, held on Friday, 20 May 1960.
5. *Ibid.*
6. *Ibid.*
7. *Ibid.*
8. DEFE 19/92. 18 September 1961.
9. AVIA 65/779. WS138A warhead information. Air Cdre D. C. McKinley, 9 June 1959.
10. DEFE 19/87. E C Cornford to CSA, 16 November, 1961.

Chapter 7

1. ADM 1/26924. Long-range ballistic rockets: policy and discussion on offensive use. JY Thompson, Director of Gunnery and Anti-Aircraft Division, 23 November 1953.
2. *Ibid.*
3. AB 15/2043 An enriched uranium reactor for submarine propulsion. J. Diamond J. Smith. AERE Harwell, September 1951.
4. AB 8/966/2 (Initial problems of the submarine PWR design and related experimental programme—Royal Naval College, Greenwich. J Edwards, September 1961.
5. ADM 1/27389. Polaris/Skybolt.
6. ADM 205/202. The British nuclear deterrent. Selkirk, 1 June 1959.
7. ADM 1/27389. Polaris/Skybolt.
8. *Ibid.*
9. *Ibid.*
10. *Ibid.*
11. AIR 20/10062. R. C. Kent, AUS(A), 1 March 1960.
12. ADM 1/27389. Polaris/Skybolt
13. *Ibid.*
14. ADM 205/202. The British nuclear deterrent. The letter is marked as a draft reply, and there is no signature, although it is quite likely that it was written by Mountbatten.

15. ADM 1/31023. The Nuclear Deterrent.
16. AIR 19/998 undated.
17. *Ibid.*
18. DEFE 13/617
19. AIR 19/998 undated.
20. AIR 20/11530. British Nuclear Deterrent Study Group correspondence: June-December. SAAM to DCAS
21. *Ibid.*
24. AIR 2/13710. R. C. Kent, 23 November 1960.
25. AIR 20/11530. British Nuclear Deterrent Study Group correspondence: June–December.
26. DEFE 19/87. Report by the British Nuclear Deterrent Technical Sub-Committee, AG Touch.
27. AIR 20/11530. British Nuclear Deterrent Study Group correspondence: June–December.
28. *Ibid.*
29. *Ibid.*
30. *Ibid.*
31. DEFE 19/87. Report by the British Nuclear Deterrent Technical Sub-Committee, AG Touch.
32. AIR 20/11530. British Nuclear Deterrent Study Group correspondence: June–Dec. Lighthill to Zuckerman, 22 June 1961.
33. DEFE 19/87. Report by the British Nuclear Deterrent Technical Sub-Committee. A. G. Touch.

Chapter 8

1. AIR 8/2256. Strategic missiles requirement: 1959/60 examination
2. AIR 10/10925. VC10: deterrent role. 'Introduction of the VC 10 in the deterrent role.' R.C. Kent (A.U.S.(A)) to A.C.A.S.(OR), 14 March 1960.
3. AIR 2/13382. AIRCRAFT: Bomber (Code B, 5/3): Operational requirement for future strategic aircraft. Science 2 Note No. 215, April 1960.
4. CAB 128/34. Meeting of 21 June 1960.
5. AVIA 65/1653. Successor to V Bomber Force, supersonic bombers: policy and finance. 14 March 1961.
6. AIR 2/13711. 'Maintenance of the British nuclear deterrent.' A paper considering the problems of maintaining the deterrent an airborne alert basis post-1970. An interim report, July 1961.
7. AIR 19/998. British Nuclear Deterrent Study Group, February 1960.
8. AIR 20/10806. SKYBOLT: compatibility with V-Bomber. Air Cdre I. G. Esplin D.O.R.(A.), 14 November 1961.
9. AVIA 65/780. Strategic capability of TSR 2. Carriage of strategic weapons on TSR 2. 5 September 1960.

Chapter 9

1. AIR 20/10638. Bombs: long-range guided (ASR No. 1182); long-range air-to surface weapons. RC Kent, in memo to DCAS, 6 June 1961.
2. AIR 19/833. OR1182 air-to-ground guided missile to replace or supplement Skybolt. DCAS to Secretary of State, 16 November 1960.
3. AIR 19/833. OR1182 air-to-ground guided missile to replace or supplement Skybolt. Undated.

4. AVIA 65/1833. Policy and financial control of long-range air-to-surface weapon: ASR 1182. Thorneycroft, 30 November 1960.

5. AIR 20/10638. Bombs: long-range guided (ASR No. 1182); long-range air-to surface weapons. Memo to Private Secretary/Secretary of State from Air Cdre G. W. R. Hughes, for D.C.A.S., 29 June 1961.

6. AIR 20/11493. Long-range powered guided bomb: future of SKYBOLT (DCAS folder). Air Cdre S. W. R. Hughes DRPS (Air) to DCAS, 16 December 1960.

7. RRE Memorandum 1825, May 1961,

8. AVIA 65/1833. Policy and financial control of long-range air-to-surface weapon: ASR 1182. CGWL, 13 December 1960.

9. AVIA 6/18920. An assessment of vulnerability of a Supersonic Flight Bomb to attack by Guided Weapon Warheads. Technical Memo No. GW 301. GTJ Pullan, March 1957. An assessment of vulnerability of a Supersonic Flight Bomb to attack by Guided Weapon Warheads. Technical Memo No. GW 301. G. T. J. Pullan, March 1957.

10. AVIA 65/1865. Comments about Minister of Defence's paper on nuclear Army weapons.

11. *Ibid.*

12. AIR 2/13710. Maintenance of the British nuclear deterrent.

13. AIR 20/10638. Bombs: long-range guided (ASR No 1182); long-range air-to surface weapons. RC Kent to DCAS, 9 June 1961.

14. AVIA 65/1833. Policy and financial control of long-range air-to-surface weapon: ASR 1182. LONG-RANGE STAND-OFF WEAPON FOR THE R.A.F. 22 December 1960.

15. *Ibid.*

16. AIR 2/14641. OR 1182: policy.

17. ADM 1/31023. The Nuclear Deterrent.

18. AVIA 65/911. Deterrent policy: CGWLs actions. Blue Steel Conference and Similar Weapons. Report by D.G./G.W., 4 November 1960.

19. AVIA 65/948. Proposals for a long-range air to surface weapon: DGGW interest. RH Francis, 21 October 1960.

20. AVIA 65/911. Deterrent policy: CGWLs actions. Blue Steel Conference and Similar Weapons.

21. *Ibid.*

22. AVRO Weapons Development Division. Interim Report on Feasibility Study to O.R. 1182. March 1961.

23. AVIA 13/1289. OR 1182. Report of a Working Group on Bristol's Proposals for a Ramjet Missile, X.12. 6 December 1960.

24. *Ibid.*

25. *Ibid.*

26. *Ibid.*

27. AIR 20/10638. Bombs: long-range guided (ASR No. 1182); long-range air-to surface weapons. Thorneycroft to Amery, 20 March 1961.

28. DEFE 7/1770. Long-range air-to-ground missile: X12. OR1182 Feasibility Studies.

29. *Ibid.*, Air Cdre S. W. R, Hughes, D.R.P.S. (Air) to DCAS, 8 June 1961.

30. AVIA 65/1583. Defence of UK: policy. Sir Steuart Mitchell to Permanent Secretary, 6 February 1961.

31. AIR 20/10638. Bombs: long-range guided (ASR No. 1182); long-range air-to surface weapons. Amery to Thorneycroft, 15 June 1961.

Chapter 10

1. PREM 11/4229. Meetings between Prime Minister and President Kennedy, and Prime Minister and Mr Diefenbaker, Prime Minister of Canada, Bahamas, Dec 1962. Ormsby Gore to Macmillan, December 28, 1962.
2. *Ibid.*
3. AIR 19/1056. SKYBOLT. Memo, 14 December 1962.

Chapter 11

1. AIR 20/7874. Evaluation of Green Satin/GPI Mark 4.
2. AVIA 26/1550. TRE Report 1083. Automatic AstroNavigation. (Blue Sapphire). AVIA 6/16432. Report IAP1458. Blue Sapphire, August 1950.
3. 'Report on Ground Clearance', Handley Page, Radlett.
4. *Ibid.*
5. T 225/1949. Skybolt missile: development in aid of the Vulcan/Skybolt installations.

Chapter 12

1. House of Commons, 30 January 1963.
2. *Ibid.*
3. T 225/1953. Skybolt and Polaris guided missiles: purchases from the United States. Memorandum for the Cabinet Defence Committee, Watkinson, June 1960.
4. AIR 20/1169. Skybolt.
5. CAB 128/34/35.
6. CAB 129/101/47. SKYBOLT, 20 June 1960.
6. PREM 11/3261. Discussions on development of medium-range ballistic missiles.
7. Rubel, J., *Time and Chance* (Santa Fe: Key Say Publications, 2006); *Reflections* (Santa Fe: Sunstone Press, 2009)
8. PREM 11/3261. Discussions on development of medium-range ballistic missiles. Record of a meeting between Watkinson and James Douglas, United States Deputy Secretary of Defence, 21 October 1960.
9. DEFE 19/76 Watkinson to Macmillan, 2 November 1960.
10. CAB 21/4979. Nuclear deterrent policy: Skybolt and Blue Steel. Watkinson to Macmillan.
11. PREM 11/3261. Discussions on development of medium-range ballistic missiles.
12. *Ibid.*
13. CAB 21/4979. Nuclear deterrent policy: Skybolt and Blue Steel.
14. DEFE 13/195. Airborne ballistic missile: SKYBOLT. Memo of 27 July 1960.
15. AIR 20/11169. Skybolt.
16. Neustadt, p. 32.
17. AIR 20/1169. Skybolt.
18. AIR 20/11493. Long-range powered guided bomb: future of SKYBOLT (DCAS folder). Telegram to ACM Sir Thomas Pike, 2 November 1962.
19. Rubel, J., *Time and Chance*.
20. DEFE 7/2160. Air-to-surface missiles: SKYBOLT. Zuckerman to Watkinson, 16 May 1962.
21. T 225/1954. Skybolt and Polaris guided missiles: purchases from the United States.

22. CAB 21/4979. Nuclear deterrent policy: Skybolt and Blue Steel.
23. CAB 21/4979. Nuclear deterrent policy: Skybolt and Blue Steel.. Minutes of a meeting of the BNDSG, 8 December 1962.
24. *Ibid.*
25. DEFE 7/2161. Air-to-surface missiles: SKYBOLT. Thorneycroft to Macmillan, undated draft.
26. PREM 11/3716. Discussions on medium-range ballistic missiles (MRBMs) for NATO: part 4.
27. DEFE 7/2161. Air-to-Surface missile: SKYBOLT. Telegram from Gp. Capt. Fryer 9 December 1962.
28. Rubel, J., *Time and Chance.*
29. *Ibid.*
30. AIR 2/15261. Strategic air-to-surface missiles: interdependence with the USA.
31. T 325/88. The Skybolt Story.
32. Rubel, J., *Time and Chance.*
33. T 325/88. The Skybolt Story.
34. *Ibid.*
35. *Ibid.*
36. Commencement address by Robert McNamara at Ann Arbour, 9 July 1962.
37. T 325/88. The Skybolt Story. Record of a meeting between the Minister of Defence and the U. S. Secretary of Defense on Tuesday, 11 December 1962.
38. AIR 19/1056. SKYBOLT. Emson to CAS, 15 December 1962.

Chapter 13

1. T 325/88. The Skybolt Story.
2. *Ibid.*
3. PREM 11/4229. Meetings between Prime Minister and President Kennedy, and Prime Minister and Mr Diefenbaker, Prime Minister of Canada, Bahamas, December 1962.
4. T 325/88. The Skybolt Story.
5. PREM 11/4229.
6. *Ibid.*
7. *Ibid.*
8. ADM 1/28839. POLARIS SSBNs—acquisition, organisation and assignment to NATO: future development/failure of SKYBOLT (air-surface missile). Brief for the Prime Minister—Talks with President Kennedy.
9. *Ibid.*
10. PREM 11/4229.
11. AVIA 66/10. 'Deterrent Gap': miscellaneous papers.
12. PREM 11/4229.
13. *Ibid.*
14. *Ibid.*
15. *Ibid.*
16 *Ibid.*
17. T 325/88. The Skybolt Story.
18. *Ibid.*
19. Rubel, J., *Time and Chance.*
20. AVIA 66/10. 'Deterrent Gap': miscellaneous papers. Report by Air Cdre Blair-Oliphant.
21. Hansard, 30 January 1963.
22. *Ibid.*

Chapter 14

1. AIR 19/1047. The Deterrent.
2. AVIA 65/1825. Directorate of Guided Weapons (Air) [D/GW(AIR)]: strategic long/short range air-to-surface weapons.
3. AVIA 65/1825. Directorate of Guided Weapons (Air) [D/GW(AIR)]: strategic long/short range air to surface weapons. Technical Memorandum WE. 1059. DJ Lyons, March 1963.
4. T 225/2547. The strategic nuclear deterrent: policy. AD Peck, 17 December 1962; AIR 19/1056. SKYBOLT. Julian Amery, Minister of Aviation, to Hugh Fraser, Secretary of State for Air, 21 December 1962.
5. T 225/2547. The strategic nuclear deterrent: policy. AD Peck, 17 December 1962.
6. AVIA 65/1825. Directorate of Guided Weapons (Air) [D/GW(AIR)]: strategic long/short range air-to-surface weapons. RAE Tech Memo WE1059. 'STOP GAP DETERRENT WEAPONS', D. J. Lyons March 1963.
7. DEFE 7/2145. Possible future nuclear deterrent weapon system. HL Lawrence-Wilson, 18 January 1963.
8. *Ibid.*
9. AVIA 66/8. Thorneycroft to Amery, 28 January 1963.
10. AVIA 65/1840. Deterrent policy: action of Controller of Guided Weapons and Electronics. BLUE WATER with the T.S.R.2 aircraft. Brochure by English Electric Aviation.
11. *Ibid.*
12. *Ibid.*
13. *Ibid.*
14. *Ibid.* J. E. Serby, 15 February 1963
15. AIR 8/2382. BLUE STEEL: development. Letter to Sir Thomas Pike, Chief of Air Staff, from P. G. Lucas of ATS Ltd. 14 January 1963.
16. AVRO Weapons Research Department Technical Report: Low Altitude Bombardment Missiles, February 1963.
17. DEFE 7/1340. RAF production programme for guided weapons: BLUE STEEL. Memo from Sir Solly Zuckerman, Chief Scientific Adviser, to Minister, October 1963.
18. T 225/2548. The strategic nuclear deterrent: policy. Undated, probably January 1963.
19. Divine, D, 'Britain without Skybolt', *The Times* (8 January 1963), p. 9.
20. CAB 131/28. Meetings: 1–12
21. AVIA 65/780. Strategic Capability of TSR 2.
22. A Survey of the Problems in Design of a Megaton Laydown Weapon for TSR.2. RAE Tech Note ARM683, January 1961.
23. *Ibid.*
24. *Ibid.*
25. AIR 2/17326. OR 1177: improved kiloton bomb.
26. DEFE 7/2145. Possible future nuclear deterrent weapon system.

Chapter 15

1. AVIA 65/1840. Deterrent policy: action of Controller of Guided Weapons and Electronics. Memorandum not signed or dated.
2. *Ibid.*
3. *Ibid.*

4. AVRO Weapons Research Division. A Review of Missile and Guided Flight Vehicle Projects Studies.
5. AIR 77/654. Minuteman as a UK Deterrent Weapon. Paper by Assistant Scientific Advisor (Operations), March 1963.
6. *Ibid.*
7. AVIA 65/1851. WS-138A: SKYBOLT policy
8. AVIA 65/1840
9. DEFE 13/619. US/UK POLARIS agreement, Zuckerman to Minister of Defence, 1 January 1963.
10. AVIA 65/780. Strategic capability of TSR2. Report dated 20 July 1960.
11. *Ibid.*
12. RAE Technical Note No. ARM. 768. Aerodynamic feasibility studies for an unpowered momentum bomb. C. W. Rhodes, November 1960.
13. AIR 2/13709. Minutes of meeting, 9 September 1960.
14. AVRO Weapons Research Division. Low Altitude Supersonic Bombardment Missiles Types W.170A and B, March 1963.
15. Neustadt, R., *Report to JFK: The Skybolt Crisis in Perspective* (Ithaca and London: Cornell University Press, 1999)
16. *Ibid.*
17. *Ibid.*
18. T 225/2923. Future U.K. Nuclear weapons policy. IP Bancroft, 2 November 1967.

Chapter 16

1. DEFE 19/77.
2. T225/2049. Skybolt trials force at Eglin air force base, USA: hiring of married quarters.
3. T 213/958. N. M. P. Reilly, 25 January 1963.
4. *Ibid.*

Chapter 17

1. PREM 11/4737. Discussions on intermediate-range ballistic missiles (IRBMs): cancellation of Skybolt; Polaris sales agreement; part 9. Sir Robert Scott, Ministry of Defence, 23 July 1963.

Appendix II

1. AIR 20/11169. SKYBOLT.
2. *Ibid.*
3. *Ibid.*
4. *Ibid.*
5. *Ibid.*
6. *Ibid.*

Bibliography

Gibson, C. and Buttler, T., *British Secret Projects: Hypersonics, Ramjets & Missiles* (Hinckley: Midland Publishing, 2007)

Gibson, C., *Vulcan's Hammer: V-Force Projects and Weapons Since 1945* (Manchester: Hikoki Publications Ltd. 2011)

Heclo, H. and Wildavsky, A., *The Private Government of Public Money* (London: Macmillan, 1974). Although it might be a little dated with respect to present-day government, it provides some excellent insights into the workings of Government during the period covered by this book, and in particular, shines considerable light on the workings of the Treasury.

Hill, C. N., *A Vertical Empire* (London: Imperial College Press, second edition, 2011). Contains several chapters on Blue Streak and its cancellation, and also on the Black Knight and Black Arrow rockets.

Landa, R., 'The Origins of the Skybolt Controversy in the Eisenhower Administration', paper published in *Seeing Off the Bear* (Washington, DC: Air Force History and Museums Program. 1995). A straightforward narrative, but with some errors.

Murray, D., *Kennedy, Macmillan and Nuclear Weapons* (London: Macmillan, 2000). An academic account but with an interesting perspective on matters on the American side, particularly the State Department.

Neustadt, R., *Report to JFK: The Skybolt Crisis in Perspective* (Ithaca and London: Cornell University Press, 1999). Richard Neustadt was an American historian who seized the opportunity to prepare a report on the Skybolt crisis for President Kennedy, who wanted to know why such a grave crisis had come apparently out of the blue. Armed with a personal letter from Kennedy, he interviewed many of the senior figures in Whitehall who had been involved in the saga, and obviously managed to win their trust, despite Macmillan's initial reaction, when he wrote: 'I do not like this. There is nothing to enquire into. The simple truth is that we naturally assumed that Skybolt would work until the American Government told us officially that it would not' (PREM 11/4737. Discussions on intermediate-range ballistic missiles (IRBMs): cancellation of Skybolt; Polaris sales agreement; part 9). Despite these initial reservations, the final report gave some valuable insights into British thinking and the workings of the British Government.

Rubel, J., *Time and Chance* (Santa Fe: Key Say Publications, 2006); *Reflections* (Santa Fe: Sunstone Press, 2009)

Watkinson, H., *Turning Points* (Salisbury: Michael Russell (Publishing), 1986). Watkinson never gave the impression that he fully grasped all the technical details of many of the defence projects he had to oversee. He saw himself more as a businessman, bringing much needed business sense to the Ministry. His sacking by Macmillan was distinctly abrupt, and this was obviously distressing on a personal level.

Wynn, H., *RAF Nuclear Deterrent Forces* (London: The Stationery Office, 1994). This is an official history, and a very thorough history, and has the strengths and weaknesses of an official history. Wynn has had almost complete access to all the relevant papers, and in this respect the book carries great authority. The problem with an official history is that it might be the truth, and nothing but the truth, but not necessarily the whole truth.

Zuckerman, S., *Monkeys, Men, and Missiles* (New York: WW Norton. 1989) Zuckerman was a man of considerable discretion, and although he spends an entire chapter on Skybolt, there are no great revelations. However, it is worth reading as an insider's view.